MODERN LEGAL PHILOSOPHY

Modern
Legal Philosophy

The Tension Between Experiential and Abstract
Thought

CORNELIUS F. MURPHY, JR.

DUQUESNE UNIVERSITY PRESS
PITTSBURGH

Copyright © 1978 by Duquesne University Press

All rights reserved. Published by Duquesne University
Press, Pittsburgh, Pennsylvania 15219. Distributed by
Humanities Press, Inc., Atlantic Highlands, New Jersey
07716.

Library of Congress Cataloging in Publication Data

Murphy, Cornelius F.
    Modern legal philosophy.

    Includes index.
    1. Law—Philosophy. 2. Jurisprudence. I. Title.
K230.M87M6   340.1   78-6437
ISBN 0-391-00859-5

Manufactured in the United States of America

FIRST EDITION

To My Mother,
and to the Memory of My Father

CONTENTS

The cognition of Law, like any cognition,
seeks to understand its subject as a meaningful whole.
                                        Hans Kelsen

Introduction

Modern Legal Philosophy encompasses a wide range of theories about the nature of law and justice. These different jural perceptions are generally understood as being incompatible. Legal positivism is antithetical to natural law. Sociologically oriented jurisprudence is opposed to both transcendent conceptions and theories which limit law to state imposed sanctions. Rivalries exist within, as well as between, the various schools of jurisprudence. As each theory gains its champions, basic differences are accentuated. A particular conception is exclusively maintained by those attracted to its method. As a consequence, the field is fragmented and it becomes increasingly difficut to understand the relative worth of any jurisprudential insight. We lack an intelligible view of the subject as a whole.

There is, therefore, a need for an integrative approach to the study of legal philosophy. If differences could be reduced, we might advance understanding of the interrelationships between the various theories and achieve a general comprehension. While eminently desirable, this task seems impossible of achievement. The divergent theories reflect irreconcilable views about the nature of reality and of our ability to comprehend it. Because the underlying presuppositions are at odds, any effort in the direction of cumulative understanding seems futile.

It may, however, be possible to approximate the integrative ideal if the problem of philosophical differences is approached from a different perspective. The prevailing theories can be understood as attempts to perceive jural reality at different levels of cognition. What at first appears as insoluble may in fact present possibilities of understanding attainable within the various degrees of human knowledge. For jurisprudential theories which are apparently at variance manifest a belief that the subject matter can be best understood when approached from the explanatory level within which each is conceived.

Within this broad frame there are potentials of reconciliation

1

which are now obscured. If we understand the various jural
theories as expressions of diverse ways of knowing, we may be able
to attain a coherent account of the entire field of legal philosophy.
Such an approach also helps us to see more clearly the advantages,
and limitations, of each particular conception. A reliance upon the
hard facts of positive law yields important analytical truths, but it
suffers the the limitations inherent in an exclusive dependence
upon legal experience. Sociological theories of law, conceived
within a broader frame, expand the relevant experience, since law
is viewed as a part of wider social processes. The subject is en-
riched; but the broadness of observation raises questions concerning the proper boundaries of jurisprudence. And, as reflections
about law and justice become more abstract, there is a need to
correlate these higher insights with the knowledge derived from
concrete experience.

As we examine the various jurisprudential theories within appropriate cognitive domains, we can also observe a certain ascent of
the mind: an upward movement from inductive and experiential
perception to the more speculative realms of juristic thought. We
begin to understand more clearly the relative merits of the different theories. The value of each as an authentic, though incomplete, perception of jural reality is confirmed. The impoverishment
which now obtains should diminish as the competition between the
various schools of jurisprudence is tempered by a deepening perception of the whole.

II.

The dominant theories within legal philosophy manifest two
themes of knowing which emerged at the beginning of the modern
age. There is in each a connection with either that appeal to experience which characterized the Baconian revolution, or the method
of recourse to abstract thought exemplified in the work of Rene
Descartes. These two themes, and the dispositions which they en-
gender, provide a frame of reference for the present study.

We begin with a review of Analytical Jurisprudence. As a theory
of positivism, it depends upon the data of legal experience as the
basis of its conceptions. In its development, as we shall explain,
Analytical Jurisprudence modifies the types of experience which
form the basis of its reflections. Nevertheless, it is appropriately

considered at the outset of our study since it is primarily an empirical mode of juristic reflection.

In the second chapter, entitled the Advent of Sociology, we examine the effect which a broadening of experiential knowledge has had upon the scope of jurisprudence. The great discovery of Comte and his followers was that social reality was intelligible; an insight which has profoundly influenced the course of modern legal philosophy. Sociology of Law emerged as a separate discipline. The discovery also created new opportunities for the extension of the Baconian method. In America, the experiential reference was refined particularly by Dewey's instrumentalism. The deepening of the appeal to experience in philosophy found confirmation in the maturing of Sociological Jurisprudence.

Jurisprudential theories derived from the new social science are evaluated both in terms of the methodological advantages which they bring to the subject, and the deeper insights which they reveal. The limitations inherent in the use of an alien discipline are particularly acute here, and are taken into account. Attention is also directed towards the problems raised by adherence to scientific models in the development of a policy science jurisprudence.

One particular assertion common to all sociological jurisprudence is that the phenomenon of law embraces more than positive rules enacted by the state. This inclusiveness provoked a positivist reaction in the Pure Theory of Law developed by Hans Kelsen. The adversive relation makes it proper to place the exploration of Kelsen's work in the chapter immediately following that which examines the Sociology of Law. The sequence is also justified because it provides an illustration of the inclination towards higher ranges of explanation which we have postulated as an animating principle. Recourse to the modalities of logic makes it possible to improve upon an earlier empirical positivism. It also provides a formidable weapon with which to combat the intrusions of a concrete sociology. Here we also consider the degree to which recourse to logic is conducive to the study of a humanistic discipline, and we explore some of the tensions which have arisen between experiential and abstract models of jural cognition.

The subject of justice has been developed by modern legal philosophers at varying levels of empirical and abstract thought. The most influential theories are within the tradition of idealism. Many believe that in order to understand the other and what is his due, it is necessary to conceptualize the problem of justice at *a priori* levels of abstraction. The fourth chapter, on Justice, documents this orientation and is placed immediately following that devoted to the Pure Theory of Law. A continuous tendency towards abstract understanding is maintained; a tendency revealed here by the movement to place the phenomenon of justice under the discipline of Kantian ethics.

In the final chapter, which addresses the problem of natural law, we undertake to explain how this question has engaged the highest ranges of speculative juristic reason. Using that impetus as the basis for our reflections we examine attempts to ground a theory of nature, in part, upon mathematical criteria. We point out the contrasting significance of traditional approaches which have been articulated upon the basis of metaphysical or ontological presuppositions. There is an explanation of the Thomistic conception of natural law and some indication of its general relevance to our comprehension of law.

III.

The structure of the book is thus corrolated with intellectual developments which have had a substantial influence upon modern legal philosophy. Placing the inquiry within the philosophical tendencies of the modern era promotes a richer understanding, as it records the tendency of juristic thought to move from empirical analyses to the possibilities of cognition within the domains of abstract thought. Each chapter constitutes a reflection upon the significance of a general theoretical development. I have tried to enter into the general spirit of each conception, extending it, in some instances, beyond the explanatory potentials envisioned by its author. Through such a procedure the objective value of each theory should emerge as part of a balanced, overall understanding. Particular jurisprudential conceptions gain an intrinsic appeal that is obscured when, standing alone, they make extravagant cognitive or explanatory claims.

Each theory reveals insights into jural reality which are of authentic merit. Yet the power to illuminate persistent legal problems is some measure of their truth. And reference to concrete questions should be required of any discipline which purports to influence human affairs. In contemporary jurisprudence questions of judicial power and authoritative decision making are paramount. They appear throughout the several chapters as we examine how each particular approach to law is able to shed light upon them.

Interrelationships between the various jural dimensions should become apparent as the study evolves. The reader can perceive connections between the different stages of reflection and evaluate in his or her own mind the degree to which each of the various theories contributes to an overall understanding. In this way, the pluralism of legal philosophy is respected and the force and integrity of each theoretical conception preserved.

The various jural conceptions speak for themselves, and no effort is made to superimpose any unitary view of the subject. Where appropriate, the limitations of a particular jurisprudence are noted. At critical junctures evaluative judgment is a necessity. It should be evident, however, that no hostility to any is intended. Every major idea of law and justice here considered contains valuable insights and I fully acknowledge my indebtedness to all whose intellectual labors have contributed to establishment of a modern philosophy of law.

IV.

This study is conceived within the Thomistic tradition of law and philosophy. The overall structure is derived primarily from philosophical principles elaborated by the eminent modern Thomist Jacques Maritain. General notions of law, justice, and prudential judgment which are also attributable to Thomism provide a certain direction and perspective. Principles of political theory utilized here also bear some imprint of that perennial philosophy.

These conceptions are not unified into a systematic philosophy of law. Some legal philosophers, of whom Dabin is the most notable example, have elaborated coherent jurisprudential theories upon Thomistic principles. However, as we have already observed, the need of our time is to advance jural understanding in a comprehensive, integrative spirit. We are at a stage in the history of jurisprudence in which mutual enrichment is of primary importance. No systematic jurisprudence is possible until we have better understanding of the whole field. And, should comprehensive philosophy of law ever emerge, it would have to assimilate a great many diverse perceptions.

Thomism is responsive to such a cognitive pluralism. Neither in its theory of natural law nor in any cognate conceptions does Thomism seek to establish a jurisprudential hegemony. Its deference follows not only from the incompleteness of its own insights, but, more importantly, from the respect for intellectual diversity implicit in the Thomistic theory of knowledge. If its metaphysical positions seem presumptuous, it should be remembered that the same philosophy affirms the mind's ability to perceive reality within diverse ranges of cognition. It thus restrains the ambitions of speculative reason while simultaneously affirming the value of other ways of knowing. This is a considerable advantage.

Legal philosophy, like many other modern disciplines, suffers from the distortions of cognitive imperialism. Limited jural insights now contend for predominant intellectual positions, asserting an explanatory power whose true value can only be assessed if the principles of intellectual pluralism are respected. It is hoped that the framework within which the study is conceived will move us towards that objective and away from the present fragmentation of jurisprudential thought. We may then gain a more coherent understanding of law and justice, and establish the importance of legal philosophy as a humanistic branch of knowledge.

Much of the basic research for this study was done while I was a Visiting Scholar at the Harvard Law School. I am grateful to that institution for the opportunity and the resources which were made available to me. Early drafts of separate chapters were read by Lon Fuller, Stanley Paulsen, Jacques Serré and Kenneth Hirsch. I am grateful for their comments but must bear full responsibility for the final product.

Judi Flynn has, again, gone beyond the call of duty in typing the manuscript. I am thankful for her effort and for the encouragement of my Dean, Ronald Davenport, as well as the faculty, students, and staff of Duquesne University School of Law.

Cornelius F. Murphy, Jr.

Pittsburgh, Pennsylvania
November, 1977

CHAPTER ONE

ANALYTICAL JURISPRUDENCE

A. *INTRODUCTION*

J urisprudence, as a scientific discipline, emerged in the nineteenth century for reasons which can be traced to the intellectual and political transformations of the modern age. Traditionally, Western Man had sought to understand the nature of law by viewing it in relation to some broader philosophy. This approach has continuing influence as can be seen in the work of Kant and Hegel. But the general scope of modern legal philosophy has been formed by a different conception of the structure and range of human knowledge.

Since the sixteenth century, a tendency to comprehend the various disciplines as separate fields of inquiry had been gaining in general influence. The idea was gradually developed that any subject of significant intellectual content was intelligible in itself, capable of being understood as an autonomous scientific subject. Analytical Jurisprudence expresses this distinctly modern idea that the various branches of knowledge are autonomous and independent. It seeks to restrict the scope of legal philosophy to the field of positive law, i.e., to the rules established and enforced by a political authority. Comprehending its subject matter without dependence upon other disciplines, it proceeds upon the assumption that the relevant data can be isolated and studied without reference to other forms of explanation.[1]

Analytical Jurisprudence is also predominantly empirical in its methodology. It appeals to experience as its source of knowledge. As it confines itself to positive law, it has as its subject matter legal institutions which exist, or have existed, within historical experi-

7

ence. It attempts "to let in the light of philosophy on these facts"[2] by isolating the distinctive notions of a legal system and analyzing their fundamental meaning. As Analytical Jurisprudence develops, the forms of experience to which it appeals will undergo change. But, in its entirety, this science of the positive law manifests the Baconian ideal of exploiting the empirical potential of a unified body of knowledge.

The political reflections of Hobbes provided a general foundation which would prove to be useful to the establishment of Analytical Jurisprudence. Hobbes was attracted to the deductive modalities of thought, but his political theories built upon precepts of psychology derived from experience and self-observation. He understood all mankind as being essentially equal in physical and mental capacities. In a prepolitical or natural state there is inevitable conflict as each seeks to improve his position under conditions of relative scarcity. But some passions, such as fear of death, incline men to peace. And laws of nature, or precepts of reason, forbid the destruction of life and impell men to work for the realization of a stable order.

In Hobbes's conception political authority was established upon the basis of a covenant by which each confers his power upon one man, or an assembly, which would possess supreme temporal power. The individual subjects, having relinquished their personal right to govern, were bound to each other in an agreement to obey the sovereign. Where sovereign power is acquired by force, he believed that the same result obtains. For in both cases supreme authority is instituted by fear. In one, a sovereign is chosen because of mutual fear among the subjects; in the other, they submit out of fear of the one who has acquired power. In either circumstance sovereign power is absolute, "as great, as possibly men can be imagined to make it."[3] The commands of this Leviathan or "Mortal God" then became the civil law of the Commonwealth.

The proximate beginnings of Analytical Jurisprudence can be found in the works of Jeremy Bentham. He had attended Blackstone's lectures, and found them wanting. Blackstone's assertion that "everything is as it should be" was particularly offensive. Experience was to the contrary, for Bentham had seen:

> [C]rimes of the most pernicious nature passing unheeded by the law: acts of no importance put in point of punishment upon a level with the most baneful crimes . . . satisfaction denied for the most crying injuries: the doors of justice barred

against a great majority of the people by the pressure of wanton impositions and unnecessary expense . . . the various rights and duties of the various classes of mankind jumbled together into one immense and unsorted heap . . . and the whole fabric of jurisprudence a labyrinth without a clue . . .[4]

In "A FRAGMENT OF GOVERNMENT" Bentham attacked Blackstone's general ideas on the nature of law and political authority which appeared in the COMMENTARIES.

Blackstone assumed that the need for government arose from the wants and fears of individuals who could only find protection in a union or community. The entire community should guard the rights of each, and, in return, everyone should submit to laws enacted by supreme authority. Some superior had to be constituted whose commands and decisions would be obeyed.

According to Blackstone, governing authority should only be entrusted to persons with Divine qualities of wisdom, goodness and power. These qualities are found in democracies, aristocracies, and monarchies, respectively. Happily, in the British Constitution they are properly combined. The executive power is lodged in a single person, with the advantages of strength found in a monarchy. Legislation is entrusted to three distinct entities: the King, the Lords spiritual and temporal, an aristocratic assembly, and the House of Commons which, as freely chosen by the people, constitutes a form of democracy.[5]

Bentham attacked this conception at several critical points. The difference between a state of nature and one of political society required greater elucidation that Blackstone had afforded. An essential distinction could be found in the habit of obedience, subsisting with reference to its object of submission. The concept was shifting and elusive, since there were innumerable situations of fact in which it was difficult to distinguish between liberty and obedience. Yet Bentham believed that it provided a characteristic mark which may make possible a stable distinction between government and a prepolitical society.[6]

Obedience is not promised to the sovereign because, as Blackstone intimates, he has undertaken to secure his subjects' rights. The relationship could be more clearly understood in the light of the principles of utility. The general happiness, which is a key to the science of ethics, provides an insight into the ultimate purposes of government. If the sovereign acts *contra* to law, he threatens the rights and privileges upon which happiness depends.

But the established law may be an impediment to happiness. On extraordinary occasions, sovereign acts against established law may be a requisite to securing the public well being. This exigency should not automatically dissolve the bonds between sovereign and subject.

The reason for continuous government is, as Hume had observed, because it is advantageous to society. To that end, Kings should in general keep within established laws and abstain from all measures which tend towards the generally unhappiness of their subjects. And, subjects should use the criterion of happiness as the measure of their obedience.[7]

Blackstone's account of the forms of government was also in error. By matching titles with qualities he assumed that departments of government *actually* have certain merits, rather than asserting that such characteristics *should be* possessed by government. In fact, Bentham pointed out, the designated qualities may be present in a branch of government other than that assigned in Blackstone's formula. A member of the House of Commons, for example, may have by reason of his own experience more wisdom to bring to bear upon a particular law than a member of the House of Lords.

By using qualities as an explanation of government Blackstone failed to observe the full significance of sovereignty and its relationship to the creation and applications of laws. The King as executive possessed the quality of power; but, Bentham asked, does the executive authority include the judiciary as well? And if it is maintained that the House of Commons, as a democratic assembly, represents the people how can it be an organ of government? If Blackstone's description is taken literally there are not subjects, and an intrinsic element of sovereign authority is absent.

Sovereignty was to be understood in terms of a disposition to obey the person or assemblage which, as a point of fact, actually possessed supreme power in the community.[8] Bentham sought to define law in a manner which would encompass the whole variety and range of human rules within a framework of sovereignty. Such a definition would not limit itself to legislation, but must include all expressions of volition, whether particular or general, which are traceable to supreme power.[9]

A law was an expression of a volition which the sovereign in a state either conceives or adopts. Its binding force was not derived from principles of legitimacy, but was to be understood in terms of the motives for compliance. Pleasure was to be expected from conformity, as pain follows disobedience. In its two essential aspects a law possessed a directive part which declared the sovereign's will and the sanctional part which intimated the motives for compliance.

Bentham's major attention was to be primarily devoted to law reform. He had, however, cleared the ground upon which a jurisprudential system could be developed. It was left to John Austin (1790–1859) to develop a theory of law which built upon and reflected these prior labors.

Austin was a Utilitarian, although he rejected some of Bentham's more radical political programs. Appointed in 1826 as professor of Jurisprudence at the University of London, he spent two years in preparation, principally in Germany, where Roman Law was an important source of research. In the Lectures he sought to delimit the field of jurisprudence by identifying it with the study of the fundamental institutions and conceptions of imposed, or positive, law. The key was to consider law as a form of command obliging to a certain course of conduct under pain or penalty of sanction in case of disobedience.[10] The organic structure which made positive law intelligible, and which distinguished it from other rules, was the sovereign subject relation. Political authority provided a determinate source to which the body of positive laws could be referred. A command of a political superior could flow from either supreme or intermediate authority, or be manifest by private persons acting in pursuance of rights granted by the sovereign. Within this framework legal phenomena could be distinguished from the Laws of God (revealed through the index of utility) or from rules of positive morality.[11]

The distinguishing mark of obedience which Bentham noted as a characteristic of the existence of government was refined under Austin's analysis. An independent political society arose where the bulk of society was in a habit of obedience or submission to a determinate and common superior, either individual or corporate. That superior, in turn, must not be in a habit of obedience to a like superior. If those conditions are met, the determinate superior is sovereign in that society, and the society is political and independent.[12] Habitual obedience, which is indispensible to the permanance of the government, is based upon a *de facto* consent rather

than a covenant. The requisite obedience is willed by some motive
which may arise from genuine attachment or from aversion to the
consequences of a violent revolution.[13]

Rules of conduct established, directly or tacitly by a sovereign
political authority,[14] were to constitute the Province of Jurisprudence. Austin saw his work as inaugurating a philosophy of the
positive law. The subject matter was clearly distinguishable from
the moral sciences designed to determine standards for determining how positive law should be made. This General Jurisprudence
would also transcend the particularities of a specific legal order and
deal extensively with the common legal principles abstracted from
all mature positive systems.

Some of the notions to be analyzed could be accounted as necessary. Concepts such as right, duty, liberty, and intent are constituent
parts of any coherent legal system. They must be carefully
analyzed, in order to trace the intimate connection which exists
between the terms as well as to discover their intrinsic meaning.
Other concepts which it is appropriate for jurisprudence to consider are not indispensible, but highly useful. Expressions such as
in rem and *in personam* are illustrative of such generalizations which
make possible the orderly arrangement of a variety of legal
phenomena.[15]

Austin's theory of jurisprudence was praised as an application of
logic[16] to law; but it was not an *a priori* science. Its subject matter
was the general body of developed law from which, by careful
observation, general conceptions could be disengaged and rationally elaborated. As understood by its adherents, Analytical Jurisprudence was to be a progressive, empirical science, a science of
legal relations abstracted *a posteriori* from law actually imposed, i.e.
positive law.[17]

As Austin's theory gained wider influence this attempt to build a
complete philosophy of law would be tested by changes in political
and legal experience. The idea of sovereignty as the foundation of
a legal system would be challenged as questions of authority un-
foreseen by Austin gained the attention of legal philosophers. The
analysis of legal concepts would develop in new directions as a
broader network of jural relations was perceived. And the demar-
cation of the boundaries between positive law and morals would be
questioned, particularly as philosophers of the twentieth century
had opportunity to reflect upon the actual consequences of absolute power. These difficulties began to arise as the new science of

positive law began to spread its influence throughout the English speaking world.

B. *THE DEVELOPMENT OF ANALYTICAL JURISPRUDENCE*

The idea of sovereign authority was difficult to apply to the American experience. For it had to be adapted to the structure of a government which was a federal democracy. Austin, in his lectures, had characterized the United States as a composite state or a supreme federal government. The sovereignty of each state, and also the larger state arising from the federal union, resided in the state's governments "as forming one aggregate body"; meaning by that expression the citizens who elect the various state legislatures. He saw a confirmation of this view in the Fifth Article of the Constitution which provides for the ratification of proposed amendments by the legislatures or by conventions in three-fourths of the states.[18]

The American legal philosopher John Chipman Gray spotted a flaw in Austin's analysis. The amending power is limited, since no state can be deprived of its Senate position without its consent. Since the existing constitution cannot be modified by majority will, the Constitution frustrates, rather than identifies, a supreme body. Should a majority force its will, the difficulties would not be overcome, since we would then be changing, rather than expressing sovereignty. Gray concluded that the Constitution of the United States was not amenable to analysis in terms of Austinian sovereignty since it would not yield a clear instance of unlimited or complete power.[19]

The methodology was also wrong. Austin had sought to discover the sovereign in society and then refer the organs of government to that authority. The first step, Gray believed, was unnecessary. It was preferable to treat the state as a postulate and then to study the operations of its organs. This will lead, as we shall see, to a concentration upon the judiciary. But it is worth pursuing the quest for location of sovereignty in a democratic society. The effort will be useful, not only in itself, but also because it will have some bearing upon matters of judicial supremacy which flow from Gray's line of inquiry.

An assumption that an electorate possesses ultimate political authority cannot be reconciled with the superior-subject aspects of Austin's theory. An electorate is obviously not in a habit of obedience to itself. The difficulty could be obviated by introducing the idea that an electorate confers powers on persons qualified in specific ways to exercise delegated power. This has the advantage of reflecting the general modern practice of limitations upon governmental authority.[20] But it does not exhaust the potentials of analysis. If, as with Gray's example, a majority should express its will against the provisions of a given constitution, the focus of ultimate authority will have shifted. And if a minority, by force, gains power and changes the basic constitution, the problems become still more complicated.

A deeper analysis would fix basic authority in society as a whole: viewing the people as the holders of ultimate authority. This introduces a consideration which, although indeterminate,[21] provides a supreme temporal measure of legitimate power. And while dependent upon political theory, it has a basis in historical experience.

The conventions by which the United States Constitution was ratified support the idea that the body politic as a whole participates in the establishment of fundamental law. Anticipating objections from state governments, the Convention provided for final ratification by special conventions in each of the states. Delegates were chosen from the community at large, in a deliberate effort to make the conventions an expressions of this ultimate political authority. The ratification was a concrete expression of the autonomy of the people, acknowledging them as the source of constitutive power:

> [T]he convention which framed the Constitution was, indeed, elected by the state legislatures. But the instrument, when it came from their hands, was a mere proposal, without obligation, or pretensions to it. It was reported to the then existing Congress of the United States, with a request that it might "be submitted to a convention of delegates, chosen in each state, by the people thereof, under the recommendation of its legislature, for their assent and ratification." This mode of proceeding was adopted; and by the convention, by Congress, and by the state legislatures, the instrument was submitted to the people. They acted upon it, in the only manner in which they can act safely, effectively, and wisely, on such a subject, by assembling in convention. It is true, they assembled in their several states; and where else should they have assembled? No political dreamer was ever wild enough to think of breaking down the lines which separate the states, and of compounding the American people into one common mass. Of conse-

quence, when they act, they act in their states. But the measures they adopt do not, on that account, cease to be the
measures of the people themselves or become the measures of
the state governments.

From these conventions the Constitution derives its whole
authority.[22]

This conception places the question of delegated authority upon a
firm basis and provides a higher perspective with which to evaluate
inevitable encroachments of governmental power. Its utility can be
illustrated with reference to the evolution of judicial supremacy,
particularly as this phenomenon has been manifested in the United
States.

In the Austinian theory of sovereignty, provision was made for
judicial lawmaking. Objections to judicial legislation were ground-
less, since the authority of courts was maintained by a tacit command. If it is understood that the sovereign wills that judicial decisions should be observed by subjects, their binding legal quality is
established.[23] Austin wrote against the background of a constitutional system in which judicial lawmaking was of limited range and
which principles of legislative supremacy predominated. As Analytical Jurisprudence developed, its exponents expressed a growing
awareness of emerging judicial power. Sir John Salmond, himself a
judge as well as prominent analytical jurist, asserted that the law
consisted of the rules recognized and acted upon by the Courts.[24]
This shifting emphasis was more fully expressed by John Chipman
Gray.

As we have observed, Gray felt that Austin's attempt to locate
sovereignty within society was futile. The state manifests itself
through its organs. If one wished to understand the nature of
positive law, the preferable course was to observe what these organs
do. *A* law may be thought of as a sovereign's command, but *the* law
was the body of rules which the courts establish and apply to individual cases. The courts create rules in the application of statues as
well as in their common law decisions. Legislative enactments are
not self-executing. They gain meaning as interpreted by the courts,
and in that form are imposed as law upon the community.

This expansive judicial power was not intelligible as the act of an agent fulfilling the tacit command of an unknown sovereign. A judge does not directly consider what would please the state; he rather considers what other judges or jurists have held with respect to the point in controversy. The rules applied by the courts are not the expression of the state's command. They are the law because they are laid down by judges.[25]

Gray believed that Austin was mistaken in teaching that law is the command of a sovereign, but the American jurist felt indebted to his predecessor for emphasizing that the law of the state was not an ideal but something which actually exists. An emphasis upon legal experience as the foundation of jurisprudential thought had brought the central position of courts into proper focus. Judicial lawmaking was creative, but it was not boundless. The power possessed by judges is measured by ideas of public policy, general custom and professional opinion.[26]

Structural analysis of the court system by analytical jurists revealed levels of vertical and horizontal authority which would also confine the power of courts. But supreme appellate tribunals have a general discretion to make law, and this supreme power can have substantial impact upon society. We have become conscious of the presence of this power in the Supreme Court of the United States in its exercise of an ultimate judicial authority which affects the meaning of the Constitution. To simply describe the process as an evolution of the law would be inadequate. Some considerations of sovereign authority become, in spite of Gray's strictures, relevant to our understanding of this important institutional development.

In its power of judicial review the Supreme Court exercises a supervisory authority over other branches of government, restraining them, in appropriate cases, from exceeding the limits of their delegated authority. It also protects the constitutional rights of individuals from the encroachments of official state power. The proper fulfillment of these functions requires the Court to consistently interpret the meaning of Constitution, and this results in a sophisticated degree of judicial legislation. The process brings the phenomenon of judicial supremacy to its highest level of expression. The power to interpret the meaning of the Constitution becomes a supreme form of lawmaking.

As the Court develops the law of the constitution, traditional values are reaffirmed and emerging values articulated. The Court plays a formative role in shaping public consensus as particular cases are transformed into a colloquy with "the judges speaking directly to the people as participants in an endless public conversation on the nature and purposes of law."[27] Some view the pedagogic role with reservations. They suggest that its actual effect is to have the Court teach from a position separate from and above the people, imposing its subjective view of a higher law upon a reluctant public.[28] The difficulties are compounded by the fact that the federal judiciary is virtually unaccountable. The judges do not stand for election, and Article V, as well as congressional regulatory powers under Article III, provide only marginal restraints.

Under these circumstances standards of authoritative decision making need to be articulated. We shall return to this important question of judicial supremacy throughout these reflections; for the present it is sufficient to note the connection between general principles of political authority and the analysis of a legal institution. While it is important to follow Gray's advice and observe what courts actually do, an adequate jurisprudence must also avert to broader criteria. In Austin's theory there was an ambivalence towards sovereignty, generated by his desire to place a political concept at the service of legal analysis. When, as with the judiciary, we identify sources of power to impose law which are not readily made accountable, we are made aware of the importance of sovereignty as a political concept. The Supreme Court has no inherent right to supreme power; it participates, in some unique way, in the right of the people to self government. A balance must be struck between its creative independence and the democratic character of its authority.

Before leaving the topic of judicial lawmaking and its relationship to concepts of sovereignty a collateral development should be noted. In his assessment of the implications of sovereignty, Austin made a clear distinction between unconstitutional and illegal acts. In every society certain fundamental principles are tacitly understood as constraints upon sovereign power. Acts of a sovereign contrary to such basic expectations would be unconstitutional, but if these same acts were subject to correction by positive law the idea of sovereignty, conceived as legally unlimited power, would be compromised. If the direct exercise of sovereign power was subject to a legal duty, the individual or collectively exercising such power would not be truly sovereign.[29]

We are so accustomed to the institution of judicial review that the force of Austin's analysis is frequently ignored. But it contains insights which any sound view of constitutional adjudication should take into account. The distinction maintained by Austin bears some resemblance to the so-called political question doctrine of constitutional law.

The power of judicial review can be conceived as inherently unlimited. In such a view, restraints on its exercise are understood as prudential forms of self limitation. The Court will refrain from adjudicating because such action would be practically unwise. But some issues in litigation can be characterized as nonjusticiable because other co-equal branches of government have a competence to determine for themselves whether their actions comply with the basic document. Professor Wechsler suggests that abstention from judicial decision in such cases is justified if the court determines that the Constitution has committed the resolution of the particular issue to another agency of government. That determination, he argues, is "*toto caelo* different from a broad discretion to abstain or intervene."[30] Austin's analysis gives some jurisprudential support to the thesis espoused by Professor Wechsler, and draws attention to the importance of nonjudicial forms of accountability in a complete constitutional system.

More direct implications of Austin's position can be seen when the objective of constitutional litigation is to directly challenge the act of the Chief Executive or the Congress. Where a subordinate official is the defendant, no great difficulty is encountered, even though the obvious purpose is to challenge the lawfulness of a sovereign act. Austin conceded that a subordinate official could be subject to legal coercion. The classic example is the so-called Steel Seizure Case,[31] where the Secretary of Commerce was restrained from carrying out the unconstitutional orders of President Truman. But where an attempt is made to make the individual or group which holds a portion of supreme power immediately accountable, the problem becomes more difficult. The federal courts have resolved the difficulties in a manner which, while honoring the perspicacity of Austin's analysis, demonstrates the limitations of his theory of positive law.

As we have noted, the people are the possessors of supreme political authority. Federal governmental organs possess delegated powers balanced, in our constitutional system, by a distribution among co-equal branches. No one branch is completely independent; all are subject to the superior authority reflected in the constitution. Within this frame of reference, the judiciary, as guardian of the basic document, has a capacity to supervise the acts of otherwise co-equal branches. Further, a wide range of legal and equitable remedies make possible the adjudication of important claims in a manner which avoids direct confrontation between the courts and the other branches which possess a measure of sovereign power.

In Powell v. McCormack,[32] petitioner, elected to serve in Congress, had been excluded by resolution of the House of Representatives. Together with some of his constituents he sought a declaratory judgment that the action was unlawful. The Speaker of the House, certain members as representative of the collective body, the Clerk, Sergeant at Arms and Doorkeeper were named as respondents. The Supreme Court held that the House Members had a legislative immunity under the Speech and Debate Clause of the Constitution, but it sustained the action against the minor officials. It also decided that the petitioner was entitled to a declaratory judgment that his exclusion by the House was unconstitutional.

The result was, in some degree, illogical. As the dissenting opinion pointed out, the minor personages over whom jurisdiction was retained were not, in any meaningful sense, executing policies of their principals. Yet the procedural techniques used by the Court majority were plausible, and provided the affirmation of right which was necessary. They also suggest the Court's sensitivity to the type of problem raised by Austin's analysis.

The justifications for judicial action in such cases has been articulated in more recent litigation involving the office of the President. In *United States v. Nixon,*[33] a subpoena had been issued in a criminal prosecution directing the President to produce certain tape recordings and related documents. The subpoena had been resisted on the grounds of absolute executive privilege as well as the political question doctrine. On the latter point the Court, in rejecting the claim, spoke of the underlying prosecution as an expression of the sovereignty of the United States. Holding that there was no absolute unqualified privilege of presidential immunity from judicial process, the court rested its authority upon the constitutional responsibility of courts to state what the law is. The decision may be taken as proving the falsity of Austin's assertion that "Supreme power limited by positive law, is a flat contradiction in terms."[34] But it could be equally maintained that the evolution of constitutional law had made it possible for courts in this country to avoid expressly disavowing the Austinian position.

In cases where Congressional or Executive accountability is the direct object of litigation, the Court, in asserting jurisdiction, is in fact making a functional distinction between the authority of its decisions and their actual enforcement. While there is language referring to compulsive process in the opinions, it is doubtful whether coercive implementation was anticipated. To put the matter more jurisprudentially, it was unnecessary for the court to determine *in advance* that a decision could be coercively enforced before it would presume to enter judgment. Pragmatically, the sanction is not, as Austin believed, indispensable; it is expected that the otherwise co-equal branch will abide by the decision. There is an appeal to the rule of law rather than an enforcement of legal rules.

Austin conceded that restrains upon sovereign power were possible, provided they were judicially enforceable. But his basic conception of the nature of positive law prevented him from fully appreciating the implicit possibilities. As sovereign commands, positive laws required the subordination of the one subject to the threat of sanctions. Assuming a diffusion of sovereign power, the one whose acts were subject to superior judgment would be divested of that independence which Austin identified with sovereignty. Such a procedure could give those exercising such judgment an unlimited power.[35] The obvious rebuttal to this line of reasoning is that in such circumstances the possibilities of abuse of judicial power is a risk worth taking, if it prevents other branches from acting arbitrarily. In fairness to Austin, however, it should be observed that he evidenced an awareness of the dangers of arbitrary government, but looked to general public enlightenment as the most effective remedy.

In a wider sense, Austin's analysis of political society, sovereignty, and positive law does not comprehend either the importance of judicial review or the status of constitutional law as a body of fundamental principles which is enforced, or at least effectively invoked, as the law of the land. While he stated that constitutional principles could be understood as a "compound of positive law and positive morality" he did not anticipate the degree to which norms having a substantial ethical content would be accounted as law. This deficiency of conception raises the larger question of whether the

rigorous distinction between law and morals as it has been espoused within the analytical tradition has any justification.

For Austin, jurisprudence should limit its attention to the commands imposed by sovereign authority; laws which actually exist in
a political community without regard to their moral quality. Many
have found in this restriction an encouragement of arbitrary
power, and there is undoubtedly some truth in the criticism. But
there were reasons for maintaining a clear distinction between positive legal rules and other normative phenomena. These reasons
make the strict separation not only understandable, but, to some
degree, justified.

In British philosophy, the drawing of careful distinctions between various standards to which human conduct can be referred
for evaluation has been an important methodological procedure.
When drawn into the field of jurisprudence, it became possible for
jurists to carefully distinguish between the types of norms which
measure human conduct. The methodological advantages corre-
sponded with a felt need to establish jurisprudence as an autonomous discipline, a task which required that the boundaries of the
new science be exactly defined.[36] In these circumstances, the separation of positive law from other standards was virtually inevitable.

There is also a tendency in British thought to identify legal rules
with prevailing ideas of justice and fairness. Hobbes reasoned that
justice, equity and other moral rules, while not properly laws in a
state of nature, become civil laws when the commonwealth is established and commands of the sovereign gave them obligatory
force.[37] Hume argued that the exigencies of social life made justice
necessary, and that the establishment of public authority was in
pursuance of that end.[38] Within this tradition, justice is not an
external entity to which positive law must conform.

> [W]hen by *just* we mean anything but to express our own
> approbation we mean something which *accords with some given
> law*. True, we speak of law and justice, or of law and equity, as

opposed to each other, but when we do so, we mean to express mere dislike of the law, or to intimate that it conflicts
with another law, the law of God, which is its standard. According to this, every pernicious law is unjust. But in truth,
law is itself the standard of justice. What deviates from any
law is unjust with reference to that law, though it may be just
with reference to another law of superior authority. The
terms just and unjust imply a standard and conformity to that
standard and a deviation from it . . . But justice is commonly
erected into an entity, and spoken of as a legislator in which
character it is supposed to prescribe the law . . . The . . . dolt
who is placed in a jury . . . will talk fiercely of equity or justice
— the justice of the case, the imperious demands of justice,
the plains dictates of equity. He forgets that he is there to
enforce *the law of the land,* else he does not administer that
justice or equity with which alone he is immediately concerned.[39]

The general conception is one which assumes that each citizen
will abide by the enacted law and that the application of such rules
will realize prevailing ideas of justice. Objections to legal rules
made in the name of justice are suspect as assertions of selfish
interest. There is force in Hume's argument that men are inclined
to choose their immediate advantage over the more general values
implied by the idea of justice. The institution of public authority is
designed to remedy the defect; the theory being that those not
having a direct interest should be intent upon a more objective
good.

Difficult questions of conscience, such as those implicit in jury
nullification and civil disobedience are not adequately dealt with
within this form of legal positivism and it is a serious defect. As to
disobedience, it is partially assimilated to the broader ranges of
positive law provided by constitutional developments. Objections to
a particular rule in the name of conscience include an appeal to
constitutional principles in the hope that the higher jural norms
will vindicate the claim. In a wider sense, sound principles of civil
disobedience may not be radically inimical to the preference for
positive law. There is a prima facie obligation to obey the positive
law. The conflict between moral and legal obligation implies a more
limited claim concerning the primacy of ethical commitments.
Moral imperatives require disobedience "at certain moments, not at
every moment, the refusal of particular legal commands, not of

every legal command."[40] With that qualification, the concern of analytical jurists that positive law should not be subject to constant revision on moral grounds can be considered as a meaningful contribution to the requirements of civilized existence.

~

In Austin's lectures the distinction between positive law and moral rules is stated with an unfortunate emphasis. In cases of conflict between the two orders he affirms the reality of the positive law.[41] Yet any assessment of his intentions should take into account the Lectures in their entirety, for they express a general subordination of positive law to higher principles. He continuously returns to the notion that Utility, understood as an index of Divine Commands, should measure the enactment and progressive development of positive law. The purpose of law is to promote human happiness. Even if we assume that such a teleological view was sincerely held, however, it is probable that the relationship between positive law and guiding principle is too remote to effectively curb arbitrary exercises of power.[42]

In Austin's theory, the existence of sovereign authority was determined by a relation of dependence. A subject populace submitted to superior power and the permanence of the bond was assured by habitual obedience. The possibility of rebellion was admitted in case the exercise of sovereign power reached a point of intolerable oppression, but the general idea was that of a unilateral projection of authority. The expectations of the citizen as to how lawmaking power should be exercised was placed at the outer margins of the theory, and there is no consideration of the requisites of an ongoing relationship between lawmaker and citizen. This conception should be compared with the idea espoused by Professor Fuller that law is a purposive activity designed to further a collaborative relationship between government and citizens with respect to the observance of rules.

The emphasis in Fuller's work is upon a procedural morality which can be observed in the workings of a legal system. He identifies principles of legality which constitute mutual expectations as to how legal rules will be made and applied. The publication of rules, the avoidance of *ad hoc* decisions, the need for congruity between rules as announced and their administration, the general avoidance of retroactive legislation, these, and comparable principles, are operative precepts within a legal order viewed as a common enterprise. They are not ultimate, external standards measuring the conscience of lawmakers. And they reveal some of the characteristics of an authoritative relationship within a politically organized society; responsibilities which interlock and must be observed if a system of human rules is to be maintained.

But what if procedural morality is not observed? Does the resulting situation deserve to be called law? Fuller insists that a *gross* departure from such principles would result in something that was "not simply bad law, but not law at all."[43] It may be objected that enforceable legal commands can in fact exist in spite of serious breaches. But this can be affirmed only if the perspective and expectations of the citizen are not taken into account. One who has experienced the extensive use of arbitrary procedures might be surprised to be informed that what had been suffered was law; he would be more inclined to the explanation that he had met with the application of naked power.

It is further objected against Fuller's analysis that a purpose may evidence the pursuit of evil as well as good. Indeed, the ruler may observe the procedural rules out of his desire to impose and maintain an efficient but evil legal system. Such criticism fails to fully grasp the moral relationship between ends and means. As Fuller has himself observed, if efficiency is to replace moral purpose, the substitution will be successfully achieved at the price of doing violence to the integrity of law. Efficiency as a purpose is most fully realized by upsetting basic expectations as, for example, in the retroactive application of criminal rules.[44]

There is a further consideration which commends Fuller's observations to a jurisprudence which places emphasis upon the observation of experience. He identifies interactional expectancies which underlies the official establishment of rules and their public assimilation; a reference not to an ideal order but to qualities of moral reason operative within legal processes. Elements of social life embedded in jural experience are revealed which impose limits upon institutional authority and power. As they are grounded upon socio-legal observation, Fuller's insights extend the Baconian method of making reality intelligible. They are in continuity with that empirical disposition which we have identified as a characteristic of Analytical Jurisprudence. Such perceptions of interactions beneath the facts of power identify aspects of authority which are not accounted for in Austin's theory of sovereignty.

C. *MODERN ANALYTICAL JURISPRUDENCE*

Analytical Jurisprudence arose in the Nineteenth Century as an effort to confine the phenomenon of law within a framework of political authority and to develop a conceptual structure on the basis of empirical criteria. This attempt to establish an autonomous science of positive law was not successful. Failure was partly the result of weaknesses inherent in the theory, and because positive law was being influenced by other modes of knowing which promised a greater jural intelligiblity. Confidence in the capacity of inductive methods was in decline and the need for more reliable, abstract criteria was keenly felt. Progressively, empirical legal phenomenon were being reduced to logical categories, a trend best exemplified by Kelsen's Pure Theory of Law.[45] The tradition traceable to Bacon was being replaced by that confidence in mathematical and logical forms of reasoning which is the heritage of Cartesian thought.

Following the Second World War, the position of Analytical Jurisprudence was precarious. Its prestige had been reduced by the Pure Theory of Law. The analytical tradition, as a form of legal positivism, also received a considerable amount of moral criticism. Natural law thought was being revived in opposition to all theories which excluded an ethical dimension from legal definition. Under these circumstances, analytical jurists had to combat two forms of abstraction. It was incumbent upon them to demonstrate that positive law could be understood according to an empirical, rather than a logical methodology and to arrest the drift towards metaphysical explanations associated with natural law.

The work of Professor H. L. A. Hart[46] is the primary example of the new Analytical Jurisprudence. Professor Hart sought to demonstrate that the older analytical positivism could not adequately explain the nature of rules. The basic idea of the Austinian tradition, as we have seen, was that law consists essentially of sovereign commands coupled with threats of sanction in case of disobedience. This implied that legal rules consisted of externally applied measures of conduct. But a good deal of legal experience would not fit this conception, at least if normal uses of language were respected.

For example, wills and contracts are acts *in the law,* expressions of powers or facilities conferred upon individuals, and not the fulfillment of imposed duties. Similarly with public power. An act of legislation is not a response to a command carrying a threat of sanctions; it is rather the exercise of an authority. In these circumstances, failure to follow the rules is not an act of disobedience. Such acts may be nullified or declared invalid, but it would be improper to equate these consequences with the imposition of punishment.

That people *have* legal powers suggests a consciousness of authority or an inward dimension to the concept of rule. How members of a group use rules is as important to our understanding of law as is the idea that rules consist of obligations imposed from without. Even the basic concept of obligation has an inward aspect since it implies a social bond existing between persons. Thus, violations of obligatory rules involve more than "bad man" predictions of what officials will do. To speak of one as having an obligation provides not only a prediction of hostile reaction. Viewed from the perspective of those who maintain rules, it provides *a reason for* the hostility.

Hart's method, particularly its stress upon the inward dimension of rules, is not without precedent. Sir Henry Maine had described the observance of rules in communities where there was no obvious political authority. Amos, building on Maine's insight, had held that the primary characteristic of laws was the manner in which rules are felt to be obligatory by the social group. The history of law was the "evolution of customary rules out of the innate genius of the people."[47] What distinguishes Hart's method is the central role he assigns to inwardness in the general understanding of law. For Amos, the rules of the group and the development of political authority were two interacting phenomena. Hart's genius consists in the fact that he pushes analysis beyond considerations of political organization and anchors the definition of positive law upon an anthropological foundation. Law as a total phenomenon arises within, and is understood by, evolutionary human consciousness.

In this view the meaning of law is derived from the development of societies. A primitive community is maintained by certain basic rules, mostly prohibitive in character. A maturing society requires some method of removing doubts as to what are the rules, means of providing for their public and private modification, and procedures for determining when the rules have been broken. Positive law, the existence of which corresponds to these needs, consists of primary rules of obligation supplemented by secondary rules of recognition, change, and adjudication.[48]

A legal system in this conception is to be understood as the group sees it, not as it might be derived from principles of sovereignty. It is grounded in concrete social life, known through the experience of all who use rules as the basis of private claims and official decisions. This change of methodology involves a profound shift in the empirical and experiential aspects of Analytical Jurisprudence. Under Austin, the science of positive law was built upon the raw facts of political and legal experience. It grew out of a mentality which emphasized the observation of external data. The new analytical jurisprudence reflects the more contemporary movement which concentrates upon consciousness as a more authentic index of meaning. In a larger sense, the new approach to the phenomenon of positive law derives from an intellectual effort to understand the being of man in concrete social existence rather than abstract thought. It is a manifestation of philosophical anthropology.[49]

Because it is not tied to a vertical concept of authority, Modern Analytical Jurisprudence is able to encompass a much broader range of legal experience than was possible through the Austinian method. Acts in the law, such as wills and contracts, gain a greater significance, and professional commitment to "private lawmaking" is brought into prominence. Seen as social bonds, rules are sustained by the commitment of citizens and officials, rather than as precepts imposed from without by threat of sanction. These insights make more intelligible many contemporary aspects of legal process which cannot be comprehended within Austin's frame of reference. The secondary rules of recognition, change and adjudication, which mark the way that evolving societies modify the primary rules to meet the exigencies of growth, are also a significant development. These are concepts of great potential which can illuminate some of the more intractable areas of legal experience.

The general method of modern analytical thought, particularly in its reference to conscious experience, has advanced understanding of the judicial process. Since the beginning of the century, explanations of adjudication have shifted from external predictions of "what courts do in fact" to an emphasis upon the decisional choices of judges. To some, that discretion was a paramount datum; others related the inner perspective to a general field of

norms. Professor Dickinson's criticism of the older theory suggests
such a balance:

> 'The view that law is a prophecy of what will be decided has
> the weakness of emphasizing exclusively the outside specta-
> tors' point of view . . . and consequently of ignoring the point of
> view of the judge . . . [t]he sound way to anticipate a future
> decision is to attempt to put oneself in the place of the judge
> who will find himself confronted with one or more legal rules
> applicable, or conceivably applicable, to the case before him.
> For him these rules cannot be conceived as mere rules of
> prediction. He is not interested in predicting what he himself
> is about to do. The standpoint of prediction is that of the
> observer; the judge's attitude towards the rule is that it is a
> guide or mandate for action. . . .[50]

If a relationship between primary and secondary rules is assumed, obedience to a superior need not be postulated in order to
understand that judges, in their discretionary use of precedents,
are responsive to general rules. Hart's conception of the nature of
positive law accounts, in this instance, both for discretion and authority. It is an improvement over the positivism of Gray as well as
that of Austin, and it provides a more subtle analysis of the lawmaking power of courts.

The degree of discretion possessed by judges depends upon the
position of their court in the judicial hierarchy. This calibration can
be better explained by an inward perspective, since the authority of
lower court judges is *subordinated to,* not *derived from* the higher
courts within the jurisdiction.[51] But difficulties remain in determining the status of the various laws applicable to decision. This is of
particular importance because as the psychology of personal judgment is accentuated, jural constraints upon discretion become
tenuous.

According to the principles of Legal Realism,[52] adjudication did
not involve the application of legal rules to diverse facts. The
search for similarity between the facts of earlier cases and those of a
present controversy was made, existentially, by each judge; rules
were *discovered* in the process of determining similarity or difference.[53] Viewed in this way, precedents are not *pre-existing rules.*
Professor Hart has pointed out that extreme realism ignores the ways
in which precedents are used as general standards of conduct. In
advising clients, lawyers have recourse to prior decisions, and,

while there are large areas of uncertainty, it would be erroneous to describe all legal advice as a service which is rendered provisionally. There is not a constant recourse to courts.

As for the judicial process, Hart contends that rules derived from decisions have a core meaning of clear application, but also a penumbra of doubt. When cases arise within the open texture of a legal rule, the judge exercises a discretionary power.[54] This position has been attacked as being incompatible with the rule of law. For it implies that when existing rules do not dictate a certain result, a judge may reach beyond the law for some other standard to guide his judgment. Professor Ronald Dworkin has articulated this criticism in a form which, while ostensibly a critique of analytical legal positivism, bears some continuity with its principles and methods.

To understand how discretion is constrained one must view courts in an institutional context. This draws attention to their role in a democracy. Litigants appear before judges not to request favors, but to demand that they be accorded that to which they are entitled by the law. As a participant in an institutional process, the litigant deserves to receive from the judge his best judgment as to what are his legal rights. Litigation raises expectations of entitlement. Even in cases where decisions are not clearly dictated by relevant statutes and precedents, the judge is bound to refer to existing law and authoritatively resolve the plaintiff's claim.

In order to establish his thesis that in "hard cases"[55] judges do not exercise a free discretion, Dworkin argues from perspectives which extend the general philosophical approach which is characteristic of Modern Analytical Jurisprudence. We have already noted how modern analyses refer to a certain inward awareness in elucidating the nature of positive law. To perceive more fully the nature of the judicial function, Dworkin relies upon an empirical self conscious; a phenomenology of adjudication which provides a philosophical explanation of how judicial lawmaking is constituted in experience.

For example, by reflecting more closely how judges use precedents one can understand that the problematic of precedent involves more than general rules inductively extracted and applied to subsequent cases. At least in difficult cases, judges disagree about what rule or principle the precedents should be understood to have established. The argument *for* a particular rule may be more important than arguments *from* that rule to the particular case.[56]

Dworkin, and others of a similar mind, make a strong case for
the proposition that the judicial process is self sufficient, and that
the judgments of individual judges, operating within this institutional framework, should be based solely upon the discovery and
extension of legal rights. It is opposed not only to Hart's theory of
discretion, but also to theories of adjudication which include social
norms within the applicable sources of decision. Whether the judicial function can be understood as excluding reference to social
standards or policies[57] is a question which we may postpone until
the second chapter, where the general influence of sociology will be
examined. Of more immediate interest is Dworkin's contention
that not only ordinary civil litigation but also constitutional adjudication can be comprehended within his model.

The latitude available to judges interpreting constitutional
norms is notorious. While recognizing the interpretive leeways,
Dworkin insists that here, as elsewhere, discretion is constrained by
law. He acknowledges the special complexity of constitutional adjudication, and advances a sophisticated exposition of judicial reflection to meet the difficulties. The ideal judge dealing with such
issues recognizes that constitutional theory is dipolar: drawn toward political and moral philosophy, but also established in institutional expression. His own selfconscious reasoning must refer al-
ternatively to each source of meaning. In deciding difficult cases of
due process and personal liberty, he cannot avoid drawing upon his
philosophical conceptions as he also seeks to gather understanding
from text and precedent. Ultimately, the judge must rely upon the
soundness of his own belief in the proper meaning of the fundamental law.[58]

Earlier, we pointed out that constitutional adjudication raised
important questions of judicial supremacy. The Supreme Court of
the United States, when it interprets the Constitution and applies it
to pending cases, is exercising a form of final authority which sur-
passes simple adjudication. In such circumstances the Court exercises a power of recognition since it must decide what are the fundamental rules. This power must be measured by some standards
of authoritative decision-making. The principle danger to be met is
that of judges imposing their own subjective views of the higher law
upon the public.[59] Dworkin insists that his model judge is projecting his understanding of *the law* and not his own personal convictions. Even in constitutional cases, the positive law rather than the
judges' unbridled will, is the authoritative point of reference.

But it is difficult to see how the Dworkin thesis restrains arbitrary decision. The judges' opinion reflects what he honestly believes the constitution requires, even if it includes his own intellectual and political convictions. This is probably an accurate self-conscious view of the reasoning process. But it does not adequately account for the political role of the Court. Dworkin recognizes that the judges' conception of constitutional law is influenced by a social *milieu,* but his insistence upon the personal quality of judgment leads him to underplay the public dimension of the constitutional process.

A Supreme Court justice may understand the due process clause as invalidating any constraint upon a fundamental liberty. Thus, he may consider an anti-abortion statute, or a law imposing the death penalty, or one outlawing certain sexual practices between consulting adults, to be unconstitutional. Such judgments would be contrary to public morality but not, in Dworkin's view, arbitrary. In such cases, he argues, the judge would not be enforcing his own opinion against that of the community, but rather would be noting the inconsistency between these specific enactments and the basic moral precepts which sustain the Constitution.

There is much force and some truth in this argument; however, it is not fully responsive to the requirements of authoritative decision-making. The Court must protect the individual from the passions of the majority, but if it is to nullify communal action in the name of fundamental law it must appeal to standards which the court and the public share. The legitimacy of the Court depends, in significant measure, upon the degree of public acceptance of its decisions.[60] To attain such consensus it must justify its interpretations of the Constitution with reference to standards of fairness and human dignity which are broadly held within the larger society. Without the larger frame of consciousness, Dworkin's theory remains subject to the criticism leveled against it by the person whose own theory it was meant to disprove. Professor Hart has raised:

> The crucial question ... whether the new theory can escape Bentham's criticism of Blackstone's theory, namely that it was a fiction which would enable the judge in the misleading guise of finding what the law behind the positive law really is, to invest his own personal, moral or political views with a spurious objectivity as already law.[61]

If we continue to inquire how modern analytical thought contributes to our understanding of courts a further observation may be made which concerns the role of the jury. Jurors, like judges, exercise a discretion. This participation of citizens in adjudication is constrained by allocations of competence and by the responsibility to exercise discretion in conformity with basic rules. But juries do render verdicts contrary to the rules, and this aspect of discretion needs to be illuminated by jurisprudential inquiry.

The discretion of jurors not to apply applicable rules is tacitly accepted, but efforts to make that discretion explicit are generally resisted. The resistance is at least partially influenced by an earlier positivism which placed jurors in a subordinate position under the commanding power of trial and appellate judges.[62] The framework which Professor Hart articulates for comprehending a legal system, with its emphasis upon conscious participation, may provide greater justification for the jury's power to deviate from existing law.

Jurors act within the category of adjudication. They are involved in determining whether the primary rules have been broken, and in applying appropriate sanctions. They are charged by the court as to what the law is; but, particularly in criminal cases, they may render a verdict of acquittal contrary to the announced rule and evidence. Is this simply the inevitable consequence of discretion, or does it possibly imply that juries participate in the other secondary rules of change and recognition? As representatives of the community, do they not modify the rules, or, in certain instances have the power to determine what are the basic obligations? Whatever the proper conclusion, there is no *a priori* reason why the exercise of this public power should not, in its own way, be as creative as that possessed by judges.

The pervasive implications of the theory of secondary rules can be perceived more clearly, however, with reference to the judicial power. Courts are obviously organs of adjudication, but, in spite of Dworkin's thesis, it is a common place that they legislate interstitially. More subtle difficulties are raised when courts are asked to assert their jurisdiction under circumstances in which such authority may properly belong to the legislature. Whether a rule of comparative negligence should be introduced by the judiciary or the legislature, whether courts are competent to abolish an immunity, or whether the legislature rather than the courts should introduce a new cause of action, are all examples of a general problem of competence which is an important part of modern legal process. In such cases there are no precise criteria for ascertaining which organ has legitimate authority. Rather determinations are made in a manner which corresponds to that inward acknowledgement which characterizes the functioning of a rule of recognition.[64] Through their mutual deferences judges and legislators manifest their acceptance of largely unstated principles by which the various legal organs are authorized to determine what shall be the law.

A further major interest of Analytical Jurisprudence has been the analysis of basic legal concepts. Austin included the study of such terms within the objectives of General Jurisprudence and he devoted some of his lectures to the analysis of pervading notions. His followers refined the meaning of basic concepts but they generally remained within a framework which assumed that legal rights and legal duties constituted the fundamental legal relations. Some development could be noted in the work of Sir John Salmond, who distinguished a range of legal advantages—rights, liberties, powers and immunities from legal burdens—duties, disabilities, and liabilities.[65] An American jurist, Wesley H. Hohfeld, made further progress in the exploration of basic conceptual structures.

To move analysis beyond the basic dichotomy of legal rights and legal duties, Hohfeld developed a scheme of jural relations, classified as "opposites" and "correlatives." The correlatives: right, duty; privilege, no right; power, liability; immunity, disability; have been influential but they have also been subject to severe criticism. The scheme has been attacked because it cannot be consistently applied to concrete cases, a fault allegedly derived from Hohfeld's interest in Hegelian logic.[66] His basic purpose, however, was to increase understanding rather to solve cases, and his capacity to differentiate legal concepts are as much traceable to developments in the scope of empirical knowledge as to the influence of logical thought.

The radical empiricism of William James, which was widely influential, was premised on the belief that an adequate philosophy of experience should take into account the relations between things as well as the multiplicity of distinct phenomena. A grasp of these diverse connections is essential if we wish to observe the fullness of any domain of fact.[67] The disjunctive and conjunctive relations between legal terms, in all their nuances of meaning, presented fresh jurisprudential possibilities.

The search for the lowest common denominator of actual legal relations was within the spirit of inquiry promoted by an American philosophy of experience. There has, however, been a tendency to reduce the multiplicity of legal terms. Using the power of logic, Kocourek produced novel insights. But his contraction of terminology shares with Goble's reduction of legal concepts to relations of power and liability a pursuit of abstract unity which overlooks the complexities of legal relations.

Even if a universal meaning cannot be predicated of particular jural terms, a more extensive conceptual vocabulary can be justified by the variety of legal experience. Inductive methodologies are no longer understood as revealing general laws which invariably apply to all occasions; yet some intelligible meanings can be derived from a limited range of concrete phenomena. We are able, as Alfred North Whitehead observed, to ascertain "some characteristics of a particular future from the known characteristics of a particular past."[68] Basic legal concepts have a relatively stable significance even if, on some occasions, a particular term develops a different meaning or is assimilated to another concept. Legal privilege and legal immunity are illustrative. Referring, respectively, to suspension of duty and freedom from liability, they possess distinct and separate meanings which legal draftsmen are, practically speaking, compelled to take into account. Within such contexts, they reveal empirical diversities which are irreducible to more basic terminology, and testify to the vitality of an empirically oriented jurisprudence.

In modern Analytical Jurisprudence, as with the Austinian tradition, there is an interest in operative legal concepts. In this regard, the new Analytical Jurisprudence has been substantially aided by improvements in linguistic philosophy. The later work of Wittgenstein was particularly important, since he came to realize that attempts to reduce language to simple logical units could not be reconciled with the complexities of empirical reality. Words and phrases have an immense range of meaning, and a proper understanding of language demands consideration of all the variants of actual use.[70] These principles were applied by Hart in his critique of Austin. By using the tools of linguistic philosophy, he was able to uncover deficiencies in the Austinian conception of positive law. The idea of obligation, for example, was significantly clarified through the distinction between the expressions "being obliged" and "having an obligation."[71] The new analytical positivism has also applied linguistical methods to illumine the ways in which legal concepts are used in the operation of a legal system. Bentham insisted that basic legal concepts such as power, right, and duty were essentially "fictions"; and that to understand what such words actually meant, one must understand what operations the law performs. "Knowing thus much we shall have ideas to our words: not knowing it we shall have none. . ."[72] Similarly, Professor Hart insists that a proper understanding of legal concepts requires that we carefully consider the function that such words perform in the operation of a modern legal order. Close attention to the varied uses of legal language restrains the urge to find a single meaning, since we become conscious of the flexible uses to which words may be put within the functioning of a legal system. The varied meanings of the concept of rule[73] is illustrative, and comparable analyses can be made of other basic terms.

The new analytical jurists have also made contributions to the difficult question of vagueness. Insisting upon a careful examination of how legal concepts are actually used, they check the desire to make an apparent vagueness of language an excuse for projecting personal or social values into the meaning of legal terms. This aspect of the analysts' work deserves more attention than it normally receives. To put it in proper context, it should be understood in its relation to American Legal Realism.

Legal Realism[74] grew out of a concentration upon the judiciary in jurisprudential thought. Gray's definition of positive law as the rules made and enforced by judges stimulated a general interest in the functioning of courts. As we have already observed, the view that precedents were a self-contained body of rules was challenged by the realists as incompatible with the discretionary character of judgment. Law, including that made by judges, was gradually being understood as a process of social decision. The relationship between rules and policy became a central jurisprudential theme. The vagueness of legal concepts, their "open texture" was emphasized. Where jural content was missing, emotional values could take up the slack.

Modern analysts have criticized this trend as being inattentive to the degree of precision obtainable where the actual use of legal

language is carefully observed. In Hart and Honore's CAUSA-
TION IN THE LAW,[75] the tendency of jurists to reduce difficult concepts such as proximate cause to matter of "policy" is countered
with examples of the range of meaning which causative language
has actually acquired within the legal process.

This reaction to legal realism is valuable not only in itself, but also
because it suggests further reflection on the phenomenon of
vagueness. There is a psychological dimension to the problem. Demands for precision of language occur in a great variety of contexts
which should be systematically examined. It is important to be alert
to the motivations which lie behind the call for clarity. Some situations evoke canons of construction expressing judicial policies favorable to a litigant. Justice Holmes' view that in criminal cases "fair
warning should be given to the world in language that the common
world will understand"[76] is a familiar example and one which has
general support. The so-called "void for vagueness" doctrine raises
more complex issues. Broad punitive language creates a strong
threat to civil liberties: consequently, demands for precision are
strong. If the operation of the vagueness doctrine was subject to
linguistic examination, a better understanding of this constitutional
doctrine might emerge.

In determining the constitutionality of a statute challenged for
vagueness, a court must imagine possible adverse applications of
the words in issue. How far such projections may legitimately be
made is difficult to determine. However, extensive evocation of
overbreadth can conceal the personal preferences of judges as
much as reveal actual dangers to litigants. The insistence of
modern linguistics that language has meaning only in context may
help form an intelligible outer boundary for the legitimate uses of
the void for vagueness doctrine. A challenged legal rule is an attempt to communicate guidance with reference to some forms of
specific conduct. The language used often has a concrete, if common, meaning. Considerations such as these are often obscured
when one freely constructs, in a vacuum, innumerable possibilities
of interpretation.[77]

The emphasis within modern Analytical Jurisprudence upon specific empirical experience can impede, as well as promote, jural
understanding. Some of the limitations can be seen in the controversy over the meaning of *mens rea* in criminal law. In developing a theory of criminal law, Professor Jerome Hall, an American
jurist, has defined this central term as consisting essentially in the

voluntary doing of a morally wrong act forbidden by the law. Professor Hart, however, would restrict the concept to the voluntary commission of a legally forbidden act.[78] This narrow reading of *mens rea,* which brings the excusing conditions into prominence, is an important contribution to the administration of justice. It rejects the emphasis upon external standards of responsibility which were part of the tradition of positivism, and asks instead whether, in a particular case, it would be just to punish an individual who lacked requisite knowledge or consent. This focus of inquiry also respects the person as a choosing being; a respect which should be reflected in the way that criminal sanctions are administered and applied. It is also preferable to social theories which would eliminate punishment entirely and replace it with a system of compulsory treatment for individuals with detectible criminal tendencies. Restricting *mens rea* to a dimension of voluntariness has these positive advantages, yet it is not satisfactory as a general explanation of the purposes of criminal law.

The basic difficulty lies in the extreme individualism of the theory. *Mens rea,* so defined, is justified as an application of Kant's maxim that men should never be treated only as means but also as ends. It also seeks to maximize personal choice. If individual decision becomes an operative factor in the criminal law, one is enabled to predict the likelihood of sanctions and can weight the prospects of punishment against the satisfactions which may be obtained from a breach. In this view, criminal laws are best understood as guides to conduct and the application of sanctions is determined by individual decision to conform or disobey.

This reasoning raises the objection that such a *rationale* of the criminal law is immoral or anarchic. Professor Hart's reply reveals the weakness of his theory. He contends that the approach is not immoral, provided that "bad" laws are considered as being within the scope of his argument. For in disobeying an odious precept the individual asserts his dignity and dramatizes the unethical character of that particular law. But if compliance with the criminal law is understood as a succession of singular choices, it becomes impossible to attain a coherent view of the phenomenon of obedience.

With respect to the more serious offenses, obedience is generally understood as not being optional. This characteristic is consonant with two primary aspects of modern Analytical Jurisprudence: the notion of primary rules and the concept of obligation understood as a bond between members of a social group. The obligation to obey is intelligible as a normal duty which can, in a given instance, be overridden by a more compelling moral claim.[79] Such an explanation of obligation is ethically cogent and is compatible with Hart's desire that one should not be punished unless his action was authentically volitional. However, if this much is granted, it remains necessary to consider Professor Hart's objection to the inclusion of a moral element in a theoretical definition of *mens rea*.

Professor Hall understands *mens rea* as the voluntary doing of a morally wrong act. Professor Hart rejects this definition:

> [I]f this theory were merely a theory as to what the criminal law of a good society should be, it would not be possible to refute it, for it represents a moral preference: namely that legal punishment should be administered only where a 'morally wrong' act has been done . . . But of course Professor Hall's doctrine does not fit any actual system of criminal law because in every such system there are necessarily many actions (quite apart from the cases of 'strict liability') that if voluntarily done are criminally punishable, although our moral code may be either silent as to their moral quality, or divided. . .[80]

The objection misconstrues the manner by which Professor Hall reached the definition of *mens rea*. The definition is *theoretical*; it is not offered as an informative report of empirical data.

In working towards his definition of criminal law Professor Hall was faced with the problem of establishing a stable generalization out of vast numbers of punitive rules within the field of criminal law. He chose a non-inclusive approach, one which included within its scope the major felonies and misdemeanors. He concluded that it was possible to define a substantive field of law, even if it required some exclusion from the resulting definitions.

The method can be defended as a legitimate means of arriving at a theoretical definition. A theory is not offered as a description of particular acts; it is rather an attempt to discover principles which account for the use of words.[81] The definition of *mens rea* expresses its actual use within the criminal law: it identifies its common characteristics, integrating the situations of its dominate usage by judges and other officials who administer criminal justice. The search for common elements is based upon an observation of jural reality. While it involves some postulation of moral purpose, the primary justification for the definition is that it describes, in a general sense, what the expression *mens rea* means in the operation of criminal law.

At a deeper level, the divergent analysis of Professor Hall and Hart suggest fundamental differences concerning the scope of jurisprudence. Modern analytical positivism is not favorably disposed towards generalizations about the nature of positive law. One may, in theorizing, miss more subtle, concrete nuances of meaning. But such objection cannot be applied in the present context. Professor Hall's definition of *mens rea,* as well as his general theory of criminal law, is not a construct of a possible, good society; it is a descriptive-normative theory of the positive law. It is certainly not immune from criticism, but it should be judged on its own premises. The definition does not purport to include every possible instance, but its generalizations are based upon experience.

To provide a systematic explanation of a particular subject, and to elucidate its basic concepts, some distinctions and exclusions are inevitable. The results are justified provided we are left with an organized set of propositions which interrelate the primary concepts so that their significance, in themselves and in relation to the entire system, are made intelligible. If the theorizing is empirically grounded and logically pursued, it should be unobjectionable even if it perceives some moral purposes at work within the positive law. To observe that ethical meanings guide the use of legal concepts does not imply approval of their interpretation or application in a given instance. But the fact that a legal concept possesses a moral connotation cannot be ignored. The alternative is an exaggerated emphasis upon empirical description which, while ostensibly inclusive, tends eventually to narrow comprehension.

The controversy between Professor Hall and Hart can also be understood in terms of a disagreement over the relationship between positive law and morals. Professor Hall sees normative elements within the empirical data. Professor Hart prefers to view moral standards as external measures by which one can evaluate the positive law. The study of basic moral concepts such as justice, liberty, and equality which closely parallel the concerns of positive law are part of the pedagogy of Analytical Jurisprudence. But a complete legal philosophy should also consider the extent to which legal concepts and institutions have within them qualities of moral import.

Basic concepts which are essential to the definition of law provoke a desire for a further elucidation which, in part, is of a moral character. Professor Hart views the concept of command as a term more suggestive of authority than coercion.[82] The distinction is well taken; but what is meant by authority? As used within the legal order, it carries meanings which, in some measure, elude empirical designation. Many central legal concepts also have an ethical component. Norms guaranteeing due process and the equal protection of the laws are obvious examples, but a moral dimension can be found in more pedestrian areas of the positive law. The concept of "unconscionability" in the Uniform Commercial Code illustrates how basic concepts can have a meta-empiric significance.

While there are moral elements within the existing law, it is important to note how the search for ethical meaning can deflect accurate comprehension. Determining the proper meaning of legal obligation is illustrative. Under the premises of analytical positivism, the validity of a positive law is not dependent upon moral criteria. To say that a legal rule is valid, is to acknowledge that it passes the tests provided by the rule of recognition. Therefore, a judgment that an organ enacting a law is competent to do so does not necessarily include reference to principles of morality or justice. Since a specific legal obligation arises upon determination of validity, it follows one may be under a legal duty to obey valid laws which are unjust. Such a conclusion appears to be offensive to moral sensibility.

In dealing with such a problem it is important to keep in mind what the definition of positive law offered by modern Analytical Jurisprudence is designed to achieve. The basic objective is to reveal an anthropological structure which can explain the evolution or development of legal systems. This concept of law is derived from philosophical reflection upon the general features of evolutionary consciousness rather than from a consideration of moral experience. Much of the criticism of Hart's theory could be moderated if this distinction was kept in mind. Further, if the concept of validity was intrinsically connected with moral criteria, many practical insights into the actual workings of a legal system would be obscured. One who is properly served with process has a legal obligation to obey the orders of the court issuing such process, even if its jurisdiction is defective. The obligation obtains until reversal by higher authority. This is a general principle of validity, which is often applied over moral objections.[83] Determinations of the competency of other legal organs are similarly made, and they are devoid of moral criteria other than fundamental considerations of order.

Conceding this, there remains some force to the objection that the concept of legal obligation needs further elucidation. The social bond which sustains obligations undoubtedly reflects a general conviction that the body of laws in question are morally defensible. However, we still remain uneasy, because without an explicit justification of specific laws we may be drawn back to the notion of "being obliged" which was the heritage of Austinian jurisprudence. It has been proposed that an ethical understanding of legal obligation can be obtained through the methods of ordinary language analysis. Situations in which one were legally obliged could be distinguished from those in which officials made conscious reference to moral principles in imposing a legal obligation.[84] In assessing the value of the distinction one should not demand too much moral explicitness from the positive law. The autonomy of the legal order does not necessarily imply that it has no valuable ends. Indeed, as a system for establishing and enforcing rights, positive law promotes important humanistic goals:

> "Rights are not merely gifts or favors . . . a right is something a man can stand on, something that can be demanded or insisted upon without embarrassment or shame . . . A world with claim rights is one which all persons as actual or potential claimants, are dignified objects of respect, both in their own eyes and in the view of others . . .[85]

Law justifies its compelling force more by reference to that objective than by explaining its call for obedience in terms of essentially moral criteria.

~

Analytical Jurisprudence began with the assumption that the nature of a legal system was intimately connected to the idea of a sovereign political authority. The relationship between ruler and subject, and the institutions necessary to enact and enforce positive law, were understood as being dependent upon the existence of an organized state. While there was some deviation from this framework—as with Amos's treatment of international law—the general assumptions persisted. Shifts in institutional direction, such as concentration upon the judiciary as a supreme power, were consistent with the original premise.

Modern Analytical Jurisprudence, as exemplified in the work of Professor Hart, constitutes a fundamental break with this tradition. The Austinian approach is considered deficient because its emphasis upon external power could not satisfactorily explain the existence of rules. To gain a full understanding of this central concept, an inward perspective has been adopted. This revealed that a shared acceptance of basic rules, and of procedures for changing them, was essential to the concept of law. These insights, of profoundest importance, were achieved by extending analysis beyond the usual postulates of political organization, and by uncovering structures of social evolution which are basic to human experience.

Positive law is now understood in terms of primary rules of obligation and secondary rules of recognition, change, and adjudication. As this conception is based ultimately upon criteria of evolution—a movement from primitive to more developed legal systems,—it attains greater depth than was possible when concepts of sovereign authority were considered indispensable to legal cognition. But it is pertinent to consider whether basic separation between the realms of positive law and political organization is either possible or desirable.

Secondary rules are described in THE CONCEPT OF LAW as powers conferred upon public officials and private individuals to achieve socially desirable ends:

> "without such private power-conferring rules society would lack some of the chief amenities *which law confers upon it.* For the operations which these rules make possible are the making of wills; contracts, transfers of property and many other voluntarily created structures of rights and duties which typify life under law . . ."[86]

It has been pointed out that rules of change supposedly conferred upon private individuals or groups refer primarily to capacities rather than powers. Marriages, wills, the formation of contracts may be done or performed by anyone provided they possess requisite abilities. Secondary rules do not, in such situations, confer powers upon individuals; they regulate a presumed capacity. Some powers, however, such as power of attorney, are directly dependent upon governmental permission.[87]

There are other situations in which the facts of political institution make a difference in our understanding of secondary rules. One illustration involves the phenomenon of nullity. A court decision in excess of jurisdiction can be quashed on review, but it is considered valid if no appeal is taken. By contrast, wills and marriages which do not comply with legal requisites are void *ab initio*. The failure to distinguish between capacities and powers, and to consider distinctive nuances is a deficiency in Hart's theory traceable to the substitution of general social consciousness for the phenomenon of political organization. If the emergence of a constitution, express or implied, rather than a shift from primitive to mature conditions is treated as the distinctive mark of a legal system, some of the confusion concerning the nature of secondary rules could be overcome.

At the global level, a stronger case can be made for the separation of jurisprudence from political theory. In international relations, there is no effective supra-national authority; but law undoubtedly exists. Some order has appeared through the evolution of customary rules and the extensive acceptance of treaty obligations. This horizontalism,[88] is reinforced by the jural structure of modern Analytical Jurisprudence.

Professor Hart contends that the absence of a supreme political authority simply reflects the fact that international society is operating, in the main, with a set of primary rules. The phenomenon may properly be called law, not only descriptively in terms of a discernible order, but also philosophically, for reasons which are based upon the evolution of social consciousness. The forms of horizontal order which exist within the international realm are law because states have chosen to obligate themselves by such restraint at this period of human history.[89]

This confirmation of horizontalism provides a deeper support for practices which, because of the absence of central authority, are necessarily precarious. The Security Council, acting under Chapter VI of the United Nations Charter, cannot *compel* disputing states to settle their differences, but it can *remind* the parties of their treaty obligation to seek the resolution of the conflict by peaceful means. The conceptual framework of modern jurisprudence also provides international law with useful analytical tools for identifying jural phenomena. Doubt as to what are the rules is pervasive, since many primary norms have not been incorporated into formal treaties. Through declarative resolutions the General Assembly of the United Nations may, under some circumstances, express the meaning which the international community ascribes to these basic rules. The purpose of such resolutions, whose content consists of customary rules or general principles of law, is to authoritatively verify whether such legal norms exist.[90]

In spite of these important contributions, modern Analytical Jurisprudence, with its apolitical premises, is not responsive to the deeper needs of the world community. For beneath the formalities of state practice there lie enormous propensities to violence which are beyond the power of horizontal ordering. Balances of terror in the field of armaments and the widespread violence both across and within the boundaries of states, are the true measure of progress in contemporary world society.[91]

That these anarchic conditions imply the need for some form of higher authority should be evident. But the imperative does not fit meaningfully into the new jurisprudence. That is because understanding is confined within an evolutionary framework, and the problematic of international authority is reduced to a question of growth. The development of international society is now at a point of history in which states have chosen to adopt predominately decentralized forms of law. For the analytic mind, considerations of supra-national authority are matters of future maturity and development: refinements towards which we are now perhaps moving, but not indispensable to sound juristic theory.[92] An evolving consciousness of movement towards maturity cannot perceive anarchic conditions as *essential* moral deficiencies.

The deeper question, however, is whether there can be law without security. It is a question which draws us back to the starting point of these reflections on the history of Analytical Jurisprudence. For Hobbes, the establishment of political authority was required by social circumstances which bear considerable resemblance to the contemporary human condition. That disposition towards violence, endless conflict, and constant defensive postures which constituted for him the state of nature have become the expectation of millions of human beings, who are, presumably, the beneficiaries of international law. It is fashionable to ridicule Austin's conclusion that international "law" is not, strictly speaking, law because it lacks coercive authority.[93] Yet the founder of Analytical Jurisprudence had a sound grasp of the requirements of order derived from his awareness of the importance of political authority.

If the science of jurisprudence is to be relevant to the exigencies of universal society it must renew its contacts with theories of political organization. Some autonomy may be lost, but the gains in terms of the relevance of legal philosophy to the advancement of life will more than compensate. This is not to argue, of course, for a literal revival of the Leviathan, but only for a reconsideration of the factors which lead Hobbes, Bentham, and Austin to believe that a substantial connection exists between concepts of political authority and the science of positive law. In the foreseeable future, a general connection between the fields of law and political theory will be indispensable to enduring reform. To see the inadequacy of a definition of law made without reference to political institutions is a necessary step towards such progress.

The history of Analytical Jurisprudence is marked by a sustained effort to separate the science of positive law from disciplines which have traditionally impinged upon it. In an important sense, modern legal philosophy is a study of how well this objective has been achieved. In this review of the empirical analytic tradition, we have considered the establishment of jurisprudence as an independent, self-sufficient discipline and the effort of analytical jurists to work out the basic elements of a philosophy of positive law. As we have seen, a paramount concern has been the desire of these jurists to distinguish their field from the related disciplines of ethics and political theory. We must now turn to a further intrusion upon this quest for independence: the influence of sociology upon the science of positive law.

CHAPTER TWO

THE ADVENT OF SOCIOLOGY

A. *INTRODUCTION*

D uring the nineteenth century, while Austin
and his successors were establishing a science
of positive law, a new science was emerging in
Europe which would constitute an important challenge to the
autonomy of jurisprudence. This was sociology, the science of society. According to its founder, Auguste Comte, sociology was to be a
complete science of social phenomena. Its arrival marked the culmination of efforts of the mind to attain a comprehensive understanding of human life. In earlier epochs, the effort was sustained
by theology and metaphysics; both, according to Comte, pseudo-
sciences which would not be replaced by the definitive science
which he was establishing.

For its methodology, the new science would draw upon the
genius of DesCartes and Bacon, "the founders of true philosophy,"
but surpass them in its techniques of cognition. DesCartes' contribution, the revival of mathematics, provided the tools for a general perspective but it was to the spirit of Bacon that Comte gave his
deepest homage. The objective of sociology was to study man in
society and for this the observational methods introduced by Bacon
would, when refined, be of primary importance. Biology was also
an important ally. Its emphasis upon the growth of living or-
ganisms provided a model for the understanding of society as a
developmental reality. Modern biology also accentuated the complexity of phenomena and the relativity of our understanding.[1]

Comte was anxious to attain a proper balance between reasoning
and observation. No proposition which was not reducible to fact
could be intelligible; but, as a science, sociology was to be composed

46

essentially not of facts but of laws. No facts were to be considered scientific unless connected with others, at least with the aid of a justified hypothesis. This method would be valid for the entire realm of social experience. The task of sociology was to observe the subtle interconnections among social facts; the laws of action and reaction within an entire social system.

Even the potentials of human development would fall within the scope of this science. The dynamic side of social life could be grasped through the use of provisional hypotheses of human progress which could be subject to positive verification. All other study of social reality was to be subordinate to the positive science of sociology. Law was a metaphysical vestige "absurd as well as immoral." In the new age of humanity there were to be only duties resulting from social functions, obligations based upon morality and love.

This cognitive imperialism was continued by Durkheim. For him, the social sciences of law and economics would become branches of sociology. Problems of epistemology could be solved only by a sociology of knowledge and sociology of law would replace the instruction given in law schools. As the new science developed these hegemonical tendencies would persist, part of a continuous struggle between sociology and legal positivism as each seeks a predominate role in explaining jural phenomena.

The basic realities of social life could be sufficiently identified by the sociological method to provide the beginnings of a general theory of law and society. In his Principles of Sociology, the Englishman Herbert Spencer revived social contract doctrines to explain the existence of political organization and its subordination to individual human happiness. But the general thrust of sociological thought was moving in a contrary direction. Durkheim sharply criticized both Hobbes and Rousseau for making individual existence the primary social fact. This, he argued, forced them to conceive of social restraint in terms of an artificial organization. Natural Law and evolutionist theories, alike in seeing social and political life as natural, were also individualistic and thus unacceptable:

> Neither of these doctrines is ours. To be sure, we do make constraint the characteristics of all social facts. But this constraint . . . is due simply to the fact that the individual finds himself in the presence of a force which is superior to him . . .

It does not derive from a conventional arrangement which human will has superimposed, fully formed, upon natural reality. It issues from innermost reality; it is the necessary product of given causes . . .

. . . [I]f . . . we say that social life is natural, our reason is not that we find its source in the nature of the individual. It is natural rather because it springs directly from the collective being which is, itself, of a *sui generis* nature, and because it results from special development which individual minds undergo in their association with each other, an association from which a new form of existence is evolved . . .[2]

As for contractual explanations, they involved a contradiction. Contracts are a result, not the cause, of society.

The political theories of Hobbes assumed, as we have seen, that society without government was chaotic. The reason for this spirit of combativeness was elucidated further by sociological theorists. From their perspective, unorganized social life is essentially a violent struggle for power and domination. The strong control the weak. But the hegemony is precarious because the instinct for emancipation is intense and continuous. Political society emerges when both realize that the struggle can only be extended at a cost which outweighs the benefits. Here force sets a limit to itself; state and law are called to life by a common interest in peace and order.

The state has a contingent and conditional existence. Society, for the sociologist, is the primary and supreme reality. Organs of government are intelligible, not in themselves, but in their organic connection with the social *milieu* in which they arise and which sustains them. The state is a social association, the forces operative within it continue to be social forces. The powers which control society control the state. All its functions, including lawmaking, are caused by the dominate social powers.

The subordination of state to society also affected the idea of sovereignty. In the earlier theories which had shaped Analytical Jurisprudence sovereignty signified absolute political authority: a right to govern unlimited by legal restraint and capable of being exercised independently of those who are subject to its commands. Metaphysical conceptions of the state developed on the Continent of Europe were, in this respect, comparable. The state, endowed with a distinct personality or collective will, pursued its own ends. It was limited only by laws which were self-imposed. For the sociologist such absolute supremacy is fictitious. Duguit expressed the opposition most forcefully. Social solidarity, a fundamental law of unity and purpose, was the primary rule of conduct. It determined the powers and duties of "social man in general, and the man invested with political authority in particular."[3] Solidarity is a law which exists outside of, above, and in a superior position to sovereignty.

The primary datum is that all life is group life. Individuals find themselves, by necessity and choice, existing within groups and associations which shape the course of their existence. The internal structure of these groups, their mutual interactions, and their relationship to the broader society were for the sociologist the phenomena of primary interest. This new orientation of thought would seriously challenge the orthodox theories of legal positivism which tried to understand law in isolation. The state and positive law were no longer self-sufficient entities. They were integral parts of broader social realities which were now becoming intelligible.

B. *SOCIOLOGY OF LAW*

The problem of positive law, conceived sociologically, was to determine the relationship between the legal order and the order obtaining within social groups. The Austrian jurist Eugen Ehrlich sought to enlarge the scope of jurisprudence by identifying the points of contact between the decisional law of the state and the "living law" of the community. The contrast was established through a demonstration of how associations create their own normative order.

Each human grouping—the family, social and religious associations, economic entities and relationships, political organizations, has an inner structure which results from the action and reaction of forces within it. Through an equilibrium flowing from relations of domination and subjection, rules are established which determine the purposes of the association and the role which each must play in it. Since the state and positive law are social institutions, the nature and limits of positive law can be fully understood only in relation to this ordering which occurs within the innumerable associations which constitute the concrete life of society.[4] To explore this relationship more fully Ehrlich made a distinction between a legal proposition and a legal norm. The former refers to all the jural precepts contained in statutes and decisions; the latter to any command which has become effective in practice. Legal propositions are largely derived from the order within associations and they can only become legal norms if effective within the association to which they are meant to apply.

The contrast between these two realms is accentuated by the fact that at any given period every society has more norms ordering its inner life than it has positive laws created by government organs. These insights into the interdependence of social and legal order constituted a repudiation of the idea that jurisprudence should be restricted to an analysis of the institutions, rules, and concepts of positive law. The task of a modern legal science was to distinguish those norms which actually regulate society from juridical propositions which purport to command but which are not actually effective.

The significance of Sociology of Law is well established and its basic insights have become an integral part of modern jurisprudence. The futility of the prohibition laws, the coordination of constitutional law with social reality, studies of actual behavior in fields as disparate as commercial and penal law, all reflect, in a fragmented way, the general influence that sociology has had upon legal philosophy. We have not, however, consistently applied a general science of societal ordering to the evaluation and appraisal of legal doctrines. Such an approach is perhaps too suggestive of ideology and incompatible with our pragmatic temperament. Nevertheless, it is important to observe some of the ways that a theoretical sociology of law can improve our understanding of legal processes.

The importance of a structural comparison between social and juridical ordering is illustrated by the development of tort law and liability insurance. With limited exceptions, it had been assumed that all controversies arising out of accidental injury should be resolved through the conventional forms of litigation. The victim was entitled to a judgment for damages suffered if he could prove both the defendant's negligence and his own freedom from contributory fault. The applicable theory assumed that the defendant was personally liable. In fact, damages were usually paid by the defendant's insurer, and if there was no liability insurance, there was often no recovery.[5]

The growth of the insurance industry has resulted in a large economic "association" which can be analyzed according to the criteria established by Ehrlich. As tort law developed, this association and the judicial process were simultaneously asserting an authority with reference to the same subject. The industry had its own order concerning which claims arising out of accidents were to be considered; this regime paralleled and, in many respects, competed with, that of the judicial system. The norms applied within the industry to claims have often been derived from positive law, but modified and interpreted to serve the purposes of the dominant power. Negligence and causation have a meaning for the insurance adjustor which is quite different from the interpretation placed on these terms by the average juror. For its part, the judicial system has generally tried to operate without reference to the social facts of insurance, leaving it to the legislatures to make fundamental reforms.

With the advent of "no fault" insurance, substantial changes are now occurring in the automobile accident arena as well as in other aspects of tort law. Here, as in many other areas of modern life, legal policy has lagged behind social reality. An earlier conscious attention to the realities of the insurance system and its actual effects upon the administration of justice could have accelerated the tempo of reform and made the relevant legal processes more credible.

A greater awareness of the general ordering within society is necessary if positive law is to be an instrument of justice and human progress. In the study of social reality, economic power is a phenomenon of primary importance. Attention to factors of domination and subordination is needed to protect the individual from exploitation by corporate capitalism. Social thinkers such as Marcuse have portrayed the plight of "one dimensional man" whose existence is threatened by large economic forces and by the dehumanizing effects of uncontrolled technology,[6] and such insights have a jural significance. They can illuminate the deeper meaning of legal controversies and reveal factors of injustice which legal formalism may not perceive.

Improvements in the law of products liability have been made possible, in part, because specific legal issues have been viewed against the background of economic realities. In *Henningson v. Bloomfield Motors*[7] the Supreme Court of New Jersey extended implied warranties of merchantability to the user of an automobile not a party to the original contract of sale. Attention to the relevant economic structures placed the controversy beyond the bounds encompassed by traditional norms of contractual liability. The court acknowledged the existence of a mass marketing system within which remote automobile manufacturers stimulated demand by advertising to attract buyers to purchase automobiles under terms set by the industry. Aware of that ordering, the court decided that the absence of privity should not prevent a producer for being liable to the ultimate user for injuries suffered because of a defect in the product.

Progress in the realization of civil and political rights is also dependent upon awareness of social facts. The pursuit of racial equality by courts and legislatures is aimed at bringing social structures based upon domination into line with constitutional ideals of equality. Consciousness of injustice is aroused when disparities are perceived between social and legal norms; between an ordering created by social forces and what is commanded by the rule of law. The most intractable problems of race relations, such as housing and school integration, are intelligible within the overall framework of a sociology of law, and a similar analysis can be made of sexual discrimination supported by traditional social norms. Women suffer indignities because their roles have been previously fixed, not only by the general culture, but by the facts of male dominance in the family and within the business, educational, and professional associations in which women seek to enhance their life prospects. An imposed normative ordering has been the social reality: it is now the task of positive law to restructure these relationships according to the requirements of personal freedom and dignity.

An adequate jurisprudence should take into account the basic elements of a Sociology of Law, since at every juncture, the legal and social orders intersect. Neither the need for, nor the limits of, legal coercion can be understood unless the social structures with which law must deal are brought explicitly into focus. A general understanding of social systems and of the forces of power and reaction within the important social associations, is essential to the progressive development of a modern legal system. While the general interactions between the legal order and social life are given, it remains to consider more closely the quality of the relationship.

In the encounter of law with social reality it is important to determine, as far as possible, the degree of mutual influence. An assertive sociology would see the legal judgment as not only re-

sponsive to, but also determined by, social forces. But while awareness of the facts of social ordering aids the administration of justice,
it does not control the decision. In the Henningson Motors case,
the court took judicial notice of the dominant position of the automobile manufacturers, but its judgment was guided by jural
principles of fair dealing. The gross inequality of bargaining position between manufacturer and purchasers made the limited express warranty unacceptable. A sociologist might argue that the
"jural" principles are, in reality, social values; norms of the broader
society by which the particular controversy must be measured. Yet
even if some social origin is conceded, the broader standard is of a
jural nature. Its functional meaning has been shaped, and re-
shaped, by the courts and the legal profession.

When matters of fundamental law are at issue, the relationship
between social and legal norms is more complex, because it involves
questions of judicial power and authoritative competence. The application of social norms to the solution of constitutional issues can
be resisted on the theory that they represent the views of a dominant majority seeking to impose its prejudice upon a persecuted or
repressed minority. In the controversy over capital punishment it
has been frequently argued that societal judgments are only reflections of the instinct for vengeance. However, the Supreme Court
has decided that at least some statutes which provide for this ultimate penalty reflect principles of retributive justice.[8] Such a con-
cession to societal precept can be taken as an abdication of the
Court's responsibility to uphold individual dignity.[9] A routine
sociological justification: that legitimate legal power must respect
social norms, is plainly inadequate. But it may be equally erroneous
to assume that a radical opposition between legal norms and social
values is necessary to sound adjudication. Some judges of the highest integrity[10] have reconciled in their own minds a deference to
social *mores* with a deep commitment to individual freedom. Without compromising the primacy of liberty they have recognized the
legitimate role which the larger society plays in the quest for the
meaning of the Constitution.

A concrete decision may be guided by jural rather than social
forces; but once the legal order ratifies an emerging social aspiration, the new value tends to have a general influence upon legal
development. In the post-Henningson era, the doctrine of implied
warranties has been extended to areas of consumer need by reason
of the impact of changing economic forces as well as through the

creative use of precedent. The consequences of social struggle for the development of law are often beneficial since the pressures for change can breathe new life into dormant legal precepts. But there are also hazards. The decision of the United States Supreme Court in *Brown v. Board of Education*, [11] signaled the beginning of a legal, as well as a social, revolution. It has brought about a wave of legislative, administrative, and judicial actions designed to realize the promise of racial equality. As part of the process, courts have reexamined existing laws and sought to impart meanings consistent with the new social aspiration. Unfortunately, in some instances, results have been obtained which compromised the integrity of the judicial process. Reinterpretation of civil rights statutes in light of the new social ideal is a case in point. For example, in *Jones v. Alfred Mayer, Inc.* [12] the Supreme Court interpreted § 1982 of the Civil Rights Statutes as barring private and public racial discrimination in the sale or rental of property. The statute was enacted in the Reconstruction era following the Civil War. The judicial decision was made while a contemporaneous Congress was passing Fair Housing Acts designed to end racial discrimination in that field. The decision was arguably consistent with the literal language of the statute, but it strains credulity to suggest that the court's interpretation faithfully reflected the intention of the 1866 Congress.

~

Legal decisions responsive to a struggle against imposed ordering are also expected to promote a new equilibrium within the relevant social association. The expansion of products liability has undoubtedly influenced changing practices within the economy such as buyer protection plans and other emerging modes of promoting consumer satisfaction, although it remains to be seen whether new marketing practices will fully satisfy the jural standards. Subject to such residual supervision, it is important that whenever positive law promotes reform the autonomy of social life be recognized in the processes of readjustment. The positive legal order must preserve its independence and integrity; so also must social groups affected by law reform be allowed a substantial measure of autonomy in their effort to adapt to change.

These complementary truths are often forgotten by reformers who, from a position of legal power, would impose a new realignment of social relations by force of law. The coercive pressures which some government agencies apply in order to achieve non-discriminatory hiring policies is a current example, and judicial policies designed to achieve an integrated society may be subject to the same criticism. A primary justification for extensive intervention is a belief that without it, existing patterns of domination cannot be transcended. Jurists, however, should not fall victim to simplistic explanations of social life. Such an assumption may betray a Nietzschean conception in which the will to power serves as the decisive explanation of human acts.[13] In such a view there is little recognition of Santayana's belief in liberty as the slow cooperation of free men.

In the process of social change, the enforcement of legal right must be supplemented by changes in social relations based upon mutual respect and good will. If, as sociology maintains, social life has its own forms of ordering, a legal solution of social conflict is necessarily inadequate. Positive law can effectively concentrate its remedial power on the rights of those suffering subjection, but it is beyond its capacity to reconstruct the underlying social relations. That full reconciliation is beyond the power of courts or legislatures is a general truth which bears upon sexual, as well as racial, relations.

The changing attitude of law towards marriage reflects a movement from imposed regulation towards a jural policy which protects the personal liberty of the parties in establishing and dissolving the marital union. Replacing the hierarchial family model, the process of equalization of the power and rights of the spouses is well advanced. The law is leaving social conduct surrounding marriage to private ordering. But there has not been any notable restructuring of heterosexual unions upon stable foundations. This failure to establish a new *social* order as an alternative to traditional marriage has led to a more pervasive intrusion by the state. Government agencies are significantly involved with the economic consequences of marital dissolution,[14] a development which indicates the dangers incident to a vacuum in social relations.

The current instabilities in marital relationships are due to innumerable causes, but a factor of prime importance is the principle of spousal autonomy. The prevailing policy of the law is to accentuate the independent individuality of the married persons rather than the community of life which exists between them.[15] This emphasis has some justification, but, pushed to an extreme, it betrays an ignorance of the ingredients of permanent union.

If the prevailing trends towards marital dissolution are to be checked, greater attention must be given to the relevant sociological data on the importance of the family. Here the emphasis is upon the creative, positive value of associational life; it is in the context of voluntary relationships of permanent intent that individuals prosper. Sociological research has shown the vital place of the family in individual motivation and achievement and the wider prosperity of social life which flows from stable[16] unions.

There is a deeper difficulty which is intimately bound up with the quest for equality and the profound aversion to hierarchial ordering which it entails. It has been asserted that *any* form of subordination is incompatible with the principle of equality, because offensive to human dignity. But the extreme leveling of differences can also flow from envy and a failure of mutual respect.[17] Moreover, the maintenance of any social association requires some allocations of competence and the family, viewed as an association, should be able to establish its inner order in terms of collaboration[18] instead of domination.

The interpenetration of jural and social phenomena also occurs upon the global plane. At the level of international society the basic insights of a sociology of law have significantly increased our understanding of its juristic qualities. By focusing upon actual behavior sociological jurists have expanded understanding of international law beyond the narrow framework provided by legal positivism.

The General Assembly of the United Nations, for example, is not empowered to act as a legislature. On strict premises of positivism, its resolutions would not possess legal significance. Yet on some occasions the Assembly exercises a rule of recognition. Its resolutions can be a means of detetermining what are the basic rules of international life.[19] Whether the Assembly has the authority through its resolutions to develop or change the rules can be answered, if at all, only on sociological terms.

If supported by a sufficient consensus such resolutions may be functionally operative even though not formally binding. They may have a legal quality when, in the interactions between member states and other officials, the norms contained in such resolutions become relevant to expectations concerning what is or is not permissible behavior.[20] The degree of authoritativeness which any particular resolution possesses depends upon contextual analyses which belong more to the practical order than to theoretical reflection. We will consider some of these details further in the chapter, in connection with an appraisal of the methodology of the policy sciences. But before leaving the field of Sociology of Law, a further bearing of its general insights upon international law should be mentioned.

Customary rules which favor the interests of developed industrial nations have been challenged by emerging nations because they were established under historical circumstances of economic and military domination. Again, structural perception: an awareness of incongruity between formal rule and social reality has profoundly affected general understanding of customary law. Discontented with an imposed ordering, they resist international prescriptions which, while ostensibly fair, reflect the interests of the more powerful states. Here, as with developments in domestic law, awareness of economic realities is essential to a just evaluation of the inevitable conflicts. Conditions of equality or inequality determine whether a nationalization program affecting foreign investment is in fact discriminatory or undertaken for an unlawful purpose.[21]

The widening and pervasive range of conflicts between the developed and developing world which now characterizes international life is susceptible of various explanations. For the Marxist, they reveal an authentic movement of history: the passage of man, through stages of exploitation and resistance, to a new humanism. An orthodox sociologist may see the deepening struggle as the prelude to a new order; one which will emerge when the cost of continued conflict outweighs the benefits to both weak and strong nations. Whether these insights will, in the long run, supply the requisite vision of lasting peace remains to be seen. Much will depend upon the breadth of conception within which one understands the phenomenon of law.

C. SOCIOLOGICAL JURISPRUDENCE

Sociology of Law assumes that a general science of society is indispensable to an understanding of the nature of positive law. By observing the structures of social organization and their capacity for ordering life the jurist can test legal rules by contrasting them with the rules of conduct obtaining within social groups. But social facts also have a direct bearing upon the administration of justice. People have desires of which they are more or less conscious and which they wish to satisfy. They make demands upon the legal order: claims that these wants, or interests, should receive jural recognition. A practically oriented jurisprudence must concentrate upon the immediate interplay between these demands and the creation of law.[22] The purpose of positive law is to establish and protect legal rights, but these rights are means for securing the interests which the law recognizes.

The basic principles of a sociological jurisprudence were established in Germany by von Ihering and transplanted to the United States by Roscoe Pound. The situation of law in America at the turn of the century made it a propitious time for new direction. The judiciary had achieved a position of eminence in both the state and federal legal systems and its posture of administration was rigid. The prevailing spirit was one which understood law as a body of self-sufficient rules from which one could inexorably derive the solution of controversies. Pound was acutely aware that this "mechanical jurisprudence" was illusory; that in fact decisions involved choices between equally authoritative, competing, lines of reasoning. He also realized that the gaps of interpretation and application were being filled with value judgments.[23]

The general pressure of social demands made upon the law was being ignored or resisted by judges not only because of their devotion to the law, but also because the interests being asserted were incompatible with the values which they sought to maintain. In Nineteenth Century America law was adjusted to an ideal of rugged individualism; the self-sufficient and responsible person provided the ultimate model for juristic effort. But this ideal, appropriate to a rural, agricultural, and expansive nation, could not be readily applied to an urban industrial society. By making specific, or cataloguing, the various interests which the law had recognized as well as those which were pressing for recognition Pound sought to bring the legal order into closer alignment with social reality.

Interests are divided into individual, public and social classifications. Individual interests are those of personality, domestic relations and "substance," i.e., claims of an economic character. Public interests include claims made on behalf of political institutions; demands made to assure the existence and efficient functioning of the State. General interests include the broad, basic values to which one should refer in seeking to make an adjustment of conflicting interests. The adjustment constitutes public policy. Six general interests are catalogued: those of general safety and order; demands for the security of domestic, religious, political and economic institutions; the interest in general morals; the interest in the conservation of resources; the interest in the advancement of civilization or general progress; and the interest in the individual life—the demand involved in civilized existence that wants be satisfied, at least to the extent of a human minimum.[24]

He also sought to improve the moral dimensions of decision making. Inevitable judgments often masked a personal preference of judges, and it was expected in Pound's reform that an understanding of all the interests involved in controversy would broaden the parameters of responsible judgment. The realization of justice had been identified with the exact application of statute and precedent. But this could not be reconciled with the growing awareness of judicial discretion. Abstract natural law was discredited, and an alternative was necessary if discretion was not to be arbitrary. Pound borrowed from Stammler the idea that those responsible for the administration of justice were obliged to make the empirically conditioned principles of law just. The objective was to achieve a relative, rather than absolute, justice; a justice for the time and place. Relativity was tempered because a personal desire to be just would be paramount. It was to be a justice according to law.

The general importance of Pound's contribution can be seen in its relationship with Analytical Jurisprudence. Pound's legal philosophy strikes a balance between sociological and legal data. He fully accepted the reality of positive law and the need for a politically organized society with instruments of coercion. Because of his insight into the social objectives of a legal system, he was able to widen understanding and avoid the dangers of isolation implicit in an autonomous positivism. And the breadth of experience upon which Pound relied broadened the inward scope of positive law. Drawing upon legal history as well as sociology, he revealed deficiencies in the understanding of human law as espoused by Austin and his followers.

Law is a part of civilization. Men and women have wants and desires which, when aggressively asserted, conflict with the expectations of others. These antagonisms must be reconciled by some measure of reason made effective by organized political force. In seeking to establish an ordered society, men have drawn upon both moral and political ideas. Their understanding of law throughout history reflects both of these influences.

To restrict the idea of law to a system of rules is inadequate because it identifies only one part of the body of precepts which courts and administrative agencies draw upon in resolving conflict. Principles which provide starting points for legal reasoning, standards for measuring behavior, and general legal conceptions are equally essential. The entire body of authoritative materials for guiding decisional acts must be acknowledged if efforts to define the nature of law are to be commensurate with reality.[25]

For the analytical jurist, it was a distinct advantage to define jurisprudence as a science of *law,* as it avoids the ambiguities inherent in expressions such as *jus, Droit,* or *Recht.*[26] But, Pound argued, the multiple meanings inherent in these expressions more accurately reflect jural experience. They manifest a historical conviction that law should conform to ideas of justice as well as embrace claims of right which a legal order makes effective.

The importance which Austin and his followers attributed to the role of sovereign political authority was also deficient in that it promoted the narrow understanding of law as a body of coercive rules. Emphasis was placed upon the imperative element, the expressed will of the lawmaker. Insufficient attention was given to juridical development, to the manner by which the practices of tribunals, the modes of thought in the profession, and the refinements of juristic science were integral parts of law. Even Gray, who understood the central role of courts did not grasp the deeper significance of judicial activity nor the extent of which habitual experience in the administration of justice was integral to juristic understanding.[27]

Nor did the analytical positivists appreciate the degree to which judges, legislators and administrative officials rely upon the ideals of the society in which they functioned. To penetrate more deeply into the influences upon decisional choice, it's necessary to take into account the jural postulates of a particular age. Law is not the application of sovereign commands, it is an effort to make adjustments to a changing and progressive ideal of civilization.[28]

When viewed in terms of its larger objectives, an adequate definition of law is a composite of distinctive jural elements. Law can be understood as a body of authoritative precepts developed and applied by an authoritative technique in the light of authoritative ideals. It provides for the adjustment of the relations of human beings and the ordering of their conduct in society.

In common law countries, pursuit of the moral objective was properly the work of judges carrying on the traditional element of law. Legislators, guided by a general ideal, exercised the imperative dimension, the power of command. Adjudication was, or should be, a tradition of experience developed by reason and reason tested by experience. Judges creating legal rights participate in the exercise of state power; but this authority cannot be understood in terms of naked force. The establishment of a legal right is the recognition of an interest, and we should always be ready to question whether, in the light of the total scheme of interests and the ideals of the epoch, such a recognition is reasonable.

The objective of the legal order in this conception is neither the pursuit of power nor the realization of the will of a dominant class. It is a matter of responsible lawmaking, especially the responsible exercise of decision making authority by the judiciary. The demands and aspirations of individuals; their claims to possess, to act, to be free from arbitrary control, to live a humane existence—these are the starting points for a modern realistic conception of the administration of justice through law. It is an eminently civilized conception. It expresses a confidence that human interests can be recognized and harmoniously adjusted; brought into balance through the wise and careful application of legal precepts to the even-changing currents of human expectation and need.

Some of the developments within this form of Sociological Jurisprudence have been of a conceptual nature. Attempts have been made to state with greater precision the various aspirations encompassed by the generic term, interests. Demands, or claims, which are amenable to objective verification, must be distinguished from the more elusive and subjective connotations of desires, wants, or needs. Such distinctions are important, if only to insure that what is stated as an interest is in fact an individual claim rather than the expression of what a particular decision maker considers to be good for those who are subject to his choice.[29]

Pound's theory of interests has had an enormous influence both upon the development of legal doctrine and the administration of justice. The interests behind legal norms are recognized in Restatements of the Law, and judges at both the state and federal level have come to understand their role more clearly as a result of Pound's influence. A deductive enforcement of legal rules has been replaced by a moral effort to recognize as far as possible important claims of an individual, public and social character.

Difficult problems have arisen, however, in the application of the theory of interests to the administration of justice. It was assumed that the judicial process would be improved by an explicit acknowledgement of interests and by the reasoned transformation of interests into legal rights. The responsibility of judges in this century was to consist of a wise weighing and balancing of conflicting interests, with a general objective of securing as many as is possible with the least sacrifice to the totality.[30] Jurists such as Cardozo developed a wider theory of responsible decision making, but a general acceptance of the sociological conception was difficult to realize. The judge, according to Pound, was to formulate just precepts according to the social ideal of his time; but such a measure, borrowed from neo-hegelianism, was vague and morally unpersuasive. Nor did the proposals satisfy criteria of justice.

Pound's theory assumed that each decision maker would actively strive to be just and that the scheme of social interests would provide a basis for elevating that aspiration into a reasoned choice. But the theory tends to make *de facto* interests the criterion of justice and fails to provide an objective measure for determining whether particular claims should be secured. These limitations are partially defensible because Pound's overall objective was to identify, through the table of social interests, the values which had become or were becoming the public policies of the legal system.[31] The recognition of interests was in itself desirable since Pound, following William James, believed that the good consisted of satisfying demands. Some sense of overall balance served as a practical restraint. Nevertheless, the basic criticism is valid at least insofar as it points to the limitations of sociological explanations of decisional acts.

The one who decides must be convinced that the demand being pressed upon him, properly identified as an interest, is *entitled* to recognition. That determination is guided primarily by the relevant constitutional principles, legislative enactments, and the cumulative wisdom of judicial precedents. It is an effort to find the

just on the basis of jural experience. But these materials are not
fully determinative. Nor can traditions and techniques of judicial
activity, of themselves, replace the personal element of decision.[32]
A choice between competing interests is, in substantial controversies, inevitable. For an interest to be preferred, it must be perceived
as the claimant's due by the one responsible for judgment. Such
perception is no doubt intuitive. The judge sees a disparity between
a claimant's plight and common ideals. But judgment also involves
an acknowledgement of, and deference to, moral entitlement.
There is a personal recognition by the one who must decide that a
specific claim possesses an ethical cogency which should be accorded
legal protection.

A connected difficulty can be seen in the general charge that the
schema of interests provides a mask for subjective preferences. The
Legal Realists, in particular, concentrated upon the personality of
judges as the crucial element of decision. They stressed the influence of idiosyncratic biases. Legal principles allowed judges to give
a formal rationalization for conclusions reached for reasons peculiar to the individual decision maker. The procedures for justification allowed them to conceal the true basis for their decisions. In
recent years these suspicions have been concentrated in critiques of
decisions made by the Supreme Court of the United States.

The idea that in constitutional litigation judges should balance
interests has provoked two major criticisms. The first is that it inevitably leads to subjective choice rather than a realization of objective ideal. A process of weighing one interest against another leads
to judgments which are too particularistic, because a decision to
prefer one interest is made with reference to standards which are
more the personal values of the judge than they are social ideals.
The second objection raises the threat to constitutional rights implicit in any system of balancing. Mr. Justice Black was an articulate
exponent of the view that valuable freedoms were compromised if
subject to comparative evaluation against interests which the state
pressed for recognition.

The search for alternatives to constitutional balancing has
brought a renewed emphasis upon positivistic elements of judicial
lawmaking. Justice Black's insistence upon literal interpretation of
the Constitution[33] is an obvious example of a general movement
which has found more sophisticated expression. Professor
Wechsler's advocacy of principled decisions, based upon reasons
which transcend the immediate case, is a more forceful expression

of the need for judicial integrity and objectivity. A call for greater
articulation of the grounds for decision, for a "reasoned elaboration" which explains decisions in a coherent manner, falls within
the same *genre*.[34]

More profound reactions to the methodology of balancing interests have also arisen which, if adopted, would basically change the
conception of responsible decision making which Pound has articulated. A theory of interests assumes that judicial discretion will be
measured by traditions which promote reasoned adjustment of
value conflicts in the light of jural principles. Contemporary skepticism and doubt would cabin that discretion within narrow boundaries.

If certain "interests" are conceived as *competencies:* expressions of
social roles allocated to individuals or groups by the Constitution,
they can be immunized from the vagaries of balancing. This approach has the advantage of making fully explicit the origins of our
liberties. A claim of free speech is not just a demand for individual
satisfaction; its meaning and justification is derived from allocations of authority which pre-date the written Constitution. It refers
to particular social arrangements which suggest preferences as to
whom, in a given area, should have decision making authority.[35]

This method, if extended to a range of claims for personal freedom, would substantially reduce the hazards to which these values
are subjected in a general balancing of interests. But in spite of its
positive features this alternative contains some of the very dangers
which it seeks to avoid. Role distribution may express structural
premises which are reflected in the Constitution; it may also include the value preferences of those who make the allocation. Since
these distributions involve broad areas of decision making authority, the potentials for arbitrary choice in the assignment of roles is
significant.

This jurisdictional process is subject to the further objection that
its use bypasses the real issues implicit in litigation.[36] The Supreme
Court's primary responsibility is that of adjudication, a role which it
can only fulfill if it addresses itself directly to the adverse claims
asserted by the parties. In the field of individual or civil liberties,
the important cases involve a conflict between individual or group
autonomy on the one hand, and the assertion of a public or governmental authority on the other. The court should measure the
asserted interests against the theories of social life assumed by the
Constitution. But if it is to *resolve a controversy* the actual, antagonis-

tic claims asserted by the parties must be the focal point of decision. Courts have a constitutional duty to protect the individual from the exercise of arbitrary power and they quite properly have a preference for liberty. This legitimate bias should not, however, be generalized into jurisdictional rules which avoid the complexities implicit in any conflict between the individual and the society.[37]

The method of balancing interests has limitations, yet it is more conducive to the responsibilities of decision than the proposed alternatives. The scheme of interests formulated by Pound refers to a wide range of claims which have received varying degrees of recognition by the legal system. The division and subdivision of interests within individual, public, and social categories provides some rational guidelines for determining the quality of claims which are asserted in constitutional litigation. Furthermore, the survey specifies with admirable concreteness many progressive values while avoiding any dogmatic generalizations as to their scope. Carefully examined, they suggest lines of development rather than static demands. It is often forgotten that Pound placed at a supreme level of social interest the freedom of the individual from arbitrary power, as well as claims for fair opportunity of advancement and minimal conditions of a civilized existence.

That some judges may inflate certain interests at the expense of others suggests personal shortcomings more than an intrinsic deficiency in the theory of interests. Pound never tired of insisting that claims must be weighed on the same plane, if decision was not to be prejudiced in advance. He also believed that whenever individual claims are asserted against governmental power the interests of both must be put in general or social form in order to properly appraise their importance.[38]

The interests at stake in constitutional litigation cannot be mechanically weighed nor can they reveal, of themselves, the proper balance of decision. Neither can the scheme of interests be literally applied to a given controversy. Sound personal intuition must at some point come into play for the "sovereign prerogative of choice" to become operative. But if the spirit of Pound's theory is maintained, if all the interests involved are at least implicitly acknowledged, the possibilities of authoritative judgment are improved. We may then have a greater assurance that a court has considered the full context of a dispute and that the inevitable choices bear a relation to the basic value structure of society.

Modern decision making is increasingly influenced by sociologi-

cal method and where deficiencies are perceived the reaction of
jurists is usually expressed in some form of neo-positivism. The
attack upon a balancing of interests expresses a preference for legal
criteria of judgment. As Sociological Jurisprudence moves into a
more scientific phase this tension will be revived. We will then have
a further opportunity to explore the varied dimensions of responsible judgment. It is first necessary to trace a basic shift in the
direction of Sociological Jurisprudence, one which substantially influenced the development of Legal Realism and which culminates
in the policy science forms of jurisprudence which are now influential.

Pound's theory of interests brought social phenomena to the
attention of jurisprudence while simultaneously maintaining the
autonomy of positive law. But the effort to strike a balance was
unsatisfactory to some who believed that the social dimension was
receiving insufficient attention. Criticism was directed at the formulation of interests as demands, but it also cut deeper. A French
scholar expressed the greater discontent when, in an assessment of
Pound's work, he concluded that "while it is undoubtedly a school
of jurisprudence it is hardly a school of sociology."[39] The characterization of interests as explicit demands made upon the legal
order was superficial; it could only record the more obvious social
facts of behavior. Comprehension of social facts in their complex
interrelations should be the objective of a sociologically oriented
jurisprudence, but such a program was beyond the scope of
Pound's conception.

These criticisms reflected a growing understanding of the extensiveness of conflict in modern life. Interests were more than *de facto*
demands; they involved very complex and dynamic attitudes taken
by individuals and groups towards a constantly changing environment. Potential for conflict increased in proportion to the rapidity
with which life styles and opportunities were being transformed by
an expanding industrial economy. Antagonisms were generated
because demands could not be equally satisfied, and because in an
increasingly pluralistic society the range of common interests was
diminishing.[40]

Under these circumstances, the development of a more accurate sociology seemed imperative. Only by penetrating more deeply into the substance of social reality could one identify the full range of interrelations which reveal the causes and consequences of conflict. In Europe, there was a renewed interest in techniques of induction; the pursuit of general laws which controlled social facts. In America the influence of the philosopher John Dewey upon the jurisprudential dimensions of social science was profound.

Dewey's instrumentalism was a continuation of the pragmatic tradition. He shared with pragmatism a strong feeling for the problematic situation and the need for contextual theories of meaning. But Dewey's larger contribution came from his grasp of the philosophical import of scientific method and its significance for the illumination of experience.

Developments in the natural sciences, especially as exemplified in modern physics, had enormously improved the capacity of man to control his environment. These successes resulted largely from the attitude taken by scientists toward reality. For them, objects of experience were not, as in medieval science, given objects of knowledge; rather they were *data,* subject matter for further inquiry and investigation. From the perspective of modern science nature was a challenge, not a completion. A given occurrence was a problem which stimulated investigation to determine the relations of interaction upon which it depends. An active search for efficient causes had replaced the attempt to explain events according to ultimate, or final, causes.

According to the canons of experimental method, knowledge occurs when a problematic situation is resolved. Reflective operations transform data into *known* objects when the interrelations upon which a phenomenon depends are ascertained and the conditions and consequences of its happening are determined. Knowing is the fruit of Doing.

This emphasis upon mental activity underscores the value of intelligence to practical accomplishment. "Reason" was traditionally associated with an immutable order of nature: a realm of higher realities subject to intellectual perception which, when perceived, regulated human actions. Intelligence, by contrast,

> ... [I]s associated with *judgment;* that is, with selection and arrangement of means to affect consequences and with choice of what we take as our ends. A man is intelligent not in virtue of having reason which grasps first and indemonstrable

truths about fixed principles, in order to reason deductively
from them to the particulars which they govern, but in virtue
of his capacity to estimate the possibilities of a situation and to
act in accordance with his estimate. In the large sense of the
term, intelligence is as practical as reason is theoretical . . .[41]

The dualism between knowledge and action is overcome. There
is now an immanence to cognition. Intelligence is a participant in
the endless interactions of existence, becoming operative whenever
it directs changes to consequential ends. An instrumental logic provides procedures for reaching reasoned decisions whose value is to
be tested by their consequences in subsequent experience.

These conceptions of science and philosophy could be applied to
the perplexing realm of social conflict. Dewey perceived that at the
root of competition ideals were in conflict. Each had a conception
of his self-perfection, and, in a changing environment, efforts to
realize potential multiplied antagonism. If left unregulated conflict
leads to chaos; to the realization of false ideals and the domination
of man by man. Dewey sought to employ the improvements in
scientific method so that the situations in which values are affected
could be subject to intelligent control. Particular antagonisms must
be more precisely understood and, as known, related to the larger
moral experiences of the collective society. This meant a transfer of
the burden of morality to intelligence: a call to develop philosophies
of social experience which were at once empirical and also committed to the conservation and promotion of the basic aims of human
culture and civilization.

These philosophical premises required a revision of the concept
of law. Law is a part of social life, intelligible only within the context
of human interactions. Dewey perceived parallels between the progress of philosophy and the evolution of law. As philosophers and
scientists turned from the contemplation of eternal truths to the
control of experience, so also had modern jurists revolted against
the domination of metaphysical theories of law and sought empirical indices of meaning. Austin's definition of law as a sovereign's
command was illustrative of this trend. Its instincts were sound but,
as part of a naive empiricism, it was mistaken in its concentration
upon a single socio-empirical fact. Developments in the social sciences revealed the importance of a wide experiential range, a consideration of diverse empirical factors as essential to adequate
understanding. Human interactions crystallize into forms of be-

havior as the needs and interests seek relative forms of stable expectations. Habits became customs and customs are the source of law. But interactivities are continuous, and law intervenes and becomes itself a social process. Law is not a separate entity; it is what it does. And its sphere of action lies in its modification of human activities as ongoing processes.[42]

The influence of operational method upon jurisprudence can be seen in the work of Karl Llewellyn both in his critique of Pound and in his defense of legal realism. The focus of law, Llewellyn argued, should be upon all points of contact between the behavior of judges and other officials on the one hand, and the public or "layman" on the other. This would concentrate attention upon particular situations rather than generalized reflections upon the nature of the legal system. It would also mean that legal rules and concepts would not be uncritically accepted. For legal scientists, "real" rules would be factual or descriptive terms which have a predictive function: legal rules and rights would be considered as existent *qua* their effectiveness; in terms of their capacity to do something about a perceived need.

Underlying interests should also be more critically examined. As they reflect value judgments, more must be known about their origins and the consequences of their use. In Pound's jurisprudence there was too much verbal comparison. Words representing interests related to formulas said to constitute a rule of law. To move beyond unexamined meaning, the specific data said to represent an interest must be compared with the actual behavior of judges. This requires a close study of the practices of courts and the social impact on those practices.

Society is in constant flux yet it moves towards some purposes. If law is to serve those purposes, Llewellyn argued, there must be a systematic analysis of interrelations in particularized situations; systematic analysis, "not hit or miss stuff, nor the insight which flashes and is forgotten, but sustained effort." And there must be an enlightened objectivity of research. In setting objects for inquiry there is a need that the observation, description, and establishment of relations be freed, as much as possible, from the preferences of the observer and what he thinks ought to be.

In this call for a more realistic jurisprudence, Llewellyn was refurbishing empirical, analytical techniques which were an integral part of the common law method. But there was something new. An application of mental energy to practical problems which echoed the procedures of modern science and which instrumentalism had applied to law could now be perceived:

> New, I repeat, is one thing only: the *systematic* effort to carry one problem through, to carry a succession of problems through, to *consistently,* not occasionally, choose the best available technique, to *consistently* keep description on the descriptive level, to *consistently* distinguish the fact basis which will feed evaluation from the evaluation which it will later feed, to *consistently* seek *all* the relevant data one can find to *add* to the haphazard single-life experience, to *add* to general common sense[43]

The methodology of experimental science was beginning to affect jural thought but its influence was fragmentary. The full impact of operational thinking upon jurisprudence[44] would arise out of the collaboration of a lawyer and a political scientist: Myres McDougal and Harold Lasswell of the Yale Law School. Beginning with a seminal study of the purposes of legal education,[45] they have combined their talents to provide a comprehensive socio-juristic analysis of legal processes.

Here a more sophisticated understanding of social conflict precedes a comprehension of the nature of law. Social observation reveals that life in society consists of countless human interactions, occurring in various forums, where individuals and groups seek to achieve a wide range of values from differing positions of power. Antagonisms arise not because of a "conflict of interests" but because some participants in these social processes threaten to deprive others of values. The conflict must be resolved and the competing values allocated.

From this perspective law is a process of decision. Legal institutions are not autonomous entities. They are decisional agencies: part of a vast social process of value sharing and distribution. In this conception of law, power and authority are crucial terms since the pervasive issue is whether decisions are authoritative. Community expectations as to who is to make decisions, the scope of their authority, and the relevant procedures are integral to legal definition. Otherwise decisions, however controlling in fact, would not be law but rather exercises of naked power.

In this form of Sociological Jurisprudence paramount attention must be paid to the policy dimensions of decision making. A democratic society seeks to distribute, as widely as possible, all the basic values of human dignity. When power, wealth, knowledge, respect, and all other demand categories are *shared* they are goods; a society in which they are widely shared is a free society. In the exercise of decisional discretion the primary purpose is to maximize values. The objective should not be to realize one's subjective preferences, but rather to make choices according to criteria of preferred public order.

This reorientation enlarges the conception of the legal profession. By drawing attention to the pervasiveness of conflict and the variety of forums in which authoritative decisions can occur, the Lasswell-McDougal approach has helped to make a law student aware that his skills of counselling, advocacy, and persuasion will have application in contexts other than court litigation or the traditional advising of clients. And he may understand his role less in terms of the manipulation of ambiguous jural symbols and more in terms of the systematic study of decisional patterns. As a student, and eventually as an attorney, one must be interested not only in a body of rules, but in a process of decision in which rules become both authoritative and controlling norms of conduct.

This subtle and continuous interpenetration between legal and social processes requires highly developed skills of intelligence which must be used contextually in an effort to determine the authoritativeness of decisions. The human interactions which constitute the foundation of conflict as well as the consequences of conflict resolution must be dissected. To know whether prior decisions are law one must first know who were the participants, what values they were pursuing, the basis of power from which they operated and the strategies employed to realize their objectives. To comprehend whether decisions are authoritative and controlling a scientific inquiry must be directed towards the aggregate consequences of choice. The ideal is one of observing and canvassing all relevant past experience. Decisions cannot be viewed in isolation. All causes and consequences of decisional patterns must be reviewed comparatively, across boundaries, and through time. Cognition of law consists of knowledge of, and in, the decisional process.

The phenomenon of change provides the stimulus for reviewing the past and for attempting to forecase the future. Values, in potency, are demands made in human relations. In the complexity of modern life there are constant changes in the perception and distribution of values. Claims for revision are made, but they are resisted in the name of prior allocations. Inevitably the prescriptions and policies imbedded in decisional patterns are invoked. The scholar, the advocate, and the potential decision maker must comprehend and evaluate the authoritative status of these prior decisions which are now subject to challenge. Each, from his own perspective, must examine the flow of decisions and observe both the subjectivities and objective consequences of particular choices. Attention must be focused upon the social as well as the jural contexts in which such decisions were made. Analysis must be correlated with the constitutive processes by which decisional authority is established, as well as with the particular decisions which emerge from the constitutive process and through which public order values are maintained, revised and extended. The labor of intelligence is crystallized in five intellectual tasks designed to assure that the search for authoritative and controlling rules will be pursued through the most economical use of the skills of thought. The clarification of community policies at stake in the particular events to which decision makers must respond, the policies sought in prior decisions, the conditioning factors affecting such decisions, a careful projection of future trends, and the invention and assessment of alternatives in policy, institutional structures, and procedure constitute the intellectual operations which should assure that inquiry will be configuratively employed in relation to specific problems in context.

This so-called "New Haven approach" interrelates legal and social processes more intimately and comprehensively than either the sociological jurisprudence of Pound or the insights of the American legal realists. By focusing upon the value options implicit in decisional choice Professors Lasswell and McDougal, and their associates, have considerably enhanced the humanistic potentials of legal action. While their work has had a general influence upon legal study and comprehension, it has been particularly fruitful in its application to international law.

The decentralization which characterizes the international community makes it an appropriate field for a comprehensive inquiry into the features of authoritative decision. There is here an essential indeterminateness which encourages analysis along a continuum of shared responsibility between national and transnational officials. Juristic observation can proceed within wide margins, and the absence of formal political authority facilitates transition from legal to non-legal data. Contextually oriented jurisprudence has significantly contributed to the clarification of basic standards and policies which constitute the foundation of international order. This has been particularly true of those which concern the use of force, expressed both in customary law and in the principles of the United Nations Charter.

Terms such as "aggression," "self-defense," and "armed attack" are often assumed to have fixed meanings and be capable of exact application. They are, however, normatively ambiguous expressions whose specific meaning largely depends upon the facts and conditions underlying a given controversy and the policy objectives of those who invoke them. Moreover, basic policies of the world community are often phrased in rhetorical terms in a way which obscures the strategic purposes of those who use them. "National liberation," for example, has been invoked not only as an authentic cry for freedom, but also as a device for concealing coercive modalities of change. In emphasizing these contingencies and highlighting the variables involved in the uses of legal language, the Lasswell-McDougal school has done much to clarify the basic issues of coercion which plague the international community.

This approach to international law is controversial, as may be anticipated whenever the phenomenon of law is approached from a novel angle. But some criticisms come from scholars basically well disposed towards the new methodology. They are uncomfortable with the preference given to *policies* at the expense of *rules*.[46] Such dissents raise fundamental questions concerning the operative limits of this jurisprudential theory. The difficulties are part of a general tension which pervades modern legal philosophy: a desire to maintain an autonomous positive law competing with a need to understand law upon a wider basis of comprehension.

More severe critics have charged that an extensive implementation of the Lasswell-McDougal method in the international realm would make policy science a substitute for legal order. In a world characterized by fundamental disagreements and antagonistic ideologies, the conception of law as a process for maximizing shared values seems fanciful if not anarchic.[47] The response is that all action is for a purpose: some policy is operative whenever law is invoked and applied. This new form of Sociological Jurisprudence prefers to make policy options explicit. By drawing into consciousness both subjective preferences and the relevant inclusive values, it is hoped that decisions will gradually reflect policies of universal import. Nevertheless, a rule oriented conception of international law has stabilizing advantages which may be lost if the discretionary freedom of decision makers is exaggerated.

The suspicion that a policy science approach to law promotes insecurity is in part due to the strong concentration of the Lasswell-McDougal school upon the decisional capacity of national actors and the relatively weak attention given to the valuation perspectives of international officials. Such emphasis upon horizontal contexts, where values corresponding to national preferences are usually invoked, is not necessarily destructive of stability. General customary rules have evolved out of the processes of claim and counterclaim which constitutes state practice. However, the emphasis does prevent emerging standards and policies of the world community from becoming as functionally operative as would be the case if horizontal and vertical orientations were in better balance. Resolutions of the General Assembly and the Security Council can have an impact upon the actual behavior of nation states only if they are adequately taken into account[48] in a systematic analysis of authoritative global decision making. The failure to afford a fuller significance to the perspectives of transnational participants may be explainable in terms of fundamental commitment to national values. It can also be explained as an inevitable consequence of an action — oriented jurisprudence.

Sociological Jurisprudence seeks to understand law in terms of a correlation between legal decision and social reality. Sociology of Law, by contrast, is concerned more with the general structure of social institutions and the significance of this structure for legal cognition. The one is activist, the other more reflective, both in spirit and method. Sociological Jurisprudence concentrates upon decisional processes, and while it may be of broad conception, it inevitably focuses upon familiar decisional phenomena. Attention to levels of authority which are beyond immediate experience rarely became explicitly and systematically part of a working frame of reference. When they are considered, it is usually only insofar as they may illuminate the choices to be made by national officials.

The policy science approach towards the interpretation of international agreements illustrates a further difficulty of its methodology. The purpose of interpretation, from this perspective, is to discover the shared expectations of the parties; an objective which requires a thorough contextual analysis of all features of their communication. If recommended principles of inquiry are followed, all relevant indices of party intention and community preference will be systematically surveyed. Such analysis covers all phases of an interdependent agreement process: from negotiation, through textual expression, to subsequent conduct; without assigning *advanced priority* to any particular feature.[49] This procedure runs contrary to traditional emphasis upon the written text as the source of common intention; a tradition which considers a responsible attempt to elucidate the meaning of the expressed agreement as the primary interpretative task.

A preference for textual meaning is rejected by the policy science method. The communications which constitute an international agreement, when examined within a broad context of sovereign interaction, include innumerable variables which bear upon intention. To make a written document the primary source of meaning would be incompatible with an objective search for genuine shared expectations. It may also lead to the imposition upon the parties of an agreement which they did not desire. The exact opposite, of course, may also result: the parties may be obliged to perform an agreement which the interpretor, acutely aware of the ambiguities of language, feels best comports with basic community policy.

These difficulties surrounding the proper breadth of the interpretative process manifests the continuing struggle between a sociological orientation and an autonomous positive law. But epistemological premises derived from the assumptions of modern science also provide some explanation of the tension. In Dewey's instrumentalism scientific method assumes that what is given in experience is *data;* a provocation, not a terminus, of thought. It sets a problem to be resolved by intelligent operations, provoking an inquiry into the causes and consequences of its existence. Something is *known* only after the analysis is completed, when all relevant variables are taken into account. These cognitive premises, reflected in a jurisprudential method, explain much of the underlying difficulty which the Lasswell-McDougal school has experienced. Legal rules, principles, decisions, legislative and judicial materials are, on its premises, inherently incomplete. They are known, or constituted as good, only when their authoritative status is determined. It is only through an extensive contextual analysis into their causes and consequences that they can become, *de jure,* law.

The effect of this absorption of scientific method into legal philosophy is a theory about law which has been characterized as "not law but sociology."[50] The judgment is extreme, but useful. It vividly contrasts the sociological jurisprudence of Lasswell and McDougal with that of Dean Pound whose work, it will be recalled, earned the opposite appraisal.[51]

Pound insisted upon the autonomy of legal institutions and the primary importance of positive law; a commitment which weakened the sociological dimensions of his theory. The present phase of sociological jurisprudence, developed at the rival Yale Law School, is the culmination of a tendency to identify law with social processes inaugurated by Dewey. It is grounded upon a conviction that legal and social phenomenon can be more closely integrated through the use of scientific procedures of inquiry. The cost of the improvement has been an uncomfortable blurring of distinctions between positive law and sociology.

Law is, in large measure, a decisional phenomenon whose understanding is improved when legal principles and institutions are viewed in the context of wider social processes. This is especially important when the authoritativeness of decisions is a central jurisprudential issue. In spite of the confusion it entails, explicit consideration of societal ideals and values are, under the terms of modern life, an integral part of the search for authoritative judgments. Comprehensive understanding of social processes is indispensable; the difficulty consists in determining what are the proper ingredients of social and jural data which may be legitimately relevant to problem solving tasks.

For Pound, interests were demands upon the legal order whose significance could be determined only by reflection upon how the legal order received them. Such a survey yielded an intelligible list of personal, public, and social interests which in varying degrees bore the imprimatur of positive law. With the system of Lasswell and McDougal, interests were replaced with values. There is a deeper penetration of the moral constitution of the relevant communities. We move closer to the idea of a *social* good, since the demands made upon law are explicitly related to democratic principles concerning the dignity of the individual and the moral quality of his expectations. The importance of this advance may be understood when related to the principles of instrumentalism.

According to Dewey, the problem of values in the modern world was posed by the expansion of secular civilization at a time when a sense of transcendental meaning was in decline. The resulting instability led to recourse to idealism on the one hand and emphasis upon behavioristic theories on the other. The latter concentration reduced the good to subjective satisfactions. But emotional satisfactions and immediate desires could not have rightful authority if they were unregulated by intelligent operations. Without thought, enjoyments are only problematic goods, and what society needs is *intelligent behavior.* By applying the methods of experimental science we can discover the relations upon which an enjoyment depends. We then learn whether what is *desired* is *desirable.* The result is a causal and operational definition. While not a value in itself, the result is yet an affirmation with objective and significant meaning.

The problematic of valuation is one of determining which interests or preferences or enjoyments ought to be preserved or realized and whether those which predominate deserve to be sustained. To pursue these tasks called for a directed reconstruction of political, economic, social and religious institutions: all with the view to determining whether particular practices and policies are authoritative. In making that determination, the fact that such practices and policies exist does not serve as a justification; we must know from whence they came, and the consequences of their continuance. Only after such inquiry can we determine whether they are *values;* that is, whether they have rightful authority in the realm of conduct.[52]

The essential value categories of a policy oriented jurisprudence are treated operationally as hypotheses, but they are not purely provisional. Rather are they the fruit of prior jural and social experience, expressing the shared expectations of the various communities and institutions in which the decision maker must function.[53] These inclusive norms both guide inquiry and are continuously developed through inquiry; their meaning and breadth continuously revealed in the nuances of contextual experience.

It was Pound's conviction that judges were capable of making decisions which allowed for the balanced realization of interests. A suspicion that the method leads to the projection of personal biases stimulated a search for more secure ways of guaranteeing authoritative judgment. But, as we observed in reviewing Pound's work, a rejection of the spirit of Pound's method can lead to formalized precepts of conflict resolution which ignore that intense clash of values which lies at the heart of social antagonism.

The decisional process should be at least in part conceived as a disciplined effort to understand and evaluate value conflicts. The policy science methodology, with its sustained effort to develop objective standards of discovery and appraisal, and its insistence upon the priority of community policies, brings to the decisional process a valuable discipline. Its contextual procedures may restrain that spirit of partisanship which too often accompanies the assumption of decisional power. And its stress upon skills of thought and systematic inquiry can also temper proclivities towards subjective choices.

In spite of these advantages, however, there are inherent limitations to the policy science method when it is applied to political institutions. The major difficulty is that it does not sufficiently consider real distinctions between various forms of decision making. Within the realm of social processes, all jural institutions tend to be indiscriminately lumped together. It is evident that the uniqueness of adjudication receives inadequate attention.

Courts do not exist to maximize social values. Their paramount mission is to fairly decide disputes according to jural criteria. This fixes attention upon factors which are not an integral part of the Lasswell-McDougal method. Legal reasoning, argument and justification, rather than a "flow of decisions," are of primary importance.[54] Whether a judicial decision is, or is not, authoritative turns as much upon satisfactory answers to these questions as it does upon the systematical analyses advocated by the New Haven School.

Even the problematic of policy is not susceptible of adequate elucidation without observation of the uniqueness of the adjudicative function. It is difficult to know when policy considerations can legitimately become part of a judicial decision: difficulties compounded by the fact that there are policies developed by courts for purposes which are distinctively legal in their range and meaning. These are policies *of the law,* having a more restricted meaning than the more flexible range of community values and goals upon which the policy science school is prone to concentrate. Moreover, the *institutional* purpose of courts is to secure legal rights. Social values and objectives influence judicial decisions, but developments in Analytical Jurisprudence reveal the pressures upon judges to justify results in terms of entitlements[55] rather than policies.

A final, more general, difficulty with the policy science form of Sociological Jurisprudence should be noted. Its primary attention is fixed not upon decisions, but upon the responsibility of the deci-

sion maker. It continues a profound concern expressed by Dewey
that individuals in the modern world are easily controlled by the
forces operative within it. As methods of rational inquiry in the
physical sciences had enabled man to direct nature to human ends,
it was hoped that an application of the same methods to the problems of the social sciences would make it possible for men to control
their personal and communal destiny.

The objective of systematic contextual analysis as a jural
methodology is to provide the intellectual tools for making rational
choices. Concentration upon all relevant phases of social experience creates a discipline which can be conducive to the making of
good judgments or decisions. Dewey insisted that a genuine practical judgment as to the worth of any particular value was possible
only when its significance was tested by an intelligence formed in
experience. He expressed this quality of evaluation as a matter of
taste:

> ... Expertness of taste is at once the result and the reward of
> constant exercise of thinking ... [I]t is the outcome of experi-
> ence brought cumulatively to bear on the intelligent apprecia-
> tion of the real worth of likings and enjoyments. There is
> nothing in which a person so completely reveals himself as in
> the things which he judges enjoyable and desirable. Such
> judgments are the sole alternative to the domination of belief
> by impulse, chance, blind habit and self-interest. The forma-
> tion of a cultivated and effectively operative good judgment
> or taste with respect to what is esthetically admirable, in-
> tellectually acceptable and morally approvable is the supreme
> task set to human beings by the incidents of experience.[56]

This extensive use of intelligence in problem solving marks the
general moral character, but it is also understood to be a prerequisite of freedom of choice. All choices are causally conditioned. The
problem for ethics and legal philosophy is to reduce the degree to
which such choices are determined by subjective preferences, or
bias. It is of particular importance to a theory of decisionmaking,
for here objectivity of judgment is a supreme ideal. Our decisions
are relatively free insofar as insight and understanding enter our
deliberations. For we can then anticipate and explicitly select among
alternative courses of action.

It is to this end that sophisticated and comprehensive procedures
of scientific inquiry are incorporated as an integral part of the

Lasswell-McDougal jurisprudence. The method undoubtedly raises consciousness of alternatives before the mind's eye; to that degree it can enhance the liberty of those who must make responsible legal decisions. But, taken in its entirety, this conception of jurisprudence does not adequately account for the inward dimensions of appraisal and choice.

The subjective, or more properly personal, side of decision was vigorously stated by John Stuart Mill, in a form which bears comparison with Dewey's conception of moral freedom:

> ... [I]t is the privilege and proper condition of a human being, arrived at the maturity of his faculties, to use and interpret experience in his own way. It is for him to find out what part of recorded experience is properly applicable to his own circumstances and character ... The human faculties of perception, judgment, discriminative feeling, mental activity, and even moral preference, are exercised only in making a choice ...

> ... He who chooses his plan for himself employs all his faculties. He must use observation to see, reasoning and judgment to foresee, activity to gather materials for decision, discrimination to decide, and when he has decided, firmness and self-control to hold to his deliberate decision.[57]

This conception of free choice is far removed, in spirit and direction, from the attitude towards legal research and action which prevails in the policy science form of jurisprudence.

While its central purpose is to enlighten discretion, the general program of policy science is incompatible with authentic deliberation and choice. Personal decision is not excluded; indeed, the recommended intellectual tasks explicitly provide for the creative invention and assessment of policy alternatives. But the overall weight of the system; its virtual obsession with scientific methodology, its elaborate schematic formulae, the rigor and extensiveness of its procedures, and its emphasis upon innumerable variables, are adverse to that personal growth in knowledge and deliberate choice which is the essence of Mill's perception.

Conformity with scientific criteria, rather than individual awareness and perception, became the measure of responsible decision. The total effect is to replace authentic choice with a technique. This is undoubtedly caused by an excessive enthusiasm for the accomplishments of science, but it also suggests a profound pessimism, a deep distrust of the individuals' capacity to make wise judgments upon matters of public importance. It assigns to a sociological method the accomplishment of tasks which traditionally have been considered part of personal excellence. In its emphasis upon concrete experience, upon causes and consequences, upon projection of trends, the Lasswell-McDougal system gathers into a scientific procedure qualities of discernment and judgment which also belong to moral character.

For the scholar, as well as for the advocate, counsellor, and judge, the presence of a legal issue presents a problem to be solved. Precedents, statutes and other jural data; the facts and normative values of the social *milieu;* all bear upon the problem from their particular levels of meaning, with varying degrees of cogency. None has the power, of itself, to determine choice. They are the elements of the problem to be solved, not the solution. What the choice shall be depends ultimately upon qualities of appraisal and insight unique to the individual.[58] The correctness of choices depends more upon his or her moral and cultural formation, than upon their compliance with scientific procedures of inquiry.

CHAPTER THREE

THE PURE THEORY OF LAW

A. *INTRODUCTION*

Modern legal philosophy has been marked by a struggle between theories which perceive law as an autonomous discipline and those which would comprehend it in relation to other social phenomena. Austinian jurisprudence was established upon relatively stable, empirical foundations, and it is a primary example of positive independence. With the advent of sociology, however, this autonomy was increasingly threatened by efforts to understand jural material within a broader framework. As sociological explanations advanced, it became increasingly difficult to maintain consistent distinctions between the two disciplines.

Part of the difficulty lay in the fact that both approaches were being developed within the same general frame of reference. Legal Positivism and Sociology of Law were antagonistic, but they were both grounded on experience. The tradition which began with Austin sought to extend understanding through an inductive methodology. Sociological explanations of law were also based upon concrete experience. Law was perceived within a web of observable social interactions and structures. These epistemic similarities provoked a reaction which would culminate in a distinctive conception of the nature of positive law.

In the latter half of the Nineteenth Century, European jurists felt strongly that a decisive separation of positive law and sociology was desirable. They also understood that it could be accomplished only by transcending the pervasive empiricism which was making the two disciplines indistinguishable.[1] In the natural sciences, the Baconian method was gradually being supplemented with and in

82

some respects replaced by the spirit of DesCartes, which stressed mathematical and deductive forms of thought. An analogous shift was beginning in legal philosophy, a movement from the concrete towards abstract forms of jural explanation. It was to draw its inspiration from the work of Kant.

In his *Critique of Pure Reason* Kant, responding to Hume's critique of causation, sought a means of imposing an intellectual order upon the manifold of phenomenal experience. Synthetic truth could be attained according to Kant only if experience was organized by forms of thought. Reason and experience could then be reconciled, even though the phenomenal world was devoid of inner intelligibility. The mind was conscious of its own universal forms of sense and its formal categories of understanding. By subsuming the variety of phenomenal experiences under *a priori* forms, stable cognition of reality would be possible.

Kant also sought certitude for the will in the field of moral judgment. In the world of phenomena, the laws of cause and effect reign, and there is no ethical freedom. But as intellectual certitudes were discoverable within consciousness, so also would moral understanding be revealed within the self. Here was the realm of the "ought," implying necessities which did not exist in empirical nature. If we are to act we must be sure that the choice is one we ought to make; a decision not made according to our feelings, but upon a principle of universal validity. This was the categorical imperative: to act only upon a maxim which will enable you to will that it be a universal law. When operative, this imperative would assure that each person will be treated as an end and never merely as a means.[2] Kant based his theory of law upon his ethics. Freedom was the central concept. Juridical liberty—the independence of the individual from the arbitrary will of another—was to be achieved under conditions which realized a general law of freedom.

In the neo-Kantian revival of the late Nineteenth Century legal philosophers perceived that the critique of pure, as well as that of practical, reason was relevant to their discipline. Indeed, Stammler criticized Kant for failing to distinguish the concept of law from that of the right or just law. A concept of law derived from the categories of understanding could, through its *a priori* forms, provide the necessary and universal elements of legal experience. It was on this basis that Stammler developed his juristic theory composed of a concept of law conceived as inviolable will, and an idea of law, as a realization of justice. Del Vecchio also stressed the formal

element in legal definition and chided legal positivists for ignoring
Kant's teaching that causal explanations were dependent upon *a
priori* form. By placing actual before possible experience they had
neglected the ideas to which the facts correspond. Because of the
exigencies of thought, "law is not law except in virtue of the ideal
form which determines it and nothing can be known as law except
in relation to form itself."[3] An adequate philosophy of law can be
established only by using the forms immanent to consciousness; by
moving from the concrete to the plane of logic where one discovers
the necessary attributes of juridical cognition. Thus for Del Vecchio the essence of law is pure form: the objective coordination of
human action, which promotes respect for autonomous personality
according to norms of bilateralness, imperativeness and coercibil-
ity.

   While both Stammler and Del Vecchio emphasized the *a priori*,
rational, aspects of legal definition they had profoundly ethical
conceptions of the nature of law. However laudable, these attempts
to ground jurisprudence in idealism would not be adequate to the
needs of legal philosophy in the Twentieth Century. They were
incompatible with the effort of jurisprudence to establish itself as
an autonomous science free of value elements. Moreover, neither
Stammler nor Del Vecchio fully grasped the power of *a priori*
thought. There were untapped potentials which, when utilized,
promised not only to free the science of positive law from alien
intrusions, but also to make possible a systematic comprehension of
legal phenomena.

   In the post Kantian philosophy of the Nineteenth Century there
was a deepening understanding of the principles of thought. After
Hegel's dialectic had assigned a positive function to contradiction, a
neo-Kantian reaction sought to clarify the logic of pure thought.
Herbart insisted that the principle of non-contradiction is essential
and that the *is* of existence and the *ought* of formal logic are inso-
lubly antagonistic. This antagonism led to a division of the sciences
which would have important consequences for legal philosophy.
The realm of concrete existence was assigned to the causal sciences,
and the ought to the normative. Within the so-called Marburg
school the philosophers Hermann Cohen and Paul Natorp developed important insights into the positive, creative nature of
abstraction which would also have juristic significance. Being is not
static; it only exists in a process of becoming which is intrinsically

related to mental activity. Being is the product of thought which progressively determines its own object.[4]

It was against the background of this philosophical experience that Hans Kelsen developed his Pure Theory of Law.

Kelsen's primary adversary was Ehrlich who, in his sociology of law, had made law dependent upon its actual effectiveness. Kelsen also had to resist ethical intrusions. It was necessary to insulate positive law from moral judgments, because jural autonomy would be compromised if the justification of law was derived from ethical ideals. The requirements of legal philosophy in the Twentieth Century called for the transformation of jurisprudence into an exact formal science, capable not only of distinguishing the sphere of positive law from that of sociology but also of purifying its essential elements of all extra-juristic influences. To accomplish this Kelsen drew upon the affirmations of intellectual power which were the primary contributions of neo-Kantian idealism. Law would be understood as a phenomenon of essence known, in its transcendental-logic modalities, through the productive power of the human mind.

The science of law would be a mental conception, but it would have empirical conditions. The Kantian notion of an intimate connection between the experienced world and the realm of understanding would be useful in relating the real and ideal elements of a legal system. As a social phenomenon, positive law was distinctive because it was a coercive order. As such, it assured an opposition between what is and what ought to be. Its normative requirements, expressed in hypothetical form, set the conditions for mutual human relations. In case of contrary behavior the norms provide that sanctions should be imposed. Through the sequence of norm, delict, and sanction the legal order could be understood as preserving its existence and realizing itself in time.

Legal norms provide that something ought to be or happen. While concentrating upon duties they also encompass permissions and authorizations. Viewed dynamically, positive law is a series of authorizations to enact or apply norms within a hierarchical structure. The system is unified and validated by the presupposition of a

basic or *grundnorm,* which authorizes the norm creating and applying power. The fundamental norm, formulated in terms that "one
ought to obey the prescriptions of the historically first constitution,"[5] makes possible the interpretation of an effective coercive
order as a system of objectively valid norms.

With the basic norm one can unify the actual experience of positive law as it is generally obeyed in a given society. And it can adjust
to changes in actual life. If a particular order is no longer "by and
large" effective, the basic norm is open to the formation of a new
order. Through this contact between the factual and the normative
the science of law is correlated with social explanations of the origin
of a legal system. When power relations are stabilized might is
transformed into law. Once established, law has its autonomous
existence, governed by the logical progression of its own normative
dynamism.

The establishment of positive law as a normative order makes
possible the separation of law from sociology. As logic takes precedence in explaining jural phenomena validity, an expression of
ought, gains a primacy over effectiveness, an expression of what is.
The reason for this supremacy can be seen in the distinction between causal and normative sciences which was central to Kelsen's
system.

Human behavior can be subject by the mind to two basic forms of
interpretation. Conceived as a part of nature the behavior is causally determined; an effect determined by preceding causes. However the same behavior can be interpreted according to moral or
legal norms. It is then understood as a compliance with, or deviation from, a normative order.

Modern jurisprudence has generally relied upon causation in its
effort to understand law. Analytical Positivism, Sociology of Law,
and Sociological Jurisprudence were all committed to causal explanations of jural phenomena, hoping to understand law through the
relations of cause and effect which constitute the structure of experience. Kelsen sought to transcend that dependence by raising
jural cognition to the plane of normative understanding. This, he
believed, was not only logically defensible but it was also justified by
the historical development of normative and causal sciences.

In primitive societies, normative interpretations were pervasive.
Not only human conduct but also the processes of nature were
explained in terms of imputation. Inquiry was limited to asking
who did something, not how it happened. A thunderstorm was the

retributive reaction of an angry deity to the misbehavior of a people. As civilization advanced nature and society were differentiated. A causal explanation of relations between things was separated from a normative interpretation of relations among persons.

Once modern science was established principles of inductive causality became applicable to modern behavior. As we have already seen, the new method was used to establish an empirical science of positive law. Sociology broadened the potentials of empirical explanation, and the use of causal methodology was intensified. As the effort to identify the causes and consequences of jural phenomena progressed sociological interpretations of law became pre-eminent. This gradual subordination of law to sociology, which began with Comte and Durkheim, and is presently continued by policy science jurisprudence,[6] is traceable to the expansion of causal explanations and methodology.

To overcome the hegemony of sociology it was necessary for Kelsen to demonstrate that for juristic purposes normative methods of inquiry were more suitable than causal explanations. The social sciences which provide causal explanations of human behavior were not, Kelsen maintained, essentially different from the natural sciences whose methodology they had borrowed.[7] The difference between a sociology of law and biology is only one of degree. Both seek to understand their subject according to principles of cause and effect. There is no essential difference between them. However, a genuine difference does exist between the natural sciences and sciences, such as law and ethics, which interpret human relations according to the principle of imputation.

Law as a science is dependent upon connections; but its links are normative. For it the meaning of an act is a norm. It describes its object by propositions in which a delict is connected to a sanction by an "ought." And the juristic significance of any act is not understood in its physical existence as determined by causality, it is rather derived from a norm whose context refers to the act:

> The judgment that an act of human behavior, performed in time and space, is 'legal' ('or illegal') is the result of a specific, namely normative, interpretation ... [t]he norm which confers upon an act the meaning of legality or illegality is itself created by an act, which, in turn receives its legal character from yet another norm ... [t]hat a document is objectively *as*

well as subjectively a valid testament results from the fact that
it conforms to conditions stipulated by [a] code. That an assembly of people is a parliament, and that the meaning of
their act is a statute, results from the conformity of all these
facts with the norms laid down in the constitution. That
means, that the contents of actual happenings agree with a
norm accepted as valid.[8]

The difference between normative and causal explanation is also
a difference of the *extent* of inquiry. In causative analyses the chain
of causes and effects has no definite limit and each specific event is
the intersection of innumerable lines of causality. But the conditions to which the moral or juristic consequence is imputed are
limited. They essentially require only the two links. Imputation
comes to an end in that specific conduct which, according to the
law, is the condition of the consequence determined by that law.
Where inquiry is pursued it concentrates upon normative
regression—determining, for example, whether one imposing a
norm was authorized to do so—rather than extending inquiry out-
ward into empirical or sociological relationships and interconnections. If specific events are juristically evaluated it is an evaluation
which asserts the validity of norms relative to the events. The
norms act as principles of selection, structuring factual inquiry and
conferring upon physical events their intellectual meaning. The
reality which is determined by causal law is reduced to normative
thought relationships.

Because it functions with criteria of imputation, the Pure Theory
of Law becomes an exclusive method for the cognition of legal
norms. Sociology of Law and other social sciences which deal with
legal phenomena have parallel responsibilities. It is for them to
inquire with causative instruments into the motivations behind the
enactment of laws and the complex psycho-physical forces which
influence decisions. They can also reveal the social tendencies
which determine the establishment of particular norms as well as
the reactions within social life to enacted norms. Yet while law has
its origins in social life, we cannot know whether any particular
ordering is law unless we first know what law is. That crucial question is answered by the normative sciences which correlate its elements by principles of imputation; to norms.

Sociology of Law is a science of social causes and effects; it studies
the realm of existence. It cannot tell us what law is. Only the Pure

Theory, which belongs to the realm of essence, understands law because it is capable of viewing law as a self-sufficient, logically consistent system of norms.

———

The fundamental distinction between causal and normative sciences made it possible for Kelsen to resist sociological interpretations of law. He also met the ethical pretensions of this adversary. Since Comte, the sociological tradition has claimed a comprehension of general laws of human development immanent in social reality. But rather than being an improvement upon the metaphysics of the past these efforts to find value within society continue natural law forms of thought which have been repudiated by modern science.

The sociological claim that there exists fundamental laws of evolution is psychologically similar to assertions that human nature has laws which reason can discover. They are both efforts to justify subjective value judgements, judgments which arise from the depths of the emotional component of consciousness. They seek to make such feelings objective by placing them upon the same level as statements about reality. Sociological ventures into the absolute are as riddled with contradictions and inconsistencies as was the metaphysical theorizing of the past. The necessary laws discovered by Comte required a life measured by social function; the immanent evolution perceived by Spencer revealed an inexorable progress towards individual liberty.

As sociology cannot gain hegemony over positive law by recourse to quasi-metaphysics so also must the attempts by natural law theories to gain dominance suffer a similar repudiation.[9] Again, Kelsen's proofs are anthropological. In his animism primitive man was compelled to substantialize reality. He imagined that nature was inhabited by spirits. Because his ego was weak he had to project his emotional states into external reality. Thus his tendency to interpret nature according to social norms, especially those of retribution. Society and nature were indistinguishable.

Causal thinking emerged only when inclinations towards pure cognition had reached a stage of development in which, independently of desire or fear, it became possible for man to comprehend

objective connections within the phenomena of nature. But the
emotional component persisted both in the effort to ground social
relations upon metaphysical principles and in efforts to attribute
the newly discovered laws of empirical nature to a Divine origin.
Hume's critique of causality undermined the latter attribution. As
there was no objective connection between cause and effect there
was no inherent substance to external phenomena. A succession of
events had replaced causal necessity and nature ceased to be the
expression of a Divine Will.

    In spite of the repudiation of inviolable law by modern science,
the desire to interpret human behavior according to absolute, inherent principles of justice remains. This search for a "natural"
order, "behind" or "above" the positive legal order has psychological as well as epistemological foundations. It continues, Kelsen argues, that distrust of the human ego and its powers of independent
thought which characterized the mentality of primitive man and
which is a continuous part of emotional consciousness.

    Such distrust is revealed in personalities who are suspicious of
experienced reality and yearn to replace it with an ideal order of
normative principles. In a more moderate form, a lack of confidence is exhibited by those who rely upon a transcendent source to
justify an existing order. A more typical personality is optimistic
about the potentials of the positive law, but is uncomfortable with
the disparity between the real and the ideal. This type balances its
desire to comprehend the positive law as just with a reliance upon a
relative natural law adjusted to the circumstances. It reflects a personality striving to compromise as it seeks to reconcile the transcendent and temporal realms.

    These dualisms, wavering between the real and metaphysical
worlds, are only decisively surmounted by scientific-critical philosophy and those who are willing to accept its implications. It requires the courage to renounce the transcendent realm as being
beyond experience and a willingness to turn towards temporal existence with full confidence in human powers. Cognition here assumes an active, productive role: creating its own objects out of
material provided by the senses according to its own inner laws of
thought. Those committed to a critical theory of knowledge are
imbued with intellectual energy; more concerned with comprehending the world than in shaping it according to instinctive
desires. The advent of critical theory signals the triumph of objec-

tivity over emotional preference, the ascension of the rational element of consciousness.

This critical reason makes it possible to end the domination of natural law. Considered logically, the natural and positive orders are incompatible because positive law is committed to relativity of normative content while natural law is committed to an absolute content of justice. If positive law were delegated by natural law the delegation would inevitably lead to a contradiction between the delegation in operation and the principles of natural law from which its authority was derived. This conclusion, Kelsen argued, is reinforced by historical experience. A positive legal order assumes an absolute power to enact laws which, in the temporal realm of existence, are increasingly relative in content. This authority follows not only from principles of sovereignty but also from the development of legal systems. When law and custom combined, the relationship between law and morals was intimate, and the arguments for a subordination of positive law to natural law had a degree of plausibility. But with the advent of conscious legislation the content of norms is only infrequently drawn from general custom. Attention is now focused upon the authority which creates the norms. The creation of positive law, as distinguished from its comprehension, belongs to the realm of will which is unintelligible. Natural law by contrast assumes that the norms of justice are evident to reason. The potentials for contradiction between the two orders intensifies as positive law works out its own characteristic of discretion. And the means by which the two orders realize their objectives are also incompatible. Natural law implies that the individual once he sees the rationality of a law will voluntarily submit to its content. For positive law, the potential of coercion is indispensable.

A confident, consistent, positivism will eliminate these contradictions and inconsistencies and treat positive law as supreme and nonderivative. The reason for its validity can be found in a postulated basic norm which not only provides a delegation of authority but which also makes it possible to comprehend the legal order as a meaningful whole. It will also require obedience to the commands of delegated authority.

In this way the autonomy of jurisprudence, understood as legal science, will be assured. Positive laws will no longer be mere empirical facts, a fragile "existence" subject to the normative judgment of natural law. Rather is the positive legal order itself normative; and, where cognition of that order is concerned, the jurist can disregard the moral dimension. Where positive law expressly refers to moral norms the traditional order of delegation is reversed. Now the positive law assigns a role to morality and the objective unity of the positive order is preserved. And where disobedience seeks justification in natural law the unity and wholeness of the positive order cannot be broken. The challenge no longer has transcendent significance; it is only a psychological fact which can be properly dealt with by the inherent order of the positive law.

—

The establishment of a science of positive law on the basis of transcendental logic constitutes a profound accomplishment of human thought. It makes possible an understanding of positive law by forms of cognition which are purified of metaphysical elements. The transcendental replaces the transcendent. The autonomy of positive law is also rescued from the threat of sociological intrusion. Validity and efficacy, although connected, are distinct, and the supremacy of the former is secured. Associations, such as corporations, which when viewed sociologically appear to be autonomous, are now comprehended as partial legal orders within a larger juridically whole. By understanding law as an exact science of normative cognition, the Pure Theory of Law is also able to surpass its Austinian predecessors.

The superiority of Pure Theory over Analytical Positivism reflects the advantages of normative analysis over empirical explanation. The ought explains the existence of law after expression of the sovereign command has lapsed. Motivations for compliance become irrelevant to cognition, since the sanction, as a norm, is set over against the fact of disobedience in a logical relation. Holmes' predictive positivism is surpassed because the relation between the delict and the sanction is understood as one of legal necessity rather than factual probability.[10]

By concentrating upon the delict Kelsen developed a series of interconnected basic concepts of obligation and liability inherently consistent with a comprehension of law as a technique of coercion. There is a considerable advance in general comprehension. As a coherent system, positive law realizes itself in progressive unity. From the basic norm which authorizes norm creating authority, through the various stages of enactment, to the execution of sanctions, positive law regulates its own creation.

Jural comprehension is enhanced when the Pure Theory is contrasted with earlier positivism, and these improvements are of great importance to legal science. By shifting jural attention from traditional preoccupations Kelsen accentuated particular aspects of an operative legal order which might otherwise be neglected. This can be seen most clearly by the emphasis given to the concept of duty. Since the delict provides the condition for bringing the legal order into operation, the duty of the official to apply the norms becomes of central importance. And the reduction of legal rights to an auxiliary function is helpful to an understanding of some difficult practical problems.

The insight of Pure Theory into concrete legal problems can be seen with reference to the phenomenon of "standing to sue." Post-Austinian analytical positivism precisely calibrated legal rights and duties and made clear disctinctions between social and individual capacities of enforcement. John Chipman Gray, for example, referred to the protection of human interests as a force which society sometimes put into effect on its own motion and sometimes on the motion of interested individuals:

> The rights correlative to those duties which the society will enforce on its own motion are the legal rights of that society. The rights correlative to those duties which the society will enforce on the motion of an individual are that individual's legal rights.[11]

Under conditions of modern law, such sharp distinctions are impossible to maintain. The circumstances under which an individual may commence a legal action include situations which lie in a "twilight zone" between a strictly personal interest on the one hand, and a societal interest on the other. Insensitivity to such nuances can have profound practical consequences. In the *South West Africa*[12] cases the International Court of Justice held by the margin of single vote that a complaint brought by Ethiopia and Liberia against South Africa challenging the practice of *apartheid* in mandated territory must be dismissed because the applicants failed to prove that they possessed a legal right in the subject matter to which a legal duty of accounting by South Africa could correspond. Understood as a jurisprudential issue, the conclusion is suggested by the methodology of Analytical Positivism. In the conceptual frame of Pure Theory however, a legal right is an authorization to institute legal proceedings, a power to put the law applying process into operation.[13] This provides a broader framework for understanding the standing to sue phenomenon than was possible under Analytical Positivism.

While the Pure Theory of Law provides insight into specific problems, its general structure has been criticized as too abstract by other jurists of a positivist persuasion. Professor Hart's grounding of legal positivism upon an anthropological foundation[14] should be understood as an attempt to provide a concrete alternative to Kelsen's normative structure. His theory of positive law as a union of primary rules of obligation and secondary rules of recognition, change, and adjudication covers, in essential respects, the same conceptual field encompassed by the logical structure of the Pure Theory. At critical junctures, Hart offers forms of explanation which he believes makes jurisprudence more congruent with the inward dispositions of those who uphold a legal order. Rules of change and adjudication are ways of understanding the delegation of lawmaking authority. The rule of recognition provides an alternative to the concept of validity. Before determining whether one norm derives its validity from another courts and other agencies of identification must first recognize the superior norm and treat its specific existence as a reason for accepting the laws it purports to validate. There is an *actual* determination that laws belong to the same system, an ascertainment of membership which is presupposed in making judgments of validity. An inwardness also reveals that a legal order may be considered coherent by its participants even if it does not operate with conscious reliance upon a basic norm.[15]

The abstractness of Pure Theory also leads to an incomplete perception of positive law. Placing duties before rights was justified by the suitability of duty for normative analysis and the deeper comprehension which results. This was a radical change since in Analytical Positivism legal rights had priority. But if the reversal can be defended, it is questionable whether the phenomenon of legal duties is intelligible without some specific reference to correlative rights.

Doubt has also been raised whether an intimate nexus between duties and sanctions is as indispensable as the Pure Theory assumes. There are legal obligations such as those of paying taxes which are intelligible even if not explicitly connected with an immediate threat of sanction. It is also legitimate to place acts of nullification, such as cancellation of a license, outside of the duty-sanction framework.[16] Nevertheless the fundamental premises of coercion adopted by the Pure Theory are sound, because logic is here reinforced by political and social fact. Centralization of power is a distinctive mark of modern states, and they maintain reserves of force which can be used if necessary to realize their juristic objectives.

Some coherence may be achieved if attention is directed towards the relationship between rights and sanctions. For Bentham and the analytical jurists the elucidation of legal rights took place with an eye towards enforcement.[17] This form of analysis closely parallels what is involved in the comprehension of justice. Justice can be distinguished from other moral obligations in that the duties to which it refers are amenable to compulsion. Justice is engaged whenever respect for a right, which for the holder is his own, should be realized if necessary by force.[18]

There is a further sense in which an emphasis upon duties is unwarranted. As a matter of general expression, we usually speak of securing rights rather than of imposing duties. This is the case when we refer to the objectives of the law; it is also congruent with jural experience. Constitutional principles are as intelligible in terms of a promotion of rights as they are as an establishment of duties. Statutory norms may lend themselves more readily to analysis in terms of obligation, but in lawmaking by courts, the priority of legal rights is a requirement of adjudicative competence. In the landmark case of *Baker v. Carr,* the Supreme Court had to decide whether a claim of malapportionment was justiciable. A crucial step in the assertion of its authority was a determination that the petitioners had standing to sue because their right to vote was allegedly being diluted:

> A citizen's right to a vote free of arbitrary impairment by state action has been judicially recognized as a right secured by the Constitution ... They are entitled to a hearing and to the District Court's decision in their claims. 'The very essence of

civil liberty certainly consists in the right of every individual to
claim the protection of the laws, whenever he receives an
injury.'[19]

The shift in Pure Theory from rights to duties is also defended
on the grounds that a preference for rights is ideological. For
Kelsen it expresses an emotional desire relative to the *ethos* of a
particular community. Kelsen was equally critical of the efforts of
capitalist societies to absolutize the value of private property and
Marxist attempts to give metaphysical status to socialism.[20] But it is
possible to perceive some objective elements in these basic social
views. The core values affirmed within these antagonistic economic
and political systems are intelligible as parts of a wider whole.

The values of human freedom enumerated in the Universal Declaration of Human Rights[21] can be correlated, in general terms,
with theories of individual liberty evolved in the Western democracies. Rights of self-government acknowledged in the Declaration also have their genesis in Western political thought and practice.
The economic aspects of this *ethos* are reflected in the recognition that
each, singly and in association, has a right to own private property.
The right is not unqualified, but as philosophers such as Robert
Nozick have shown, its importance is fundamental to a sense of
human dignity.

The Declaration also affirms the economic, social, and cultural
rights of man. The major impetus for these values is derived from
Marxist-Leninist thought and the spirit of the October Revolution.
They are not exclusively dependent upon such inspiration, but
socialist countries have made the advancement of these values a
dominant purpose of their policy.

Considered in its totality the Universal Declaration of Human
Rights can be understood as encompassing different aspects of a
general humanism. Such an observation does not ignore the extraordinary practical difficulties which are encountered in attempting to reconcile the various rights referred to in the Declaration.
Yet, while a considerable divergence of interpretation is assumed,
there is no *logical* inconsistency between the basic value segments.
More importantly, they interpenetrate.

There is considerable evidence that values which were once believed to be part of exclusive ideologies have in fact a pervasive
human quality. Reaction against economic injustice is no longer a
Marxist prerogative, for in the traditional democracies, critique of

private property and power have increased. Comparatively, the experiences of Sakharov and Solzhenitsyn eloquently testify to the trans-ideological character of human freedom. They reveal underlying unities which elude the rigorous abstractions of Pure Theory.

~

The rigorous distinctions which the Pure Theory makes between norm and behavior are also too dogmatic and abstract. The concrete action which is the condition for the application of a norm is treated as a simple occurrence or event. Motivations for compliance or deviation are irrelevant to legal cognition, although they are important as collateral information as to the general viability of the norms. As attribution replaced causality the concrete act which provides the condition for the application of a norm is decisive.

The separation of normative significance from subjective disposition is valuable, particularly in the contractual sphere where objective meaning is of great importance to the stability of expectations. But it is insufficient, and indeed inaccurate, as a general explanation of the legal relationship between norm and act. From the perspective of Pure Theory, it has been said that:

> The judgment that attributes a guilty act to a person takes no account of psychic processes in that person's life. It implies only that there is a norm which punishes that act... The murderer is punished not because he has killed someone but because his conduct goes counter to a norm which attaches a penalty to murder. To put it generally, punishment is imposed not because there is guilt but because there is a norm which envisages punishment as a consequence of certain conduct.[22]

But where personal responsibility is in issue, as in most of the criminal law, the ability of a person to accomplish the norm is integral to the inquiry. Judicial proceedings which may here terminate in a determination of delict take psychic processes explicitly into account. An advocate of Pure Theory may argue that whenever intent and will are taken into account by the positive law they are juristic, and no longer psychological concepts. But that explanation will not do. Psychological factors are dealt with directly on their own terms even though their operative influence is limited by the legal order. Voluntariness of conduct is normally a prerequisite to criminal responsibility, and inquiries into states of mind occur in other branches of positive law. Extensive probing of motivation is precluded, but this limitation can be explained as much by practical, as it can by normative considerations.

As for institutional relationships, concrete observation reveals a more complex reality than can be perceived by the abstract normative analysis of Pure Theory. This is especially true of the relationship between courts and legislatures. Pure Theory has deflated the exaggerations of judicial supremacy, and its vision of law as a hierarchical structure draws attention to ways that courts are subordinate to legislatures.[23] But the relationship between the institutions is also in many cases one of *concurrent* authority, and this important aspect of institutional relations eludes the scrutiny of logical thought.

A relative hierarchy is accentuated by Pure Theory but there are collaborative dimensions which are at least of equal importance. The legislature may make certain conduct criminal without providing a civil remedy for those injured by the prohibited behavior. If a court should create a remedy in such circumstances it is not uncommon for it to understand its role as one of joint responsibility; part of a common duty to implement social policy.[24] These features can perhaps be reconciled with the modalities of normative cognition, but their full import falls outside the range of Pure Theory. They are parts of a legal process whose structure can only be comprehended by observation of the actual behavior of legal organs. More significantly, they involve operations that can be understood in terms of the purposes which the different institutions are expected to perform.

The variance between Kelsen's concept of interpretation and actual practice points to more fundamental issues which a reference to purposiveness inevitably evokes. In the dynamics of a legal order the need for interpretation arises as legal organs seek to determine the meaning of the norms which they must apply. That determination is essentially incomplete not only because the organ in the act of application creates an individual norm but also because there is inevitably an unintended indefinitiveness. The limitations of human communication are such that linguistic expression may be ambiguous. Further, a discrepancy may be perceived between expression and actual intention. And norms which are equally valid may be, in whole or in part, contradictory. From the point of view of Pure Theory, interpretation, as a legal phenomenon, is restricted to the cognition of these possibilities. "The law to be applied constitutes only a frame within which several applications are possible, whereby every act is legal that stays within the frame."[25] The choice among alternatives is an act of discretion about which jurisprudence can offer no possible guidance. If the selection is made with reference to some standards they are norms not of positive law but of legal politics. Morals, ideals of justice, or social utility may enter the interpretative process; they can only be characterized negatively, that is, as not positive law. Once the possibilities of interpretation of positive norms has been ascertained the choice among them is discretionary, unless positive law has itself transformed metalegal norms into the fabric of the positive legal order.

This analysis of interpretation is an advance beyond an earlier legal positivism which refused to admit that legal norms could be expressed with imprecision. The basic distinction offered by Kelsen: between the cognition of possibilities within the legal material, and extra legal justifications for choice among such possibilities, substantially clarifies the structure of interpretation. It is a particularly powerful remedy for use against social policy models which indiscriminately mix the components which he carefully separates. But because of the basic dichotomy into which it splits the interpretative process the approach of Pure Theory is insufficient. Limiting reason to an understanding of possible jural meanings, and then shifting attention to the discretion of the interpreter, Pure Theory ignores other important dimensions of the interpretative process.

Where the range of a statute is unclear a judge must try to ascertain the overall purpose which the legislature was aiming to achieve. It is obviously possible for him to attribute his own subjective preferences to the legislature. But professional interpretation is generally understood to consist in a search for a rational pattern or purpose which can be fairly attributed to the lawmaker. There is not a two step process by which perception of statutory ambiguity is followed by an exercise of interpretive will. The perceived lack of clear intention is normally accompanied by an effort on the part of one responsible for interpretation to rationally complete what the legislature began.[26]

Where a statutory directive is framed in general language the possibilities of extra legal interpretation are admittedly high. But even in these situations rigorous distinctions between objective legal possibilities and subjective legal politics overlook matters of jurisprudential importance. A federal agency, for example, is commissioned by Congress to grant certain licenses only "in the public interest." The phrase "public interest" is extremely vague, but it can have institutional meanings as part of its content. It has been held that such a commission requires administrative agencies to take positive steps to determine what are the public needs rather than limit its role to the passive reception of evidence by interested parties.[27]

These dimensions of the interpretive process assume that the business of applying norms includes at a least a minimum inquiry into what the norms are for; of intent *as purpose*. That this is essential can be gathered not only from the phenomenon of statutory interpretation, but even more forcefully from the interpretation of private agreements. Where the meaning of a contract is unclear, the parties seeking an interpretation are in many cases asking a court to facilitate their transaction. Some effort to understand what arrangements they were trying to make is integral to the resolution of the problem. Moral and social norms may have their influence, but the primary task of the interpreter is to try to determine what the parties wanted to do. The framework of interpretation includes this form of inquiry; it is not limited to the perception of ambiguities.

The omission of these features from Kelsen's understanding of interpretation is a further illustration of the proclivity of abstract thought to overlook the concrete aspects of a legal process. But it also emphasizes the limited conception of rationality presupposed by the Pure Theory of Law. An effort toward meaning is conceded, but only as a function of the principle of noncontradiction. In actual legal experience, reason has a much broader, pervasive significance. The purposive dimension is one manifestation which is expressed most dramatically in the historical effort to restrain arbitrary will.

Absolutism is opposed by law which presupposes a life, and a legal order, measured by reason. The difference between a narrow and broadly conceived understanding of reason in the law also reflects differing epistemological positions. In the Pure Theory, the range of reason is confined to the modalities of logic. This conception is an outcome of the post-Kantian philosophy and is traceable to the influence of Schopenhauer. But in the same period of philosophical activity important reformulations of the scope of reason were being made which have a direct bearing upon the development of legal philosophy.

Kant conceived of reason in terms of *a priori* forms of thought or categories of understanding. The conviction that logic is the supreme measure of intelligibility is in continuity with this conception. In the Nineteenth Century, it provoked reactions in which efforts were made to transcend this rationalism and the division of knowledge it required. Attention was drawn towards a conception of man as a being which seeks to understand himself in history. Here cognition could not be obtained through *a priori* forms of thought, but only through the categories of historic reason; reason engaged in understanding and interpreting history. Dilthey, a major figure in this movement, argued that only in the natural sciences could one legitimately deal with phenomena out of context as an abstracted system of relationships. The human sciences, by contrast,

> "... dealt with a human world, the product of an active mind with free will; they studied and interpreted phenomena as expressions of an inner spiritual reality. The human sciences could not remove phenomena from their historical context, as it was the context which gave them meaning. They had to be studied in their historical setting as part of the pattern of meaning and value which they formed ...[28]

This human world was the matrix of reality; a structural complex whose wholeness was constituted by action and thought working in unison.

For the natural sciences man is a detached object understood as it were from without. But in the cultural sciences he is understood from within; through his personally lived historical experiences. The cultural sciences understand historical reality as variants of the pursuit of life; modalities of existence which it seeks to penetrate with categories of meaning such as value, purpose, development, and ideal. The philosophies of Rickert and Hartmann provided complimentary insights. They saw the self as engaged in the pursuit of values, seeking to bring together the ideal and empirical worlds as he attributes valuational significance to concrete events.[29]

This change in the humanistic study of man was reflected in new jurisprudential conceptions. Radbruch, for example, placed law within the concrete realm of the cultural, rather than the abstract plane of the normative sciences. As a phenomenon of culture law could be understood as value related, involving the pursuit of justice although not its perfect realization. The thought of the Latin American jurist Recaséns-Siches is similar. For him the field of human existence is a realm of action, basically different from the domain of pure knowledge. As action, it moves beyond the scope of systematic logic yet still lies within the range of reason. Reason includes every intellectual operation which brings us in contact with reality and there is a *logos* of human action to which the law belongs.[30] Jurisprudence encompasses human reason in the making and interpretation of the law; concentrating upon the logic of the reasonable rather than upon a rationality of abstract logic. This understanding of law as a phenomenon within history and culture limits Kelsen's effort to disengage law from existence and understand it as an exact science to be known in its abstract normativity.

The contrast between experience and abstract thought is even more sharply drawn when the methodology of Pure Theory is compared with the philosophy of experience which is reflected in modern Sociological Jurisprudence. From the policy science perspective, as we have seen, reason is intimately bound up with experience. It serves to further the adjustments required in a concrete environment of human conflict. And it assumes, as Dewey argued, the evolution of intelligence as a positive factor within experience; capable, at this level, of connecting and unifying the realm of concrete life.[31] "Reason" is here not a remote faculty which imposes its forms upon reality. As intelligence, it is employed from within to enrich and expand experience.

B. *VALIDITY AND THE BASIC NORM*

The idea of validity is bound up with a hierarchical conception of the legal order, one which continually renews itself and regulates its own creation. The validity of legal norms does not depend upon their content but upon the way in which they are created. The reason for the validity of a norm can only be the validity of another norm referred to, figuratively, as a higher norm. This conception makes it possible to determine the competence of various public and private lawmaking activities and to coordinate, in a logically coherent way, the various levels of authority which function within a legal system.

Infinite regress is avoided and ultimate justification provided by a presupposed basic norm or *grundnorm*. The posited, *i.e.,* positive norms of a legal order must be created by a specific process which has historical origins; but we must move back to an assumed starting point if we wish to fully understand the nature of law creation:

> . . . [T]he basic norm is that norm which is presupposed when the custom through which the constitution has come into existence, or the constitution-creating act consciously performed by certain human beings, is objectively interpreted as a norm creating fact; if, in the latter case, the individual or the assembly of individuals who created the constitution on which the legal order rests, are looked upon as norm creating authorities. In this sense, the basic norm determines the basic fact of law creation and may in this respect be described as the constitution in a logical sense of the word . . . in contradistinction to the constitution in the meaning of positive law. The basic norm is the presupposed starting point of a procedure: the procedure of positive law creation. It is itself not a norm created by custom or by the act of a legal organ; it is not a positive but a presupposed norm . . .

> If the question as to the reason for the validity of a certain legal norm is raised, then the answer can only consist in the reduction to the basic norm of this legal order, that is, in the assertion that the norm was created—in the last instance—according to the basic norm.[32]

As a presupposition the basic norm makes possible the interpretation of an effective coercive order as a system of objectively valid norms. Primary law creating authority is conferred by the basic norm and the subjective acts of will by which the norms of positive law are created and applied obtain from it their ultimate justification.

It has been objected that the postulate of a basic norm is unnecessary because the norms of a legal order can be identified by other means. Inwardly, by criteria of recognition, we can determine whether particular norms actually belong to a specific legal system. Once the composition of the system is known the norms can be

ordered into a comprehensive whole by arranging them with reference to a basic temporal authority.[33] This procedure is arguably
more plausible than the invocation of a basic norm because the
number of norms issued in an *actual* legal order is necessarily of a
finite quantity.

Kelsen's advocacy of abstract regression culminating in a basic
norm is however not simply a systematizing convenience. Rather, it
has its roots in Kantian epistemology, especially in the separation of
the ought from existence. As an ought cannot be derived from an
is, so also no norm can be created by a human act alone. Legal
norms only come into being through a combination of specific
human acts and other legal norms. This conception accords with
the deepest levels of juridical consciousness and its innate tendency
towards abstract correlation. And it reveals the cognitive structure
of the transcendental ego as it is understood in Kantian thought.
Yet Kelsen's conception of validity is vulnerable because norms do
have concrete as well as abstract dimensions. More specifically, they
have imperative, as well as logical, characteristics.

Norms can command behavior and engage obedience.[34] The
basic norm does not satisfactorily explain the nature of legal obligation. Methodological, the basic norm makes possible the rational
cognition of a positive legal order. But it also functions as an imperative. It directs that one ought to obey not only the effectively
established constitution but also the norms created in conformity
with it. Kelsen's treatment of the moral basis of obedience is ambiguous, and at times supported by specious reasoning. To fully
understand his position one must take into account his explanations of the basis of political authority.[35]

Desires for freedom and equality constitute two of the primary
instincts of man. They are also the essential characteristics of
human nature as it is understood by philosophical relativism. Reality, from this perspective, exists only within human cognition; it is
relative to the knowing subject. The absolute "thing in itself" is
inaccessible, beyond human experience. This limitation however
has positive significance for it respects the position of man as the
creator of his world. Through his fidelity to the normative laws of
thought man is creative and free, for the world is then constituted
by his own cognition.

From this freedom of cognition there follows certain postulates
of equality. Perception of the absolute is impossible but philosophical relativism compensates for this deficiency by assuming that all,

as knowing subjects, are equal. The various cognitive processes within each are, unlike their emotional states, identical. It is therefore intrinsically possible for their intellectual perceptions to converge. Thus on an epistemological plane philosophical relativism reconciles the plurality of individuals in the existent world through their common dignity as thinking subjects. When transferred to the realm of political theory, this insight into the human condition resolves the fundamental antithesis between freedom and order.

The desire for freedom expresses itself most clearly in its reaction against compulsion, for submission to an alien will is instinctly felt as incompatible with liberty. But life in society inevitably leads to impositions because living together requires an ordering of behavior. As civilization advances tensions between liberty and order increase. The more the individual becomes conscious of his own worth the more he resents the pretentions of others to represent superior values. This negative idea of equality when combined with the essentially negative idea of freedom contains within it the seeds of chaos.

The exigencies of social life require some submission to authority. If it is to be achieved some positive conception of the reason and value of order must replace structural antagonisms. Freedom must be transformed: it must cease to mean a negation of social order and come to be understood as a specific method of establishing social order or government. To make social life tolerable some normative order regulating the mutual behavior of men *must be valid,* i.e., the domination of man over man through that order must be accepted.

If we must be dominated we prefer to be dominated by ourselves. To realize this desire natural freedom must be transformed into social or political freedom. Political freedom requires obedience to a normative order but it must be an order of our own, and not that of an alien, will. Liberty and restraint can be reconciled if the subject participates in the creation of the law to which he must submit. Under any system of political absolutism this is not possible for the people are subject to rules without participating in the power of enactment. But the ideal of freedom can at least be approximated under the institutional conditions of representative democracy.

A modern democratic state reduces the tension between the individual and social will by applying the principle of majority rule to its legislative institutions. It also acknowledges, more authentically than theories of social contract, the actual condition of man. In the reality of our social experiences there is no original creation of social order. The self is always born into an existing social *milieu* and usually into a form of government whose beginnings predate his existence. The development of this order is the crucial question of political life, and representative organs make participation in these transitions possible.

Here philosophical relativism comes to the aid of democracy because the cognitive premises of relativism reinforce political postulates of equality. The combativeness and domination of man by man which has plagued political theory since Hobbes, is neutralized by the precepts of relativism. For relativism couples recognition of the other with an affirmation of cognitive freedom. The one who experiences and assimilates these philosophical truths experiences the other not as an enemy but as his friend; indeed, he recognizes himself in the other. He acknowledges his fellows as co-collaborators in the creation of a democratic order. And, if he has made relativism his *credo* he can overcome the will to power. Conscious of his limitations, and of the relative status of his value structure, he is more tolerant of others, more ready to compromise and to accept the possibility of change should the calculus of majority rule turn against his interests.

Relativism thus gives a philosophical justification to democratic practices. Likewise, democracy contributes to the humanistic goals of relativism. As modern government moves from natural freedom without government to political freedom through a participation in government, it reserves zones of civil liberty which allow the autonomy of reason to flourish. Political liberalism requires that there be no interference in spheres of precious individual values. By respecting the rights of minorities against the arbitrary rule of majorities, it preserves intellectual as well as political autonomy. Thus the ideals of political democracy and philosophical relativism coalesce and, in combination, they establish the foundations of political and legal order. They also provide an ultimate justification for the obedience to normative commands which is a necessity of civilized existence.

By grounding democracy in philosophical relativism Kelsen provides a rationalization of obedience which is preferable to reliance upon a presupposed basic norm. However the connection between the intellectual premise and actual political life is too tenuous to be convincing. If the normative order emerging from representative government is in fact acceptable, it is so for reasons which have more to do with the emotional than the cognitive capacities of men. General obedience can also be more plausibly explained on the basis of social facts than through the postulates of pure reason: through a conviction within the general community that the existent legal rules are, at least by and large, morally valid.

The weakness of Kelsen's analysis lies in its philosophical premises, but it is also traceable to his operative conceptions of legal validity. Content to ask whether a law emanates from an *authorized* power, he fails to inquire whether the exercise of the power was *authoritative*. Validity includes delegation but it is much more than a transmission of power. To determine whether an act or decision is lawful involves considerations which are not reducible to a purely regressive analysis.

Authority implies a right to be followed.[36] It supplements a mere act of will—or delegated power—by adding reasons. And it assumes a reciprocal rather than a unilateral structure of government. It requires communications between the rulers and those who are ruled. Genuine authority can exist only if citizens understand and participate in the reasons why they are being asked to obey. It involves, in Acton's phrase, a freedom which is "not the power of doing what we like, but the right of being able to do what we ought."

An authoritative communication relates the exercise of power to a broad framework of reason. In addition to the rationality of logic it includes reasoning which calls value judgments into play, and relates lawmaking acts to the values of the community. The judicial process, for example, is not fully intelligible without reference to pressures for justification which transcend delegation of power. Revelation of all the basic grounds upon which decision rests is a requirements of intelligent discourse.[37]

Derivational validity, the justification of decisions by reference to higher norms, nevertheless accounts for a considerable portion of lawmaking activity. At the highest levels of executive, legislative and judicial power, actions are defended by recourse to superior norms, particularly those contained in a basic constitution. Where supreme power is subject to examination in the light of higher norms issues of validity are raised which are of profound importance.

The institution of judicial review is in this respect significant because it provides practical experience of the range of considerations which are relevant to judgments concerning constitutional validity. It is also important because the institution of judicial review is itself a source of controversies which promote reflection upon the nature of valid power. Modern jurisprudence seeks to determine how the power of judicial review, particularly when exercised by the Supreme Court, can be reconciled with the premises of democracy.

Here the problem of authoritativeness and obedience is acutely raised since the people, rather than the Court, are presumed to be sovereign. As an organ of government it participates in the right of the people to self-government. It has been delegated an authority, and if the assumptions of democracy are to be preserved it must be accountable for its use.

By calling their lawmakers to account through the electoral process the people preserve their autonomy. Yet the distinctiveness of the national judiciary lies in its independence. In terms of constitutional structure, the Supreme Court is virtually unaccountable. Neither the amending power under Article V of the Constitution nor Congress's regulatory authority under Article III provides more than minimal supervision. Nor do they reach the deeper problems of accountability and authority.

In structural terms, the Supreme Court has virtually unlimited power. But it is functually accountable to the people because of their expectation that its decisions will be authoritative. The Court has no inherent right to be obeyed. It can only expect general acquiescence if it acts within its jurisdictional competence and if the meanings which it attributes to the Constitution are justified by the fundamental values and the purposes of life in a democratic society.

We have already noted how Austinian legal positivism, with its emphasis upon sovereign power, is unable to give a satisfactory account of supreme judicial authority.[38] The Pure Theory of Law cannot measure the accountability of the Court and the ultimate validity of its constitutional judgments because of the radical dualism which Pure Theory maintains between valuation and cognition. From its perspective, all values are relative to the subject and not amenable to rational cognition. This position engenders a skepticism which has, as a positive consequence, the promotion of tolerance for another's views. But it is not responsive to the requirements of authoritative judgment. For here reference to values is an integral part of the quest for validity. Kelsen recognizes the existence of value systems and he acknowledges that in a given social context certain values may be generally accepted. But he also insisted that as a social phenomena they are a product of, and are relative to, a particular society.[39] Being subjectively grounded they are not jurisprudentially significant.

But the importance of democratic values can only be understood when they are considered as elements of moral experience. No agreement upon an absolute standard is required or implied. There can, however, be a practical convergence, from different philosphical perspectives, of basic perceptions of the good. Here as elsewhere, concentration upon abstract universality leads the Pure Theory of Law to overlook some essential elements of legal and political philosophy. The thought processes of pure reason do not reach the domain of concrete, functional assent to core values which make a democratic and human existence possible.[40] These considerations are of practical import because concrete valuation advances moral progress while avoiding extremes of judicial absolutism on the one hand, or the perpetuation of injustice on the other.

As a political institution the Court is under considerable pressure to bring its judgments into correspondence with prevailing social standards. Yet there is an inevitable tension between existing *mores* and what judges may perceive to be the requirements of justice. To give their intuitions normative sanction, insight may be transposed into constitutional command. When judicial perceptions surpass majority consensus conformity to higher law justifies the disparity between the ought and the is. Yet constitutional norms are notoriously vague, and reliance upon them as a justification is easily subject to abuse. There is a vast discretion within which judges may attribute meaning to the commands which they purport to follow. It is therefore of primary importance that they augment with reasons what is otherwise an act of will.

The reasons accompanying decision must demonstrate not only the institutional authority of the Court but also the relationship between the values being asserted and the deepest moral objectives of a democratic society. The need for this communicative process is now particularly acute for there is meager social consensus to which reference can confidently be made. No general agreement exists upon which to base solutions to the more intractable problems of individual and minority rights, nor are there accepted standards for the full elimination of discrimination. In these circumstances the Court must appeal to the deepest meanings of liberty, equality, and freedom; values which are within the conscience and consciousness of each citizen. Without such a decisional orientation, it is impossible to establish lawful authority.

In projecting a new affirmation of values the Court cannot be expected to completely articulate the premises of judgment. There must be room for a "creative ambiguity" as it moves towards a contemporary renewal of established values. Yet if authoritativeness is to be approximated there must be a continuous effort to convince the people that the standards towards which they are asked to aspire lie within the deepest levels of their moral experience. In default of such effort, the dangers of that absolutism which Kelsen deplores are very real. The temptation to replace the people's conscience with one's own is strongest when one has a low opinion of the moral capacities of those subject to one's power. When the public colloquy is not an appeal to responsible freedom it inevitably tends towards the coercive imposition of a platonic ideal. The consent of the governed is only operative through participation—not only, as Kelsen believed, in the creation of political institutions—but in the actual assent by the bulk of the population to the fundamental changes of constitutional order which the Court has power to promote. Such assent, and the communications which precede it, constitutes the inner substance of validity.

C. *THE STATE AND INTERNATIONAL LAW*

As conceived by Pure Theory the state is the unity of its legal order.[41] This conception has distinct advantages over both empirical and metaphysical definitions which have had an influence upon modern legal philosophy.

Definitions of the state in terms of specific attributes of people, territory, and power are premised upon assumptions which are no longer valid. They arose when geographical boundaries were relatively clear, national sentiments fixed common loyalties, and when populations were relatively stable. The pervasive indeterminateness of modern life has undermined these premises, dissolving the elements of stability and predictable jurisdiction upon which the understanding of the state was originally based.

Under these circumstances, the mutual relationships which constitute the material for law can only be satisfactorily understood in terms of a legal connection. People may or may not possess traditional loyalties, but if they are bound by a legal order they belong to a juridical community called the state. Shifting from what was essentially a political to a more rigorous legal definition, the Pure Theory transforms the empirical elements into abstract spheres of cognition.

The power of the state becomes the validity of an effective national legal order. The physical evidences of its power are simply indicia of its effectiveness. The range of state authority, now understood in terms of a spatial sphere of validity, encompass both the vertical and horizontal dimensions of jurisdiction. It provides a more comprehensive definition than is possible when legal thought is dependent upon the facts of natural geography. States, like men, are mortal; they are born and, if not always subject to absolute extinction, they may undergo a mutation. The state has a temporal as well as a spatial existence; when it comes to be and when it ceases to exist cannot be determined by natural facts. These existential elements involve matters of independence, termination, and succession which are only intelligible within the abstract frame of jural cognition.

The purpose of the Pure Theory as advocated by Kelsen is not just to make the life cycles of states more intelligible. It is also an attempt to overcome the pretensions of power which have been encouraged by metaphysical reflections on the nature of the state. Independence, traditionally linked with absolute sovereignty, is now stripped of its transcendental connotations. The independence of a state as a valid legal order simply means that it is not bound by any other national legal order.

The pretensions of political absolution can be limited further when law is understood as a dynamic process of norm creation and application. The tension between the autonomy of the individual and the heteronomy of law is often conceived as a relation between rules and those subject to their authority. The hegemony is accentuated by political conceptions of government and law, and, as we have seen, the Austinian version of sovereign authority was here open to abuse. But viewed on the plane of abstract juridical method government is a mode of law creation. Of particular importance are the innumerable administrative and judicial decisions on the one hand, and the realm of legal transactions, or private contracts, on the other.

Tradition positive law, influence by Hobbesian theories of sover-

eignty and Hegelian notions of the state, tended to treat the realms
of public and private law as clearly distinct. The one, a realm of
power domination reflected the imposition of the state's will. The
other was a field of coordination of the wills of legally equal subjects. In such a conception, the norms of public law are essentially
different from those of private law. They do not arise out of a
relation of mutuality. Rather they exist because qualified officials
have the power to obligate subjects by the unilateral projection of
their wills. But if public and private law are treated as analogous
phases of law creation within an entire legal order, the differences
between them are substantially reduced. Some technical distinctions remain but the tendency towards absolutism which is characteristic of modern governments can be arrested. The contrast between the two fields becomes relative and technical. What is of
supreme importance is the fact that in both fields the principle of
law is binding. In public law there may be more discretion, but
there is not *freedom from* the law.

The solution of the Pure Theory consists essentially of comprehending the state as an activity rather than as a metaphysical
entity. The inquiry becomes a search to determine whether a particular function rendered by an official can be attributed to the
state. As a modality of a normative order, attribution means that
the function is determined by the national legal order which constitutes the state as a *juridical* community.[42] The legal significance of
public and private behavior is ascertained by the same criteria. The
state is not the personification of a particular class; it is the personification of a legal order. If the state *qua* administrative machinery is distinctive, it is, like the corporation, a partial legal order.
It holds its authority as a delegated power. Supreme power is subordinated to law because acts of sovereign will are comprehended
as actions determined by a valid legal order which legitimizes all law
creating acts.

Through these rather complex reflections on the nature of the
state and law Kelsen provides the jurist with intellectual weapons
with which he can defend the supremacy, as well as the autonomy,
of the positive legal order against the assaults of political absolutism. Through this theoretical argument he also reveals his lack
of confidence in a concept of validity understood as a delegation of
power. The analysis of the state in Pure Theory is interesting as an
intellectual exercise, but it lacks the moral cogency and persuasive-
ness which is essential to accomplish the actual restraint of power.

In this respect, it is submitted that analysis of the phenomenon of authoritativeness along the lines we have suggested offers greater prospects for assuring the rule of law. Moreover, by reducing the problem of state power to a juridical conception, Kelsen ignores manifestations of the state as a political reality which legal philosophy must take into account.

In our review of Analytical Jurisprudence we observed that the datum of political organization was of primary importance to legal theory. In Pound's Sociological Jurisprudence the state as a form of political organization was also indispensable to a realistic understanding of positive law. The original connections between jurisprudence and concepts of sovereignty were maintained. In Pound's work, the acknowledgement included, but went beyond, the data of power. The state was considered as having distinctive interests which were essential to its normal existence.[43]

The integration of the state as a concrete phenomenon within the scope of jurisprudence also conforms with elementary facts of consciousness. Without postulating a metaphysical substance, we are aware that whenever public authority is operative factors are engendered which are not reducible to individual consciousness or other forms of social interaction. Acknowledgement of these differences is necessary if we are to adequately grasp the structure of the external objective world.

The application of the legal order to the exercise of state power is not straightforward. A complex mosaic of distinctive jural concepts must be taken into account in order to make sovereign power subject to law. One must come to grips with distinctions between proprietary and governmental functions and take into account privileges and immunities which attach, in varying degrees, to all levels of government and ranges of official behavior. State interests may be transcended for reasons of justice or social policy,[44] but a sound jurisprudence cannot ignore their existence.

The Pure Theory's conception of the state is also inadequate at the theoretical level. The basic problem is one of political theory. It will be recalled that the origins of democratic government were traced by Kelsen to individual consciousness of intellectual freedom and the efforts to balance liberty with order which flowed from that awareness. Organization was understood in terms of the possibilities of each participating in the formation of the legal order to which he must submit. That participation, through representative institutions, constituted the crucial element of life in a politi-

cally organized society. Upon this narrow base a juridical edifice
was constructed which absorbs within itself the idea of the state.

A more substantial understanding of the realities can be obtained
through reflections which are grounded upon socio-moral factors
of experience. Politically organized society can be more realistically
understood in terms of the pursuit of a common life by concrete
persons willing to live together under just laws. The state, as a
specialist in law and administration, is a part of that large whole.[45]

In the evolution of modern societies, the facts of centralization,
both of power and administration, has given a certain dominance
to the organs of government. But, if topmost, the state is still a part.
Its constituent organs are accountable, under democratic principles, to the people. By viewing the essential elements of the state
and political society in this way is it possible to overcome the separation of the state from the body politic which is the heritage of
Hobbesian and Hegelian theories, without dissolving the structure
through logical fictions as is attempted by the methodology of Pure
Theory. And within this larger framework the basic insights of
Pure Theory concerning the normative coherence of positive law
can be preserved.

~

The absence of a supreme political authority led Austin to conclude that international rules were not, strictly speaking, positive law. Kelsen believed that international norms could be understood juristically if the international realm was seen in its relation to
the general evolution of legal orders. National and international
legal orders are both coercive. International law simply lacks cen-
tralized organs for the enactment and enforcement of law. Delicts
can be met with sanctions imposed by authorized states acting
individually or through forms of collective security. International
law is thus similar to the law of primitive societies, since both rely
upon self-help for the application of their sanctions.[46]

As a dynamic order international law is a system of legal norms
created by the custom of states, by international treaties, and by
international organs created by treaties. The norms are established
in a hierarchial relation. Customary international law, which
creates obligations or rights for all states, includes, among its

norms, the principle *pacta sunt servanda.* As this forms the basis of treaty law, the two lawmaking procedures have a relation of higher and lower authority within a hierarchy. A third level is evidenced by the lawmaking of international courts and other international organs created by treaties.

The international and national legal orders form a unity; the norms of the former determining what ought to be done, national law determining who is to perform or observe the prescribed forebearance. The relationship is one of delegation, similar to that of the relation between the national legal order and the corporation. If the behavior of a national official constitutes a delict, it is attributed to the state on whose behalf he acts. Collective responsibility is incurred. If sanctions are contemplated they will be applied against the members of the state except in the limited circumstances where individual liability obtains.

The primary problem of modern international law is that of justifying its prescriptive character. Modern theories of the state accept international law as a valid legal order, but often insist upon state sovereignty as its foundation. On such premises, jurists in the latter part of the nineteenth century promoted a dualistic conception which conceived of national or municipal law as derived from the will of a particular state while international rules had their source in the common will of states. The two legal orders existed on different planes and they did not interpenetrate. For an international rule to have effect within a state, it must be transformed into a rule of municipal law by an act of national legislation.[47] It was Kelsen's contention that the international and national legal orders could be comprehended in unity and their mutual validity affirmed.

In its domestic law, a state may enact legislation or issue orders inconsistent with its international obligations. If this conflict were unsolvable, the existence of international law would be threatened. For international and national law cannot be both valid independently of each other. But national law which is incompatible with international obligations does not present a genuine conflict between norms of a lower and higher order. Within the domain of logic, where the principle of non-contradiction holds sway, it can be demonstrated that such apparent conflicts are not real.

Such repugnance between lower and higher norms means only that the validity of the lower norm *may be* nullified or the one responsible punished. Procedures for annulment, such as a process

for declaring the unconstitutionality of statutes, exist within national legal orders. At the present stage of international law there
are no established procedures for annulment, although such inconsistencies are often denounced. In such circumstances the national
norms retain their validity. Yet logically there is no contradiction
since the repugnant state norm bears the potential of invalidation.

If the two normative orders of national and international law are
to be validated as one system they must be justified by some controlling principle of reason. According to Kelsen, this can be done by
either one of two monistic constructions. National legal orders can
be comprehended as subordinate to the international legal order
on the grounds that the reason for the validity of each national
system can be found within the structure of international law. If a
political unit meets prerequisties of population, territory, and effective control, the status of statehood is conferred by international
law. The spatio-temporal conditions of statehood and the range of
legitimate jurisdiction are all determined by international rules.
These legal orders can be conceived as delegated by international
law. They are partial legal orders in a constitutive sense: validated
by, subordinate to, and included in a universal world legal order.
From this monistic perspective, international law is understood as a
supra-national legal order. Only it is fully sovereign. National legal
orders do not have unlimited competence; states are sovereign in
the sense that they are only subject to the international legal order.

An alternative monistic construction is more deferential to advo-
cates of state supremacy, yet it avoids the contradictions implicit in
theories of auto-limitation.[48] If the national legal order is presupposed as supreme, international law becomes valid for the state
only if it has, expressly or by implication, recognized international
law as binding. From this perspective, international law is a legal
order delegated by the national legal order; a normative regime
which becomes binding for a state already conceived of as a valid
legal order.

International jurists favoring state sovereignty would only allow
for subordinations to a superior law which were created by a state
through its capacity to bind itself. Any obligation not derived from
free volition was contrary to the premises of sovereign power. But
in this form the doctrine of the primacy of the national legal order
is unacceptable to the Pure Theory of Law.

International Law cannot be defined according to the object regulated by its norms. Further, not only the behavior of states but also,

in certain circumstances, the behavior of individuals is regulated by international law. As a system, international law can be defined solely by the manner in which its norms are created. The reason for the validity of international law is not auto-limitation; nevertheless, it can be found within the national legal order. It is legitimate to postulate the supremacy of the national legal order so that norms created at the international level will be regarded as valid only following the initial recognition, but this process is justified only if the ultimate reason for the validity of international law is the presupposed basic norm of this national legal order. When intellectual presuppositions are brought into play, the inflated position of states is transcended. By logic, rather than power, the fundamental unity of national and international law is established and preserved.

It is possible to establish the validity of international and national law by either one of these two monistic constructions. The choice of one or the other does not affect the content of international norms, which are obligatory regardless of one's ultimate perspective. The Pure Theory of Law, as a jurisprudence premised upon philosophical relativism, treats both as justified systems of reference. From the heights of dispassionate reason it describes the cognitive presuppositions of each and points out how an emphasis upon either betrays emotional preferences.[49]

Here, as with other aspects of the Pure Theory of Law, the abstract character of Kelsen's thought conveys an incomplete perception. The difficulties are manifested when logical analysis seeks to sustain the supremacy of international law. Those who presuppose the primacy of international law often assume that any norm of national law contrary to international law is null. But such norms are, as has been indicated, only annullable. Whether or not they are in fact annulled is a matter of procedure. The absence of such machinery, Kelsen insists, does not essentially affect theoretical analysis. It is crucial to his thesis that the logical unity of international and national law can be preserved even if a norm of the lower, national law is contrary to international norms.[50]

But international law purports to invalidate norms which are inconsistent with the obligations which it imposes. This is so even though there are no institutional procedures for nullification. Article 103 of the Charter of the United Nations is to this effect, as it provides that in case of a conflict between the obligations of members under the Charter and obligations under other international agreements the former shall prevail. There are analogous rules within the general law of treaties. It is arguable that, in these circumstances, the conflicting norm is invalid. The conflict between the two orders may, of course, remain. One may be required, in fact, to obey the law which is ostensibly invalid. And the actual power of states to disregard superior international responsibilities remains uneffected. They may choose to ignore the inconsistencies and conduct their affairs as though the conflicting norm was fully viable. Nevertheless, if we observe what hierarchical subordination actually exists, the closer contact with realities adds to the understanding of international rules. The verticalism of Kelsen's Theory is here impotent, since it assumes that circumstances of conflict may arise without violating the logical coherence of the national and international legal orders.[51]

At a deeper level of analysis, Kelsen shares with other modern legal positivists the ambition to comprehend law without reference to facts of political organization. We previously observed how Kelsen sought to understand the state as its legal order. He also contends that it is possible to understand the nature of international law without taking into account its foundations in political theory. In this sense Kelsen's thought parallels that of H.L.A. Hart. Kelsen's error is the more egregious however, because he conceptualizes international law *as if it were* a meaningful superior reality. With great mental facility his thought struggles to control the anarchy of states. But he ends by reifying the superior order of international law. According to Pure Theory, the international legal order validates, delegates authority, and imposes its norms. At bottom, the theoretical construct is an imaginary personification of a mental process.

The intellectual range of logical positivism makes Pure Theory superior in many respects to Analytical Jurisprudence. But Austin's refusal to give international relations the status of positive law retains a certain cogency. For Austin, international precepts had obligatory force as moral, not legal rules. This sharp distinction is now unacceptable, if only because customary and conventional norms are constantly referred to as legal obligations. There is also evidence of the willingness of peoples to live under rules which they regard as binding. In this sense international law, particularly in its customary form, is functionally comparable to commanded law. However, the Austinian insight persists. At essential junctures, where vital interests are engaged, the absence of coercive machinery is a fundamental defect. It is at this point that considerations grounded upon political theory become operative. There can be no positive international law, in the strict sense, until norms are established by supreme legislative authority which are indisputably binding and effectively enforced.

Considered from another angle, Kelsen's analysis of international law is flawed because he uses conceptions which are only applicable to a complete legal order. Acutely aware of the importance of enforcement, he retains coercion as an integral part of legal definition. Giving authorized states discretionary power to apply sanctions of war and reprisal makes up, as it were, for the absence of political organs. The primary difficulty is the precarious and potentially arbitrary enforcement which it implies. But, of more importance, is the model of law as coercion which permeates the theory. In the jurisprudence of Pure Theory positive law is essentially a coercive order; a quality which distinguishes it from other forms of social ordering. When seeking to understand a national legal order, the definition is cogent. But when transferred to the international realm, the distortions are considerable.

At its present stage of development, international law and organization is not moving towards collective security. This is particularly true of the United Nations. For the foreseeable future disorder will be overcome primarily by noncoercive means. The prevailing insights of political science suggest a "reconciliation" model as the appropriate means of understanding authority within the United Nations Organization. The characteristics of such a model, which include a pursuit of ends with minimal coercion and primary reliance upon negotiation and bargaining, are more likely to assure pacification than possible applications of force against force.[52] Even the potentials of the Security Council, which has coercive authority, can be better understood in noncoercive terms. As an organ of collective conciliation its primary effectiveness will depend upon its ability to skillfully promote the peaceful settlement of disputes.

CHAPTER FOUR

THE PURSUIT OF JUSTICE

A. *INTRODUCTION*

I n his Pure Theory, Kelsen provided a positive, logically grounded alternative to the Sociology of Law. In his conception of justice, he again responds to a sociological challenge. For the school of Sociological Jurisprudence, the purpose of a legal order is to satisfy the interests and demands made upon it. Unless these are satisfied, law cannot endure.

This orientation implies the primacy of peace. But in the satisfaction of demands there cannot be, in a strict sense, justice. Justice is a dimension of social happiness, a need felt whenever there is a conflict of interests. Such conflicts do not admit of objective resolution:

> [W]hich human interests are worthy of being satisfied and, especially, what is their proper order of rank? That is the question which arises when conflicting interests exist, and it is with respect to the possible conflict of interests that justice within a social order is required .... A conflict of interests exists when one interest can be satisfied only at the expense of the other; or, what amounts to the same, when there is a conflict between two values, and when it is not possible to realize both at the same time; when the one can be realized only if the other is neglected; when it is necessary to prefer the realization of the one to that of the other; to decide which one is more important, or, in other terms, to decide which is the higher value, and finally, which is the highest value. The problem of values is, in the first place, the problem of conflicts of values, and this problem cannot be solved by means of rational cognition. The answer to these questions is a judgment

of value, determined by emotional factors, and, therefore, subjective in character—valid only for the judging subject, and therefore relative only . . .[1]

Justice is subjective; a desire enveloped in relativity. This is not, for Kelsen, the same as arbitrariness. Values are shaped in a social context, and particular statements about justice may well reflect a general consensus. As law is related to morals, a given legal order bears an ethical relationship to the society in which it functions. But this is a connection with only one, historically conditioned, value system; a socio-ethical regime with only relative moral significance.

For Pound, the subjectivity of justice was a positive quality. The desire of judges to be just in the administration of law could, he hoped, bring about that equilibrium of interests which was the mark of a progressive civilization. For legal positivism, however, justice would be transformed into legality. Aspirations for justice could then be fulfilled through the conscientious application of the positive law:

> [I]t is 'just' for a general rule to be actually applied in all cases where according to its content, this rule should be applied. It is 'unjust' for it to be applied in one case and not in another similar case. And this seems 'unjust' without regard to the value of the general rule itself, the application of which is under consideration. Justice in the sense of legality is a quality which relates not to the content of a positive order but to its application . . .[2]

Justice under the law is a commitment of ethical import. Fidelity to positive rules has a moral value, for the ideal of the just man includes adherence to authoritatively enacted law. Similarly, a commitment to the general principles of a legal system is a mark of disinterested impartiality. And the principle of legality incorporates the moral ideal of equality, however much it may be insisted that legality is only the objective meaning of positive law.

Kelsen's approach to the problem of justice emphasizes the separate reality of positive law. But, if the distinction is relentlessly pursued, there is an inevitable reappearance of subjectivity. Literal interpretations of the Bill of Rights, for example, can set the objectivity of positive law over against the public passions of majorities. But literalism can also become a technique for avoiding the reality of value conflict; and when these complexities are evaded, the bias of the interpreter, rather than the impartial majesty of positive norms, begins to take precedence.

The equal application of legal norms is only a part of decision making in the law. Judges and lawyers understand that the *corpus* of law applicable to decisions include principles of justice as well as precise positive rules. There is also as we have seen, an extensive interpenetration of social values and juridical precepts. This intermingling of rules, precepts and interests, and the margin of discretion which modern lawmaking assumes, requires a more extensive elucidation of the relation between law and justice than that provided by the reductionism of Kelsen's positivism.

Throughout this century, political and legal philosophers have sought to enlarge our understanding of justice by appeal to empirical, rather than logical thought. Through a comparative empiricism, Arnold Brecht developed universal postulates of justice ostensibly based upon the general experience of mankind.[3] Julius Stone, assuming like Brecht that the content of justice is derived from social experience, purports to have discovered quasi absolute precepts of material justice. Beyond the perimeters of positive law Stone explicates normative qualities which have emerged from Western man's historical efforts to be just. These are, he believes, of sufficient merit to be *for us* absolutes, even if not further identified with a transcendent order of reality.[4]

Some of these reflections have a direct bearing upon Kelsen's theory of legality. From the experience of history Stone extracts a standard of equality which requires that whenever jural action is undertaken it should affect all equally, and equally with others affected by previous action in similar circumstances—unless there are sufficient reasons for doing otherwise. Where extra-legal values become influential, the margin of discretion can also be restrained by principles of justice. Brecht insists upon a standard of generality: a just judgment must be based upon a general scheme of values rather than upon particular norms arbitrarily selected for the case at hand. Similarly, Stone contends that one deciding between competing claims must gain, as far as possible, a grasp of all relevant facts and values, especially those competing against the ones being asserted.

A general structure of justice also emerges from modern reflections. Hart notes that, as a distinctive part of morality, justice has two primary connotations.[5] In ordinary language it is normally discussed either in the context of sharing social burdens and benefits, or with reference to the redress of injuries. Among Stone's

quasi absolutes is the precept that where there has been a serious
disturbance of normal equilibrium, some form of redress is required in the name of justice. On the societal plane, contributions
to the body politic must be appropriately acknowledged. A serious
infringement of socially accepted values, or distributed advantages,
may be met by punishment provided the dignity of the individual
and standards of proportionality are respected.

These ideas have broadened the scope of justice, but it is doubtful whether they are fully responsive to Kelsen's critique. In large
measure they refer to moral dispositions of the judging subject;
refinements of interior attitude which are a necessary part of impartial decision. There is also much that is purely formal, as in the
drawing out of a general structure of justice. And, when these
empirical reflections touch upon sociological data, deeper weaknesses are revealed.

From sociological experience, Stone includes the free assertion
of interests as a quality of material justice. To give to each his due
demands, at a minimum, that each be accorded the liberty to define
his own interests, express them, and compete openly for their acceptance in the community. The precept is morally cogent, but
when we approach situations where freedom may be restricted, our
convictions become less certain. It is unjust to arbitrarily interfere
with freedom, but the standards by which we are to judge arbitrariness are largely derived from social norms. Brecht maintains for
example that if freedom is abridged because of a conflict with other
values, such action can be characterized as just only if it is in pursuit
of values considered higher under the axiological scheme within
the relevant society.

A lack of certitude also surrounds the concept of equality. If
unequal situations can be treated differently, there are not substantive standards to measure the appropriate classification. One can
commend fidelity to truth, but we cannot ascertain from experience the necessary criteria for determining when such requirements have been met.

It was inevitable that within modern legal philosophy attempts
would be made to establish justice on super-empirical foundations.
In the pursuit of justice there has been a turning inward, an orien-

tation which suggests that what it means to give another his due is more likely to emerge from reflective self-consciousness than through a consideration of empirical evidence. The legal philosophy of Gustave Radbruch[6] is illustrative of this tendency towards a subjective understanding of the meaning of justice.

The thought of Radbruch exhaustively divides the boundaries between the objective world and the perspectives of a thinking subject. For every given aspect of existence there corresponds an interior mental attitude which establishes our relationship to reality. These variations are intelligible when we understand the extent to which a value element is or is not involved.

The primary confrontation with the natural world is value blind. We bring order to the phenomena of natural existence through the imposition of our forms of thought. A second basic attitude towards existence is evaluating. We are conscious of the fact that at certain times we confront nature, and the world, armed with explicit norms or standards of evaluation.

There are also processes of thought and will which lie between the mental attitudes identified as value blind and evaluating. They encompass the fields of value related phenomena, of which culture is the primary instance. Never pure value, it is rather a mixture of civility and barbarism, human realization and failure. Although not an accomplishment of righteousness, its significance for the thinking subject lies in the manner that it reflects a striving for the realization of the good.

Law is a phenomenon of culture. As such, it is neither devoid of value nor the fulfillment of righteousness. Being value related it does not have an autonomous existence. It is rather grounded within human consciousness. Man creates and maintains positive law in order to realize justice. In terms of the structure of consciousness, it is preferable to comprehend law as a value-related phenomenon rather than as a construct of pure logic. The ought is not determined by positive law, for law is dependent for its existence and orientation upon the autonomous human spirit which breathes purpose into its structure. So strong is this subservience that the very concept of law contains *a priori* dimensions which determine the primary characteristics of a legal system.

Justice, as a personal quality, shapes relations between men by way of equality, and all legal orders reflect this imperative in their inevitable tendency towards generality. Basic legal concepts prove, upon examination, to be prejuridically determined by subjective pointers towards justice. Legal right and duty, rule, even legality itself are fully intelligible only when law is understood as a cultural phenomenon intrinsically bound up with an interior determination to give to each his due.

But the analysis of law in these purposive terms reinforces the premises of moral relativism presupposed by legal positivism. Law as a cultural phenomenon is value-related. But the range of value preferences is so immense, and so susceptible to ideological manipulation, that it is impossible to speak with confidence about the moral content of the rules in which these values are expressed. At the point of decision making, where value conflict is acute, jurisprudence can only illustrate the options available to choice. And in making imperatives concrete, there is an inevitable aspect of expediency, *i.e.*, suitability to purpose, which is inimical to objective moral certitude. Further, as a mode of culture, law must promote certainty as well as justice.[7]

By transferring the problem of justice from the empirical realm to the plane of abstract philosophy, Radbruch demonstrated a connection between the autonomous spirit and jural reality. But the quest to place justice upon unshakable foundations, and to attribute to it a more than formal meaning, remains unsatisfied. One alternative is to derive a meaning of justice from components which involve emotion.[8] Nevertheless the main thrust towards a modern understanding of justice has been towards abstract levels of cognition. The dominant themes reflect currents of idealism traceable to the Kantian noetic. Radbruch's thought is partially within this tradition, but there have been fuller expositions of this tendency to search for the objective meaning of justice within the subjective recesses of the human spirit.

For Kelsen, the fact that justice has a subjective quality meant that it was an irrational ideal. Only the normative legal order, as comprehended by logical forms of thought, was subject to cognition. This view was derived from Kant and philosophical developments in the post-Kantian period. But within the same tradition of idealism there has arisen a conviction that justice can be established upon firm normative foundations. This development can be seen primarily in the thought of the Italian jurist, Giorgio Del Vecchio.

B. *JUSTICE IN IDEALISM*

As the subject is himself the center of cognition the world reflects ideas which have an origin within consciousness. The external realm, the objective order of nature, appears as a field of physical and social facts which are governed by criteria of causality and finality. But these qualities are inborn, proper to our intellect; ideal imprints given *a priori* in our consciousness which are also found in the objective order of the universe.

In Kantian epistemology there is thus an interplay between the forms of thought and external phenomena. To bring the relationship between thought and nature into perspective it was necessary to establish the independence of the conscious subject and his cognitive ability. To prove the autonomy of legal cognition Kelsen separated the normative processes of the mind from the causality of nature. For Del Vecchio, it was necessary to demonstrate that man, although affected by physical laws, has as an intelligible being an inward power and potential to determine his own existence. His noumenal being, and the transcendental ideas of which he is in possession, make it possible for him to affirm personal responsibility and rise above empirical laws of cause and effect:

> The faculty of abstracting and recognizing oneself outside of physical nature, the faculty of referring to the ego, by ways of ideas, all the reality which converges in it, constitutes for the subject his proper and specific being, that which is preeminently his *nature.* And this faculty or vocation reveals itself to every man in his never failing consciousness of his power of free choice and of the responsibility which attends thereon. . .
>
> To act as a subject and not as an object is for man not merely a psychological possibility. It is also an ethical requirement which imposes itself on his conscience and does so all the more clearly and strongly the more sensitive and alert his conscience has become. If man were simply a phenomenon, he would not be confronted by the problem of ethics and the notion of an imperative would have no meaning for him, because human actions as phenomena, being always and necessarily in conformity with nature in the objective sense, would not be susceptible of any further critical examination or evaluation. Fact would be, as in the physical sciences, the criterion of truth. But since man, while belonging to the phenomenal order, is, and feels intimately that he is, something more than a phenomenon, the fulfillment of his own essence and realization of his nature is for him not a mere fact but a problem and a task which is continuously set before him so

long as he lives—that is, so long as he exists as a subject.
Indeed, the notion of an imperative depends precisely upon
this peculiar condition of man by which he participates in two
natures or, to put it better, belongs to a double order of reality, the physical and the metaphysical. From the latter aspect,
each of his actions has its origin in man himself and thus bears
the mark of an absolute beginning.[9]

   This ideal sets before man the duty of subduing his passions and
physical affections and transfiguring his contingent individuality in
the forms of ethical universality. The ideal is to pursue the supreme norms of morality which corresponds to our spiritual essence, especially those norms which pertain to justice. These obligations can be discovered within the depths of self-consciousness.
   An act of self-consciousness, or thought about oneself, necessarily involves some form of relation. To posit the self involves an
assertion about what is not the self. According to critical idealism,
by this process of self-reflection we can establish the reality of the
external world. Arising from the inner exigencies of the spirit, it is
deduced *a priori* independent of any perception of particular objects.
   The methodology has for Del Vecchio an application to the problematic of justice. For to be conscious of the self necessary involves
positing an other, or others, different from oneself. The other is
recognized as a subject, another self, known in a relationship which
is intra-subjective rather than antithetical. The self, rather than
being an isolated individual, is conscious of his involvement in a vast
network of intersubjective relationships. These relationships are
not imposed from without, but are rather established within our
own awareness as an immanent and irrepressible mode of behavior. The coordination of subjective selves with each other becomes the basic objective of justice.
   Out of our encounters with others there arise potentials for conflict. The measure of these encounters lies in an inward bond of
reciprocity and mutual respect. And the standard of right does not
depend upon the arbitrary will of the acting subject: The other is
intrinsically and intimately bound up in any evaluation of our conduct, since other selves are integral to our thought.
   By fully acknowledging other selves within our consciousness we
recognize the paramount value of personality. The other is seen as

an autonomous person and the quality of personality in oneself, as in all others, becomes a firm measure by which to judge interactions between subjective beings:

> In the form of law, the supreme ethical rule requires the reciprocal recognition of the absolute character of personality. Hence is derived a series of correlative claims and duties equally founded on that same presupposition and therefore universally valid. Every man, solely in virtue of his nature, can claim that no other shall treat him as if he were nothing but a means or an element of the sensible world, but rather shall behave toward him with respect for that ideal principle of autonomy which is implanted in his very nature. Under this aspect there is among all men a fundamental equality, whence it follows that the liberty of each should be harmonized and raised to the universal according to the idea of a possible coexistence . . .[10]

From this deontological perspective one can also gain a deeper understanding of the role of law in human history. In its positivity law is intimately linked with other phenomenon of human life, subject to the vicissitudes of progress and regression which mark man's journey through time. But human history has a general direction. Within each epoch, in spite of contradictions and failures, there is a discernible effort to realize human values. These values—of order and liberty, security and freedom, are, when subject to the passions and interests of individuals and nations, contradictory; but this unpleasant observation does not require surrender to ethical relativism.

Beneath the turmoil, a unitary development is at work. Principles of moral law, the ideal vocations of man, are slowly, but inexorably, being realized. Conscience has a duty to cooperate in the fulfillment of justice and this obligation finds its juridical manifestation in law. Moreover, on the ethical plane, there are ideal universally valid principles by which to judge the degree of justice within the political and juridical institutions which arise in the course of history.

In its formal significance, the inward perceptions of justice are externally expressed in positive law. The structure of a legal system reflects the *a priori* characteristics of justice which are innate to consciousness, especially the correlation of claims and obligations which constitute the frame of justice. But these innate principles also have a substantive content which remains unitary and immutable in spite of the variable elements which appear in every concrete positive legal order.

The idea of justice appears within consciousness not only in the universality of its form but also as ideal ethical standards. This ideal content feeds the actual claims for justice which arise in the course of history and also provides normative standards upon which to measure and evaluate varying degrees of juridical experience. This ideal criterion is a categorical requirement, demanding the complete recognition of personality *in oneself, as in all others* as the foundation of all possible interactions between human subjects.

Each must be recognized as the author of his own acts, prohibited from ascribing to others the consequences of his own volition or from acquiring for himself the benefits of acts which are authentically the fruit of another's efforts. A 'right to solitude' must be acknowledged, which affirms and develops that element of autonomy which is the essence of personality. And, in mutual dealings, the trans-subjective meta-empirical quality of human nature must be respected, excluding all inequalities in such relationships which are not grounded upon the genuine being and acting of each.

The ideal content of justice also gives a deontological value to the natural rights of man, as they are expressed in the Universal Declaration of Human Rights. To discern and declare such rights is a task of pure reason which is capable of reducing the manifold expression of rights to their essential unity. The ethical significance of human rights is revealed when they are viewed neither separately nor in their cultural origins, but as they are precisely derived from the essence of the person.

Understood subjectively, from within the depths of consciousness, justice becomes an ideal objective of man as he pursues that ethical perfection which makes him distinctively human. Self consciousness includes an affirmation of other selves, and upon this perception Ethical Idealism builds a structure and content of justice. Traditional attempts to establish justice upon natural foundations are surpassed and the modern challenge of moral relativism is overcome. Seen in this light justice, rather than being an irrational ideal, lies at the summit of moral reason. Recognition of the absolute personality of ourselves and all others becomes the foundation and objective of human justice.

When reciprocity is at the full, we acknowledge what is distinctive about a human being: his capacity for behavior and performances of his own, and his ability, as well as our own, "to pursue rational ends, to follow rational principles, and to engage in rational actions."[11] We then begin to realize the Kantian ideal of never treating others as mere instruments of our own ends and establish that *alteritas* and the *suum cuique tribuere* which is the essence of justice. This conception of justice bears contrast not only with Logical Positivism, but also with the problem of justice as it arises within Sociological Jurisprudence.

One consequence of concentrating upon demands made upon the legal order has been a tendency to assess human interests in behavioral terms. Ethical Idealism makes possible a more elevated conception of human interaction. Interests and demands are intelligible with reference to the ends we pursue. Where our actions impinge upon others, there are latent moral purposes at work which sociological methodologies often fail to observe. Viewed from the heights of ethical theory, some actions are seen as being performed for their own sake, as ends in themselves. They may reveal a pursuit of rational objectives and the acceptance of moral principles. And the desires which constitute our instinctual life can be understood as emotional dispositions to pursue, in particular contexts, ends which have a moral value. A rational ordering can be present even when our instinctive life seems to be imposed upon us by non-moral elements of our nature.[12]

When our relations with others are governed by moral reason, reciprocity replaces the instinct to dominate and exploit:

> By the concept of reciprocity a person recognizes another person from the same perspective as he sees himself, and from the same perspective as that other person sees himself—that is, in terms of that other person's ends . . . each person recognizes as most important in others just what he recognizes as most important in himself, and just what they recognize as most important in themselves.[13]

Moreover, an emphasis upon personal autonomy provides an effective counterweight to those pressures for uniformity and absorption of the individual within the group which has become one of the themes of modern sociology.

By affirming the intrinsic worth of personality, and pointing up the juridical implications of such acknowledgement, ethical idealism provides a creative alternative. But, although it provides some standards to which one can refer, it does not adequately resolve the problem of value conflict. Order and freedom are *both* elements of that bilateral justice which a legal order must strive to implement. Within limits, a respect for legality is a requirement of justice; part of the subordination of the self to transubjective standards. This qualified acceptance of positive rules by idealism can, however, accentuate value conflict. For social antagonisms often reflect pressures for change being applied against an established order.

Radbruch saw that the concrete meaning of justice was dependent upon value preferences which were often incompatible. He also understood that positive law included elements of suitability and order as well as those of normative justice. Subject to a moral minimum, he concluded that law could only be comprehended as a value-related phenomenon, serving a complex of values whose hierarchical ordering could not be definitively established. Radbruch was also convinced that jurisprudence should elucidate, as far as possible, the value options which were available for choice by decision makers.

The general thrust of jurisprudential thought has been in continuity with Radbruch's insight. It can be seen, for example, in Perelman's idea that the problematic of justice is essentially a matter of argumentation. Justice is significant as a principle of action even though it has no objective meaning. Equality, understood as a formal quality rather than as an objective aspect of existence, becomes the measure of operative justice. Choices made within that framework, which involve value preferences, must be defended by techniques of reasoned justification. Values are secured insofar as we are able to persuade others of their importance.[14]

This line of development accentuates the general weakness of idealism as a moral philosophy when it is confronted with the reality of value conflict. It also invites comparison with the methodologies of Sociological Jurisprudence which we surveyed in Chapter Two. Pound sought to give interests some objective basis by observing the degree to which they were assimilated into the

positive legal order. More directly relevant is the policy science
jurisprudence of Lasswell and McDougal, which reflects the influence of Dewey's instrumentalism. By intelligent operations, demands are related to indicies of preferred public order, and by
such procedures it is hoped that value distributions will be made
upon an objective basis.

Such rigorous empiricism may yield more practical certitude
than theories of idealism which hope to ground justice within the
moral imperatives of autonomous individuals. However, a fundamental criticism which we have made concerning policy science
jurisprudence applies, with equal force, to the subjective theories of
justice. Like sociological jurisprudence, ethical idealism does not
fully encompass the moral dimensions of judgment.

Kantian ethics understands imperatives, and the ordering of actions by general principles. It also can uncover an internal structure
of moral life, revealing how ethical principles have a pervasive
influence upon all of our actions. But it does not reach decisional
problems; matters of judgment when, in some public capacity, one
must choose between competing values. Within idealism there are
important insights into the field of jural actions, in terms of the
individual's duties towards positive law and the fidelity of judges to
existing law. But in serious matters of value conflict the autonomous moral conscience, responding to inner imperatives of justice
and coherence, is the measure of choice. These formulations are of
profound importance, but their tendency towards transcendent
universality is an obstacle to an ethic of decision making. They do
not adequately account for the immensely difficult concrete moral
problems which persons in authority must face if they are to con-
scientiously make proper choices under the exigencies of practical
life.

Requirements of rational justification, such as those elaborated
by Perelman, are valuable; but their paramount purpose is to condition the external projection of an inward conviction. What is
needed is a conception of good judgment which subjects choice to a
broader discipline. The gap may be filled by that practical wisdom
which has traditionally been associated with the virtue of prudence.
This moral concept has been aligned with expediency, and abhor-
rent connotations such as using others as a means of furthering
one's own interests. With its emphasis upon contingencies, prudential morality lacks the rigorous rational coherence and absolute
righteousness which are characteristic of Kantian ethics.[15] Yet, at

least in its Thomistic formulations, prudence implies personal moral excellence rather than ego-centric preference. The supreme practical virtue, concerned with the requirements of concrete choices, it acknowledges the specific complexities of decision.

A manifest injustice can never be excused. But the great bulk of juridical decisions are in fact choices between competing values. In Kelsen's terms: "What human interests are worthy of being satisfied, and what is their proper order of rank . . .is the question. . . ." The resolution of this question ultimately depends upon an assessment of specifics by the one who is authorized to decide. Considered as a matter of prudence, the ability to make wise choices depends upon one's openness to all truths which bear upon the decisional problems of law and value for which one is responsible.[16]

Impulses towards justice arising within the self do not, of themselves, constitute virtue. Good judgment in the law—jurisprudence—assumes that the one having authority to make decisions has a sound moral character and is aware of the limits of his authority. Only those with developed moral and intellectual faculties are able to bring to the situation of choice that ordering of values which constitutes the most complex dimensions of human justice.

The insecurity of values with subjective idealism is also traceable to its epistemological foundations. Central to the idea of justice is the notion of *alteritas,* the other; an involvement with and concern for another's good traditionally has made justice a complete virtue. As formulated by Del Vecchio, some concern with others was intrinsic to the nature of thought, since to be conscious of the self necessarily involved thinking of another or others different from oneself. In the depths of consciousness one is aware that he is intimately bound up in an immense number of interpersonal relationships. Consideration of another's good would necessarily follow upon any evaluation of one's own conduct. From such reflective awareness one becomes aware of his personhood and that of others, and out of such recognition there arises the imperatives which govern social conduct.

But this is a precarious basis upon which to secure fundamental rights. The high moral tenor of idealism in its purest expression is exemplary; but if we consider this orientation of thought in its entirety, justice is in constant danger of becoming an utterly subjective or purely formal concept. Understood as equality, it becomes, for Perelman, a logical quality immanent to the human mind. More importantly, even if justice is assumed to have some objective content its obligations are conditioned by a willingness of the subject to embark upon a vocation of morality:

> And so to the question why should we be moral, I would answer that no obligation to be moral can be adduced. One either is or is not moral, with all the ensuing consequences for the individual and his relations. But if one is moral, then categorical obligations relevant to all one's ends arise. Obligation and its categorical quality arise out of the concept of morality; they do not precede it. If one asks 'why should I be moral,' the answer is 'you are under no obligation to be moral, but if you are moral, these and these are your obligations.'[17]

It is difficult to reconcile this conception of our duty toward others with general understanding of the independent importance of human rights. The most valuable freedoms and liberties are those which we can plead against, or demand from, the state. The judge or other official before whom such claims are made has some conscious awareness of their ethical import; he may even identify them as part of his own moral freedom. But a theory of human rights implies some sense of *extra subjective* entitlement; implying obligations which must be acknowledged, whether or not we identify with them as intrinsic to our own moral code. Fundamental rights exist, in a decisive measure, independent of our thought; grounded upon the being of those who may justly demand their protection. Because of its radical commitment to the subjective roots of moral thought,[18] Kantian idealism does not reach this measure of objectivity.

C. *POLITICAL THEORY AND DISTRIBUTIVE JUSTICE*

The imperatives of duty, guiding all who seek to be moral, are inevitably externalized in social life. The will and conscience of each subject is, therefore, the primary source of positive law. But, to be fully effective, a legal order must be independent of the will of an individual. In cases of conflict the rule of law must be enforced against his interest. There is a need for a super-individual volition, a constant will which can effectively regulate social life.

In the evolution of social existence a common denominator of volitions is gradually developed. The coercive authority characteristic of modern legal orders is the result of this formation of a common or unitary will; a will which asserts itself, through its juridical organs, as preponderate power. A subject with a supreme autonomous will emerges. This subject, which realizes its will through enforced rules, is the state.

The state is not, as Kelsen believed, the unity of a positive legal order. It is that subject of will which imposes a juridical order. As an autonomous will it is not subordinate to another. It is, therefore, sovereign. But, if sovereign, the state does not have the right to be arbitrary. Its authority arises from a preponderance of will but this is an ethical as well as a sociological *datum*. The state is ultimately subject to those norms of justice which have their source within the conscience and consciousness of the entire body politic.

As a confluence of individual wills, the state differs in degree, and not in kind, from individual wills. Juridical relations can develop between several individuals, as can be seen in the phenomenon of contractual agreements and the manifold forms of associational and corporate life within a modern society. The state may set terms for the validity of such arrangements, but it is in fact acknowledging the will of others. Juridical determinations reflecting the actualization of obligation by individual wills are referred to the state as an ideal point of convergence.

The state is not a real entity. It is rather the expression of spiritual forces of right and justice which it constantly draws to itself. When it realizes its ethical mission it is fully operative; justly balancing individual and general will, and positively advancing the value of human personality.[19]

This ethical conception of the state is an integral part of Del Vecchio's theory of justice. The exalted mission which he assigns to it requires the active cooperation of all within the body politic. In modern thought this fundamental need has also been conceived as a basic problem of political theory. From this perspective the origins of social life, rather than the nature of the state, has been the basic point of reference. Within the current of idealism the starting point for these reflections is the thought of Rousseau.

Rousseau's thought can be best understood by contrasting it with the political conception of Hobbes. For Hobbes, the relationship between men in a state of nature was one of irreconcilable conflict. There are no bonds of right or sympathy. Everyone, on his own initiative, seeks what will preserve his existence. To overcome such anarchy it is assumed that a covenant was formed transferring authority to govern to a supreme power or "mortal god." His rule was assured by the mutual promise of each to obey his decrees. Since the sovereign would assure peace and security, the establishment of a supreme political authority was for Hobbes a solution to the fundamental instability of social life.[20]

Rousseau agreed with Hobbes that in a state of nature there are no bonds of union. But Rousseau did not believe that man in a natural state was aggressive. By nature, the ego is passive; it is only after man enters society that instincts of greed and domination make their appearance. The tranquillity of the Leviathan can be accompanied with tyranny and oppression, which does violence to the paramount value of liberty. This elementary freedom, which demands that one not be subject to the will of another, could never be relinquished. Any covenant which purported to do so was void as against nature. The establishment of sovereign authority and the enactment of positive laws did not, therefore, resolve the problem of legitimate government. We must still inquire: by what *right* do the governors govern.

The basic question is to determine how one can be both free and also a member of a political society. In a Hobbesian framework one must choose between liberty and subjection. Locke's solution was to assume a social contract the purpose of which was to establish government in order to preserve freedom. But this solution ignores the malignant consequences of social life of which Rousseau was acutely aware. In particular, the preservation and extension of economy liberty leads to a tyranny of private power, the exploitation of man by man.

Locke failed to resolve the basic difficulties because he was unable to form a moral conception of liberty. For Rousseau, freedom consists as much in not subjecting others to our own will as it does in a freedom from the domination of others. Under the conditions of a common liberty, no one has a right to do what the liberty of others forbids him to do. There is thus an intimate connection between liberty and justice, a connection which leads to the primacy of law. It is only by submitting to law that man becomes a moral person. As law implies restraint, the objective of liberty can only be preserved if in submitting to law men are actually ruling themselves. To understand how this can occur, we must move beneath the level of juridical analysis and consider the political foundations of social life. We must examine the act by which a multitude becomes a people.

To preserve themselves men must unite their separate powers.

They can then act in concert and with a general motive. To accomplish this each, without exception, must totally alienate himself and all his rights to the whole community. Rousseau insisted that no *a priori* rights could be claimed, because if the establishment of rights were left to individuals each would insist upon being his own judge of its scope, and tyranny would resume.

The proposed alienation appears extreme, but it is an advantageous exchange. By giving oneself to all, one gives oneself to no one, and one gains the same rights that others gain over him. This is possible through the profound union which results from the social pact:

> Each one of us puts into the community his person and all his powers under the supreme direction of the general will; and as a body, we incorporate every member as an indivisible part of the whole.[21]

A public person is formed: a body politic which, in its passive role, is the state but actively is sovereign. Insofar as they share sovereign power individuals are citizens; insofar as they put themselves under the laws of the state, they are subjects. Each, as it were, makes a contract with himself and finds himself doubly committed. If he is to enjoy the rights of citizen, he must do the duties of a subject, which is to obey the general will. If he refuses, he may be compelled to submit his interest to the common good. He shall then be forced to be free.

By living in society under conditions of the social contract man has an opportunity to realize his human nature. He gains rightful possession of his property because title is based upon law rather than might. The whole power of the community will protect his legitimate interests. It is now also possible for him to transcend his egoism. As justice replaces greed as the rule of conduct, one's actions gain a moral quality. The voice of duty becomes operative and man is compelled to consult reason rather than follow his passions. Moral faculties are exercised, mental powers enlarged, the spirit elevated. As I become good, I become free.

This conception of the potentials of human nature found a sympathetic audience in Kant, who related Rousseau's insight to more general aspects of moral worth. Morality is the authentic condition of a reasonable being; by being moral, one becomes an autonomous member of a realm of ends. True virtue will be realized when universal good will has become the principle of human actions.[22] However dubious the social contract may be as a matter of history, it is valuable as a pointer to genuine moral aspirations. Mankind possesses dignity insofar as it is capable of morality, and this end can only be achieved if social life is transformed so as to realize the highest ethical purposes.

～

The social contract suggests goals towards which men should strive if they are to be autonomous members of a realm of ends. Conjoined with moral theory, the idea of a social contract indicates the only acceptable way that a *de jure* union can arise in human relations. The Theory of Justice recently developed by John Rawls is an extension of this tradition.

For Rawls, the problem of justice arises out of the difficulties of human cooperation. Society exists for the mutual advantages of its members. Each has his own life plan, which leads to incompatible demands upon available resources. Social life is thus essentially marked by a conflict of interests. These circumstances call for fundamental principles which can impose an ordering upon conflicting claims. In this view the primary subject of justice is the basic structure of society: a determination of fundamental rights and duties and the proper division of the advantages of social cooperation.

The idea of a social contract provides a useful perspective from which to determine the nature of social justice. Basic principles must be acceptable to all, and congruent with basic understanding of moral worth and human good. A contractarian thesis includes a hypothetical initial position from which each must determine upon an agreed scheme of conduct compatible with a rational plan under reasonably favorable circumstances.

Placing the problem of justice in this perspective accentuates the value of personality and the equality of each member of society. Assuming an original position of equal liberty, the inquiry becomes one of determining those principles which rational men would most likely agree to as to the basic rules of social existence. Once determined, such first principles will constitute a moral constitution for a well ordered society. The principles then can be thought of as the public charter of a society in perpetuity: universal and timeless, applicable to everyone in virtue of their being a moral person:

> Once we grasp this conception, we can at any time look at the social world from the required point of view.... Without conflating all persons into one but recognizing them as distinct and separate, it enables us to be impartial, even between persons who are not contemporaries but who belong to many generations. Thus to see our place in society from the perspective of this position is to see it *sub specie aeternitatis:* it is to regard the human situation not only from all social but also from all temporal points of view. The perspective of eternity is not a perspective from a certain place beyond the world, nor the point of view of a transcendent being; rather it is a certain form of thought and feeling that rational persons can adopt within the world. And having done so, they can, whatever their generation, bring together into one scheme all individual perspectives and arrive together at regulative principles that can be affirmed by everyone.....[23]

To gain the requisite objectivity and unanimity, the deliberations leading to the conception of justice are assumed to occur behind a veil of ignorance. Agreement would be impossible if the parties were aware of the contingencies which generate antagonism. It must be assumed that no one knows his actual social position, his genetic endowment of abilities or limitations, or even the generation to which he belongs. Without such knowledge one is unable to tailor principles to his advantage; he will rather assent to principles which are compatible with a rational plan of life and his moral personality. To make the contract hypothesis plausible, certain assumptions are indispensable. A theory of justice must be rooted in human aspirations and feelings; it must, in a positive way, correspond with fundamental desires. Certain primary goods, necessary to the successful execution of a rational life plan, are therefore taken for granted. Whatever else he may desire, a rational person is presumed to want an increase of liberty and opportunity, income and wealth, and self-respect.[24]

Finally, the conditions for agreement must account for the general disparities between persons, in order to assure that the principles of justice would be agreeable to all. One must take up the position of certain representative individuals and consider the potentials of agreement from their perspective. This is necessary not only to assure liberty, but also to assure that the principles of justice are responsive to the pervasive problem of inequality. Each must be thought of as being a citizen and holding a place in the distribution of wealth and abilities. Relevant representative men imaginatively represent the various levels of social well-being. Combining these perspectives it is possible to appraise the social enterprise from the vantage points both of equal citizenship and the various levels of wealth and income.

Within this framework, Rawls develops his theory of justice as fairness. The relevant assumptions surrounding the agreement yield two basic principles. The first, of equal liberty, requires that the fundamental liberties of the person be protected and that political and legal procedures be just. Each person is to have an equal right to the most extensive system of basic liberties compatible with an equal liberty for all. Social and economic inequalities must be arranged so that they are to the greatest benefit of the least advantaged and attached to offices and positions open to all under conditions of fair equality and opportunity.

Equal liberty has precedence. At least when a basic level of material well-being has been reached, further material advantage cannot justify a loss or infringement of basic personal liberty. Social and economic policies must seek to maximize the material prospects of the least advantaged, but this objective is subject to the maintenance of equal liberty. The relation between the first and second principles are lexical because the demands of liberty must be satisfied first. Within the scheme of liberties, a less extensive liberty must strengthen the total system of liberty shared by all. A less than equal liberty must be acceptable to those so disadvantaged.[25]

The two principles of justice are thought of as the content of an original agreement defining the conditions under which equal persons will engage in social life. Grounding claims upon these principles will assure a genuine reconciliation of interests.

Steps by which the parties implement the agreement can also be imagined. From an original position they may be thought of as moving to a constitutional convention. The veil of ignorance is partially lifted, and delegates now understand the relevant general facts of their society: its natural resources, level of economic development, and its political culture. On such information they must choose a constitution which will satisfy the principles of justice and lead to effective and just legislation. Such a constitution will incorporate and protect the basic liberties. At the level of legislation the second principle of justice becomes operative. A full range of general economic and social facts are made known in order that statutory policy may maximize the long term aspirations of the least advantaged. At the final stage the rules are applied to particular cases by administrators and judges. As the rules are applied, the veil is completely lifted. Now there is no reason to withhold knowledge of particular contingencies which would otherwise be a source of antagonisms.[26]

The Rawlsian conception of justice brings to a high point of development the contractarian ideas of Rousseau and Kant. The principles of justice reveal the ultimate basis of our beliefs of moral worth and the significance of personal equality. They are chosen, on an ethical plane, under circumstances which characterize men as free and equal rational persons. The mutual disinterestedness of the parties allows for one to pursue his own good within a framework of principles of right. By adjusting one's conduct to these principles one acts autonomously, expressing most fully his noumenal self.

And all are treated equally as moral persons. When the two principles are publicly recognized, others are treated with self-respect, and the potentials of social cooperation advanced. Within the basic structure of social life we embody a desire to treat one another not as means only, but as ends in themselves. If others are treated simply as means to our ends, we would not hesitate to impose lower life prospects upon them, if so doing would increase our advantages. When they are treated as ends in themselves, we are willing to forego gains which do not contribute to their representative expectations.

Through this, and related forms of moral reasoning, Rawls preserves the elements of private gain and initiative traceable to Locke's political philosophy, while meeting the objections raised by Rousseau. Men may enter society to preserve and extend their property. In fact, the strong tend to exploit the weak, or are indifferent to their welfare. The Rawlsian ethic, expressed as the difference principle, allows for inequalities of wealth and position but subjects them to moral restraint. They are permitted only on condition that they are to the advantage of the least favored members of the relevant society.

The power of this conception is evident when it is contrasted with prevailing views of well-being. Actual disparities of wealth and income, such as the profitable advantages of large corporations, are thought to be justified since they may arguably promote a general prosperity. But under conditions of modern industrial life those furthest down the social ladder tend to be left behind, clearly disadvantaged by the abundant well-being of others. Rawls also provides a penetrating critique of meritocracy, which has been one of the more pernicious effects of expanding opportunities. Opening careers to talents would appear to be fair, but it often leads to the establishment of technocratic elites whose power and prestige sets them apart from those with lesser abilities. The second principle of justice corrects these disparities. It can, when suitably adjusted, be also used to scrutinize the particular advantages which members of the various professions enjoy as a consequence of the services which they provide.

Rawls' approach also gives renewed significance to our convictions of equality and right. By connecting, for example, a right of political participation to the premises of equal liberty he draws attention to the imperative need for public financing of political campaigns. Heretofore public resources have not been devoted to maintaining the institutions required to assure the exercise of such rights.

But in spite of these positive qualities, the Rawlsian theory of justice has serious limitations. As a work of moral philosophy within the tradition of idealism it is grounded, at critical junctures, upon ideas too far removed from concrete social reality. A connected difficulty is the aspiration towards a pure ethics which vivifies the overall conception. In both instances, a detachment which is otherwise laudable lessens the cogency of the theory.

For Rawls, society is a venture undertaken by individuals for their mutual advantage. As each pursues his own end within the framework of justice, personal fulfillment is beneficial to all. This conception of society contrasts sharply with that of sociology, which considers life in groups to be the essential datum. Rawls acknowledges the existence of associations, but only as moral instruments shaping a concern for others which one must possess to fulfill his general duties to justice. Sociological perspectives upon the relationship between the individual and particular groups are less benign. Domination and subjection; the power relations within the family, the church, the corporation, or labor union, are the elements of juristic significance.[27] Rawls' failure to take these factors into account is not fatal, since he has chosen only to emphasize that part of associative existence which is of relevance to his individualistic theory. But there are some points where the theory of justice makes essential assumptions which are sociologically implausible. This is apparent in his idea of economic freedom.

A market economy is endorsed as being conducive to values of human liberty. Allowing prices to be freely determined by supply and demand not only promotes efficiency, but it encourages independence of decision by individual households on the one hand and firms on the other. Freedom of occupation is the rule and, when the mechanism is operative, governmental intervention is minimal. All regimes, whatever their ideology, rely upon these principles as a means of distributing consumer goods. The maintenance of a competitive economy is set as an objective to be pursued in either a private capital or socialist regime.[28] The ideal cannot be fully realized, but the objective sets a standard by which to judge existing conditions.

The differences between socialism and laisse faire capitalism are more profound than Rawls assumes. Ownership of the means of production is but part of much deeper disagreements between the two systems concerning the nature of work and the structures of social life. The communal theme, which pervades all forms of socialism, has an intimate impact upon a conception of economics. Such organic link between the individual and the broader society is the premise of socialist policy, and this general connection cannot be fully reconciled with Rawlsian individualism. In socialist theories the advancement of individual well-being is recognized, but the progress of the whole is the dominant goal. Some form of group commitment and consciousness replaces rational self-interest as an explanatory mechanism. These differences are not limited to a particular ideology, they can be found in non-marxist forms of socialism such as those now being developed in Africa.[29] Without attempting to evaluate these economic conceptions, it is sufficient to note their existence in order to question the universality of the premises which Rawls uses to illustrate his thesis.

There is no moral evaluation of the market economy in Rawlsian theory. This can be traced to his conception of the good, which is defined only in terms of what a rational person would desire. Participation in the economy as a consumer or producer is compatible with such rationality, at least to a point below gross materialism. The essential normative concern is protection of the least favored; a concern reflected in the difference principle. But a strong case has been made that the consumer economy, as it functions in all advanced industrial societies, is inimical to human freedom. Sustained by endless production and consumption such economic systems, by their own momentum, level human existence to a plane of material satisfactions; excluding, or at least suffocating, higher aspirations. The individual is hardly treated as an end in himself. Some of these criticisms, such as those of Marcuse,[30] may be extreme; but they highlight certain basic flaws in a modern consumer economy which no ethical theory can afford to ignore. Fundamental aspects of Rawls' market conception, such as the pervasive notion of consumer choice[31] are also undermined by the force of social criticism. The general structure of the economy, and the pressures of advertising, make unreal the suggestion that genuine selection is a normal mechanism. Freedom of choice may be a factor in the market, but it is too fragile to explain the foundations of an economy.

Rawls' attempt to give an idealistic interpretation of economic reality fails because it does not grasp the significance of technology and the forces which technology generates. Modern consumer economies have destructive consequences because they utilize largely impersonal forms of power in productive technique and marketing. These forces give a structure to the economic system which bears heavily against Rawls' abstract ideal. Such forces can also change, or at least modify, legal policies which in Rawls' framework would seem to be obviously desirable.

Under modern conditions, a few large firms tend to dominate particular industries, a fact which distorts the ideal market mechanism. Appropriate government action would apparently be to apply anti-monopoly legislation to the extent feasible. Historically this has been the appropriate remedy. To elevate it to a truth of moral philosophy however, would be an error. Concentrations of capitol, technology, and managerial skills in a relatively small group may yield efficiencies which, from the point of view of the public interest, outweigh the benefits gained from breaking up the conglomerate. Whether or not antitrust policy should be applied in such circumstances is a matter of judgment.[32] Nor can it be assumed that such concentrations of private economic power are necessarily detrimental to the least advantaged. They may or may not be detrimental, depending upon the policy adopted. Breaking up a monopoly is but one response; the concentration may be accepted as given, but then subject to administrative regulation to assure the supremacy of the public interest.

Rawls' detachment from social realities becomes more serious when it involves ethical postulates. The difficulty can be seen in the distinction drawn between legitimate expectations and moral desert. Distributive justice is understood by Rawls as the creating of conditions under which individuals can pursue their ends subject to conditions of equal access and the difference principle. Legitimate expectations to a share of social goods arise when those making such claims comply with the principles of justice and their duty to uphold just institutions. Distributive advantages are not rewards for personal merit, except in the limited sense that those who uphold just institutions by acting upon the two principles of justice can establish legitimate expectations.

Moral worth, in a broader sense of a recognition of moral character and accomplishment, is considered arbitrary. One's initial endowment of abilities and his social situation are contingencies over which he has no control. To the degree they are favorable, he can claim no credit for them. Even the effort that people are willing to make depends upon the opportunities available, and those better endowed are more likely to strive for achievement.[33]

There is, of course, much truth in these observations but as absolutes they are not persuasive. Idealistic ethics involves a striving to surmount contingencies by an effort of personal will. To see virtue in one's tendencies to act upon the principles of justice, but to deny its presence in an effort of self-improvement and advancement seems inconsistent. We can agree with St. Paul that our abilities are endowments, without excluding genuine moral significance from the ways in which we make use of what we have.

Rawls reinforces his exclusion by distinguishing between the good and the right. The distinction is maintained since the good understood as maximizing desire can, in a utilitarian calculus, lead to the satisfaction of majority preferences at the expense of minority rights.[34] But to contrast goodness understood as rational desire, with virtue understood as adherence to principles of right, is too extreme a dichotomy. It prevents us from seeing how the developments of one's potential can involve the exercise of virtue. There are reasons for not making personal merit an explicit part of distributive justice; but the breadth or narrowness of one's understanding of moral worth has a bearing upon evaluation of expectations actually generated within social life.

In modern life there are pervasive incentives to "get ahead" many of which propose transitions to areas where there is better housing, schools, and other public facilities. This has generally in-

volved a movement from decaying cities to more attractive subur-
ban areas. Such forms of social mobility raise expectations; whether
these are legitimate is a major question of contemporary public
policy. Undoubtedly much of the attained advantages cannot be
justified since their preservation is incompatible with the aspirations of others in less fortunate circumstances. But the advantages
can be held to be without foundation only if one maintains an *a priori*
conception of moral worth and takes a dogmatic view of human
accomplishments. Conflicts of expectation can be measured by first
principles of justice, and they can provide a framework by which to
evaluate antagonisms generated by social mobility. But to view conflict only in this light inevitably leads to misperception.

   In a Rawlsian world, conflicts of interest are conflicts of incompatible desires. They arise when each wants the same things, or
when some want their desires satisfied under circumstances which
lead to some basic deprivation of others rights. At best, this analysis
touches but a part of the problems of distributive justice. The poor
in the cities and the affluent in the suburbs both want good schools
for their children. The latter's present advantages may be indefen-
sible, but a just solution must satisfy the aspirations of both groups.

   The reform of health services provides a more pertinent illustration. Physicians and suppliers now have advantages which cannot
be reconciled with the difference principle. But the vantage point
of the least representative man is not the pivotal point of social
policy. If not all, at least the vast majority are adversely affected by
existing arrangements, and the governmental objective is to devise
a solution which corresponds with the broader need. The same can
be said of many areas of reform from auto insurance to taxation.
The essential point is that distributive problems are of such complexity that they cannot be fully evaluated on the basis of a single
principle.[35]

   Social conflicts are conflicts of value as well as conflicts of interest. They may call for an ordering of priorities rather than a resolution of competing claims with reference to ultimate principles of
right. This dimension escapes Rawls' thesis because conflict is
thought of as an opposition between the desires of separate persons. If the distinction between persons is not taken seriously
human rights are not secure; but when the distinctions are rigorously followed and used as a model of all social conflict, the overall
picture is distorted.

   Conflict often exists under circumstances where a choice must be made between values which are presumed to be common. Increased production may bring more material abundance, but it may be incompatible with environmental protection. By what standard can the choice be made? It could be argued this is a problem of policy and not of justice, and that the proper choice would be made by a rational person consulting his own advantage. However, a clear distinction between policy and justice can be sustained only upon the assumption that legal philosophy is concerned with individual rights and not with a common good which is irreducible to individual advantage. Moreover, the individual, qua individual, cannot be expected to choose the better policy, since he will incline to his immediate advantage. The dimensions of the problem are transpersonal rather than intersubjective.

~

The general detachment which Rawls maintains from social reality tells against the theory of justice because some of its essential assumptions cannot be reconciled with experience. The detachment is considered necessary, however, in order that our moral insights may have a philosophical justification. Rawls does not deduce the principles of justice from axiomatic postulates, rather his entire work is an attempt to give a fully rational account to our considered convictions of fairness and right. The analysis seeks a higher unity grounded on ultimate principles because a lower level of justification would be considered arbitrary and useless.

But this assumes that without an agreement on ultimate principles, moral consensus is impossible. Ultimate principles of right, based upon a hypothetical social contract, are proposed as a means of filling a moral void. The operative premises of a democracy, however, assume that some common conceptions of right can be formed within the boundaries of experience:

> The pessimism which is an important ingredient of our constitutional thinking is balanced by an optimism—a faith that men can work together to achieve common goals in a society held together by a sense of civic righteousness.
>
> ... [I]n the end the institutions we deem important and the significance of the rights we assert must rest upon some con-

sensus in the public mind respecting the values we deem important . . . . [T]his reduces itself to shared moral perceptions and understanding.

. . . [T]he conscience of the nation lies outside the Constitution and supports it. The conceptions rooted in common understanding are the stuff of a nation's aspiration and moral vision. It is in the shaping of a common ethic of the people which draws its inspiration from religious, moral and philosophical sources. . . .[36]

~

The practical grounding of values implicit in the quoted remarks of a constitutional scholar, can be expressed philosophically by distinguishing the convergence of principles which form a common ethic from the theoretical perspectives by which they are ultimately justified. In a pluralistic society, the higher justifications reflect diverse religious and philosophical premises which vivify and give coherence to the common core of moral ideals. When deference is not given either to these operative premises, or the range of explanatory principles which support them, there is an inevitable tendency to impose a moral code upon the public conscience. A potential for such imposition can be seen in the projected implementation of the principles of justice.

Through the vehicle of a social contract, idealism seeks to establish the moral foundations of political life. Justice is no longer an optional vocation. Duties of justice and mutual respect follow upon the acceptance, in the initial situation, of the two principles.[37] Duties to uphold just institutions flow from our responsibility to ourselves and to others as enduring selves. The perspective of the original position allows us to prescind from our particular preferences and attachments. We can, at this height, view society and our place in it objectively. Henceforth, the value of our interests will depend upon their relation to the antecedently chosen principles.

The contractarian theory is an ethical undertaking to move, as quickly as possible, towards the establishment of just institutions. The four stage sequence, from constitutional convention to the application of just rules, is an integral part of ideal theory.While not dependent upon social consensus, the theory of justice envisions a sequence of moral development which will strengthen in each person the desire to comply with the basic principles. Within the family, one receives love, which arouses one's sense of value and the beginnings of a desire to realize selfhood. Our understanding of the requirements of morality increases as, in the course of life, we move through a sequence of positions which require us to see things from another's point of view. Our capacity to perceive the desires of others gradually matures, we become more considerate of their wants, more willing to give reasons when our actions affect them. Bonds of friendship and trust slowly, but surely, form.

It is when we recognize that we are the beneficiaries of just institutions that our sense of justice is engendered. As the principles are put into practice we become aware of how we, and those we love, are the beneficiaries. We desire to do our part, and to honor our duties and obligations. A bond between citizens is forged by a common allegiance to public principles of justice.

The practices of moral instruction which inculcate the appropriate sense of justice are not, Rawls argues, incompatible with human freedom:

> [I]n agreeing to principles of right the parties in the original position at the same time consent to the arrangements necessary to make these principles effective in their conduct. Indeed, the adaptability of these arrangements to the limitations of human nature is an important consideration in choosing a conception of justice. Thus no one's moral convictions are the result of coercive indoctrination. .... A person's sense of justice is not a compulsive psychological mechanism cleverly installed by those in authority in order to insure his unswerving compliance with rules designed to advance their interests. Nor is the process of education simply a causal sequence intended to bring about as an end result the appropriate moral sentiments. As far as possible each stage foreshadows in its teachings and explanations the conception of right and justice at which it aims and by reference to which we will later recognize that the moral standards presented to us are justified.
>
> ... Following the Kantian interpretation of justice as fairness, we can say that by acting from these principles persons are acting autonomously: they are acting from principles that

they would acknowledge under conditions that best express their nature as free and equal rational beings . . . Thus moral education is education for autonomy. In due course everyone will know why he would adopt the principles of justice and how they are derived from the conditions that characterize his being an equal in a society of moral persons. . .[38]

Insofar as the ideal of moral instruction depends upon circumstances of private life, it is unexceptionable. But as instruction occurs in the public realm, the justifications become questionable. The weakness here is that Rawls views authority as a purely moral conception. But for purposes of legal philosophy it is important to maintain some distinctions between moral and political authority.

Public officials participate in the people's right of self-government. This authority is a moral power. Those holding public office are entitled to pursue justice and advance the common good. But such authority is, in each case, a specific form of authorization, a commission conferred under concrete conditions. Legislators, administrators, and judges do not have a "roving commission to do good." Their competence is defined by the nature of their office and the particular delegation of power which they have received. Political authority, in all its forms, is circumscribed authority. It has a moral component, but this dimension is not unbounded. Only through an awareness of this complexity can we trace the outlines of a just authority.

The restraints upon public officials which flow from the actual constitution of political life are not imperfections; a falling short of an ideal. They are in themselves of moral significance, relevant to an assessment of the means by which we strive for desirable goals. And they affirm the sovereign autonomy of the people; a body politic which delegates authority for specific purposes, subject to an accounting for its use.

It is difficult to determine the boundaries between actual and assumed authority, especially where officials are authorized to act within standards which have a broad moral latitude. The authority of federal judges to interpret and apply the constitution to judicial controversies is an apt illustration. We have already examined several ways in which this power, particularly at the level of the Supreme Court, raises some profound issues of public authority.[39] Some of the problems involved with Rawls' conception of authority can be seen in cases where the court must determine whether the acts of state legislatures are compatible with the standards of the Equal Protection Clause of the Fourteenth Amendment.

The relevant parts of Rawls' theory of justice are the concept of equality and the difference principle. Equal justice is owed to all who have a potential to participate in, and conform to, the principles of the original position. Men may have varying abilities, but they are one in their capacity for moral personality. When basic rights are at stake, each is entitled to substantive equal treatment. We must give justice to all who can give justice in return. Distributive inequalities are justified if, and only if, they are to the advantage of the least favored. These principles place restraints upon those who would use their greater natural abilities to make a stronger claim upon available resources than can be allowed under the principles of justice.

Moral equality is a principle of substantive force. It affirms the ideals of mutual respect embedded in the concept of equal liberty, and assures that the distribution of primary goods is controlled or measured by the needs of the least fortunate. Equality is more than a procedural principle, preventing inequalities in the absence of compelling reasons; it is a rigorous normative standard which fulfills, at the highest level, the ideal of reciprocity.

By contrast, judicial administration of the Equal Protection Clause involves restraints of institutional competence as well as the pursuit of moral ideals. The constitutional standard has an ethical content, but its meaning is also shaped by the gloss of precedents and legal reasoning. The Court must also acknowledge the legitimate authority of the states, and the elements of discretion which it implies.

As moral perceptions evolve, the Court brings a closer scrutiny to bear upon that discretion, nullifying inequalities or requiring, in some instances, a positive justification for a disparity of treatment. But, as an ongoing process, the constitutional realization of equality involves a much wider range of authoritative considerations than are envisioned by the imperatives of Rawlsian justice. Adjudication is a mixture of moral and institutional authority, demanding a balance which is very difficult to achieve, especially when a claim for relief is ethically compelling.[40] But a comprehensive understanding of legitimate authority is required, not only for the fair administration of justice, but also to assure that social stability which is a paramount objective of Rawls' thesis. It is also necessary if we wish to prevent institutions having a limited competence from becoming surrogates for a general will.

~

Rawls' theory raises our judgments of the primacy of civil and political rights to a level of philosophical justification. It also measures social and economic disparities by the needs of the disadvantaged. The theory is offered as an alternative to utilitarianism which allows for the subordination of the rights of individuals to a greater sum of general satisfaction. If we contrast the principal features of utilitarianism with the Rawlsian counter-thesis, the essential structure of distributive justice may be brought into clearer focus.

Utilitarianism is teleological. The good, understand as the satisfaction of rational desire, is maximized. Thought of as a sum of individual goods, the ethic is substantially material in content. The net balance of the pleasures over pains of the members of society defines the good.

Utilitarianism retains the primacy of the whole which traditionally was essential to distributive justice, but does not have, strictly speaking, a *common good*. Its detailed empiricism replaces that inclusive moral dimension, which includes tangible criteria but also reaches intellectual, spiritual, and moral goods.

A related weakness of utilitarianism is its conception of society. It is understood as an organism. Man is thought of only as a social animal, and a certain analogue with the animal kingdom is maintained. The individual is a part, and *only a part,* of the whole community. The total effect is to make the individual intrinsically subordinated to the measurable satisfactions of the whole.

Rawls' thought moves in an opposite direction. Here there is an ethical interpretation of social life. The right defines the terms of social union, and the good, relegated to subjective rationality, becomes morally neutral. Discrete individuals join in a common venture for mutual advantage. The individual is, ideally, not subordinated to the whole, and there is a genuine community of free and equal moral persons. The assumed unanimity is a collective expression of our noumenal selves. The self is realized in the activities of many selves as the abilities of each redound to the benefit of all. It is a society of Pure Persons.

Both theories reflect essential features of distributive justice, but each has basic flaws. One lacks an adequate conception of a common good; the other depends upon a purely moral, and atomistic, conception of social union. In utilitarianism, the intrinsic worth of the individual is not fully acknowledged; in Rawls' thesis, the intrinsic worth of the individual is the exclusive consideration.

A deeper comprehension of both the nature of the human person and of the purposes of social life may lead to a more balanced view of the nature of distributive justice. Political theory can be built upon a conception of the person, but it requires fidelity to Aristotle's dictum that man is a rational animal. The person subsists spiritually, through the operations of intellect and the exercise of moral freedom. But each is also a fragment of the human species, subject to the determinations and the contingencies of the physical world and nature.

Society is a consequence of personality.[41] Societies arise to meet the needs of the individual, to fulfill what is lacking in the physical or material side of nature. And they provide opportunities for those positive communications of knowledge and love which are necessary for the spiritual realization of the person. Society, from this perspective, is natural rather than contractual in origin.

The reason for the existence of society determines the structure of its distributive advantages. Its stock of goods: the physical and spiritual accomplishments of the group, its range of opportunities, must benefit all. This subservience of the whole to the parts or members is what distinguishes a human from an animal society. In the latter, the parts serve the whole. If members benefit, it is only so the whole can subsist. In a human society, the common good benefits the members for their own sake.

While human society exists to serve, it is not *reducible to* its members. The whole is distinct from, and, in some sense, superior to its parts. This distinction is reflected in the traditional idea that distributive justice encompasses relationships between the group and its members. Within such a distributive scheme, the individual has rights but they are the rights of a member. Utilitarianism imperfectly retains this conception;[42] Rawls, in effect, rejects it.

Rawls' position accords with modern understanding of social justice, which is concerned more with opportunities than with an allocation or division of goods throughout society. The legitimacy of

claims is judged by the principles chosen in the original position.
Distributive justice is a conception of individual rights, rather than
one which accounts for the relative position of an individual in
society. The relational conception derived from the Aristotelian-
Thomistic tradition makes individual contingencies of aptitude,
material need, and social circumstances integral elements of distributive justice. The justice of social benefits and burdens in this
view depends, however, upon the claimants status as a member of
society. Having an ontological component, it can also be defended
on the basis of its explanatory power. The justification for progressive income taxation for example, is ultimately based upon
relational advantage and, not, as Rawls maintains, solely as a correction of injustice. In imposing such burdens, all who benefit
should pay; that ability to pay should be the determining principle,
however, is morally cogent. Conversely, disadvantage is, *of itself,* a
legitimate grounds for the exercise of distributive justice. The
geometric proportion of distributive justice encourages deviations
from arithmetic equality when necessary to meet the needs of all,
who, because of their relative position or circumstances, have a just
claim upon the resources of society.[43] This aspect of relational justice provides a more comprehensive understanding of a wide range
of distributive policies than is possible under Rawlsian principles.

The value of the traditional approach to distributive justice can
be seen when it is compared with more recent alternatives to the
Rawlsian conception. Robert Nozick, for example, advances a
neo-Lockean theory of social life which offers as an allocative principle the disparate acquisitions and voluntary exchanges of separate individuals. This specifies an ongoing *historical* process:

> ...There is no *central* distribution, ... What each person gets,
> he gets from others who give to him in exchange for some-
> thing, or as a gift. In a free society, diverse persons control
> different resources and new holdings arise out of the volun-
> tary exchanges and actions of persons ... The total result is
> the product of many individual decisions which the different
> individuals involved are entitled to make ...[44]

This theory of entitlement, necessarily leads to distributional inequalities. But they are unassailable unless the result of theft,
fraud, or the forceable exclusion of others from the process. If the
principles of acquisition and exchange are violated, rectification

comes into play. In the terms of Nozick's theory redistribution—unless it is to rectify an injustice—violates another person's rights.

Nozick is opposed to Rawls' theory of justice, because of its 'end result' principles: an external structure of moral criteria which determines, in advance, the outcome of social interaction. It is also objectionable because, when transferred to the legal order, it gives enforceable claims to each to some portion of the total social product. This destroys the self-ownership of classical liberalism, since it results in the partial ownership by others of one's acts and labor.

The radical concreteness of the entitlement theory may check some of the excesses of abstract ethical idealism. It does not of itself, however, provide a viable system of distributive justice. Consider problems of preferential treatment. As a means of correcting past wrongs, they may call for the application of the principle of rectification. But, as Nozick concedes,[45] it is very difficult to determine the precise limits of such a restitutionary ideal. Furthermore, in practice, the invocation of the principle tends to be expressed in terms of unqualified claims and demands. A more flexible approach would recognize historical inequities, but not as giving rise to absolute entitlements. Rather, they may be acknowledged as substantial factors which, among other considerations, must enter into allocative decisions concerning social positions or opportunities.

The theory of distributive justice developed by the Thomistic tradition has, in this regard, distinct advantages, since it respects the general concerns manifested by Nozick, while attending more realistically to the overall features of these problems. The attention here given to the relative position of the individual in society, including the recognition of disadvantage as a reason for deviating from formal equality, is balanced with a respect for natural aptitudes and personal accomplishment. This provides a more subtle range of moral criteria which can be brought to bear upon such allocative decisions.[46] It also avoids the simplicities implicit in the rigorous application of the difference principle as it has evolved in the Rawlsian theory of justice.

A Thomistic theory of distributive justice seeks to balance the positive idea that societies exist to serve individuals with the limiting notion that the individual is a part of society. This conception, if at all plausible in economic or social affairs, may be deemed incapable of providing philosophical security for human rights. The objections raised against utilitarianism would apparently apply *pro tanto* against any theory which comprehends the person in a context of a larger society. The objection is serious. It can be met by examining how a commitment to individual rights becomes part of a theory of justice.

Human rights are recognized in moral conscience. They attain a primacy in political life in the degree to which the spiritual value of the person becomes part of a common ethic. Such a development is precarious and needs to be strengthened by philosophical reflection. But where such reflection is confined to the depths of subjectivity, the resulting conceptions lack social foundations. Reviewing the idea of right in modern Analytical Jurisprudence, we criticized the phenomenological movement, exemplified in the work of Dworkin, to ground rights in judicial introspection.[47] The same criticism is now being made on a more abstract plane. To establish rights authoritatively, there must be *shared* perceptions. Rights are truly secure only to the degree that they are in fact acknowledged, and idealistic philosophy cannot substitute for concrete awareness and assent.

Further, where abstract inviolability is *theoretically* opposed to a general good, it becomes impossible to measure the legitimate range of individual liberty. The ownership of real property, for example, is subject to innumerable restrictions which are justified by reference to some notion of a general interest. To say that liberty is here restricted for the sake of liberty would serve to explain some, but by no means all, such infringements. The relevant good which constrains private property is frequently of a more general and abstract character,[48] such as aesthetic and historical values in land use control or, on the international plane, the objective of national self-determination, set over against the expectations of foreign investors.

When personal and intellectual freedoms are threatened with limitation, the opposition between the individual and the group is intensified. But, if we are to avoid emotionalism, the actual extent of the antagonism must be carefully explored before absolutes are invoked. Freedom of expression can be conditioned by the right of others to be informed; a limitation which points to considerations of a general or common good. In matters of intimacy, personal respect and inviolability should predominate. But it does not follow that any prevailing conception of a moral good inexorably leads to a serious infringement of individual freedom. Public morality is a persistent aspect of social life, and it inevitably has some legitimate bearing upon judgments of law and policy.[49]

Sociological insight reveals a very complex tension between individual and group life, a tension which, as Durkheim observed, cannot be over simplified by moral postulation.[50] The precept that liberty can be restricted only for the sake of liberty is of great practical value. It encompasses many concrete issues and tends to insure that if freedom must be infringed, the imposition is carefully circumscribed. But when projected as a universal truth of moral philosophy it becomes subject to a general charge, leveled against all theories of justice: an accusation that what is offered as objective truth is, in reality, an ideological and subjective preference.

Chapter Five

THE PROBLEM OF NATURAL LAW

A. *THE ATTRACTION OF MATHEMATICS*

I n modern legal philosophy both inductive and deductive modes of knowing have been used to understand the meaning of law. The inductive has predominated. Empirical observation has been the rule, either in the relatively narrow frame of Analytical Jurisprudence or in the broader observations of a sociologically oriented conception. Dewey, whose instrumentalism influenced the Policy Science Jurisprudence, was a strong critic of purely abstract thought which he saw as a flight from the uncertainties of experience. Yet, as the last two chapters demonstrate, there are inexorable trends towards jural knowledge in which cognition beyond experience plays a significant role. These speculative efforts cannot be reduced to desires for security. They rather evidence inevitable urges of human reason to comprehend ultimate causes and purposes.

In modern times, the upward trend of thought has been exemplified by logic and pure mathematics. At those levels it has been possible to elaborate ideas without an intrinsic dependence upon observations of fact. Such speculation yields quantitative forms of order by which physical nature has subsequently been interpreted. The extraordinary success of this deductive modality has not been limited to physics. Its cognitive potentials have been extended over wide ranges of human concern in which a need for ultimate explanation has been felt. Kelsen's Pure Theory of Law demonstrates the power of logic to illuminate the structure of a positive legal order. In the work of F.S.C. Northrop, logico-mathematical forms of thought have been applied to the basic questions of human nature which fall within the concerns of a philosophy of law.

Northrop's contribution can be best understood in its relation to Sociology of Law and Sociological Jurisprudence. Sociology of Law is concerned with group life, the composition of social structures, and the function of law within this broader experience. The search for an "inner order" leads beyond an analysis of particular groups to the ultimate foundations and overall ordering operative within a particular society. An effort is made to penetrate the basic core of symbols and beliefs which, as the elements of a common social philosophy, constitute the ultimate basis of social norms.[1]

However successful such methodologies, they do not provide a measure of what ought to be. The "living law" of a given society at a specific time may be identified with the high frequency overt behaviour of a majority of its citizens. From a sociological perspective, a positive legal rule corresponding to such high frequency behaviour is objectively appropriate. But the need for ethical evaluation remains. The standards of a society must be true, as well as immanently normative, if our sense of right is not to be repelled. The perception of immanent norms marks the limits of sociological discovery, but it constitutes only the beginning of philosophical reflection. The key variables, which indicate the ethos of a people or its dominant ideology, need to be validated by forms of higher explanation which the methodology of a Sociology of Law cannot supply.[2]

The need for further determination also arises out of a fundamental weakness in Sociological Jurisprudence, especially as it has been influenced by Dewey's scientific method. Dewey's method of inquiry begins with the recognition of a problematic situation and observation of the constituent factors which are settled in existence. The terms of the problem, secured by observation, suggest a possible solution whose ability to resolve the problem is determined by tracing the logical consequences of its application. Facts given in observation and the ideas suggested by the hypotheses function operationally to resolve the problematic situation with which the inquiry began. A standard is evaluated in terms of the consequencss of that standard when acted upon; consequences recognized or revealed through the resolution of a experiential problematic situation. But if the criterion is the ability to resolve problems, the solution of the problem in the problematic situation becomes the criterion of the good. The need, however is for a method for determining whether a given standard is worth implementing.

The difficulty is not resolved by the Policy Science Jurisprudence of Lasswell and McDougal, who are methodological heirs of Dewey. The value variables which they designate may be verified by social observation, and inductive data may clarify and operationally confirm their existence. But no invarient, objective schema is offered which can specify the inner order of the specified values. Within the policy science approach, a preferred public order provides an ultimate standard to which positive law should conform; yet as an element within social experience, these overriding preferences do not necessarily constitute the good. Disciplined inquiry may lead to objectivity of social research, but there remains the question whether the discovered values ought to prevail.[3]

For Dewey and his followers, science meant the triumph of practical reason; the application of intelligence to the requirements of the concrete. It also constituted a repudiation of that theoretical reason which, by means of intellectual perception, sought to uncover an immutable order of nature. Abstraction was not self-sufficient; it was intimately tied to experience. Neither the normative nor the logical could be understood outside of concrete nature. For Northrop, this interpretation of the significance of scientific method was only partially true. Its limits could be seen by a more thorough understanding of the stages of inquiry suggested by the problematic of ultimate good.

The question of the truth of standards or values is raised insofar as they assert or imply propositions about the nature and destiny of man. Because they touch ultimate values, the relevant modes of verification are unique. As theories of human nature they introduce factors which are unobservable; referring to concepts which are, in the strictest sense, postulated. Such concepts possess only those meanings which the postulated deductive theory from which they are derived confers upon them.

This conception of the problem of values points up a methodological error of Dewey and his jurisprudential disciples in their approach to public values. The quest for meaning cannot be fulfilled by a closer analysis of variables. The ultimate presuppositions of a society point to theoretical conceptions of the good which transcend experience. Since the nature of the problem does not refer to identifiable entities and relations, one cannot verify the postulates by directly observing what they affirm. This limitation of pragmatic cognition is true, *a fortiori*, of radically empirical theories of meaning which depend entirely upon experienced data. Both fail to understand that the problem is essentially metaphysical:

> The good is neither a fact nor a meaning; it is a set of philosophical presuppositions... there is no such thing as ethics...there are no purely ethical facts, as there are no purely ethical meanings. There is only the nature of things and one's basic theory concerning what it is...'Good' is merely a single word for this basic theory...[4]

Operational theories of value are tainted by culture bias and they fail to yield a consistent, immutable content of natural law. The solution to the problem of values is to found within the field of science; not science in its inductive, experimental stages, but at the level of deductive power exemplified by pure mathematics and formal logic.

Modern physics begins with the epistemological premise that the direct observation of external objects does not yield public, invarient knowledge. The relativity of empirical data provokes a drive for a speculative knowledge which can correct the inadequacies of perception. The progress of knowledge is seen to lie in the independent construction of intellectual forms.

In mathematical science it is possible, through the creation and manipulation of forms, to make connections between things without a dependence upon sense data. Concepts are postulated which designate basic entities and relations different from those which are immediately observed. It is a way of knowing of great explanatory power. Mathematics provides an unmatched universality, and its laws are analytical because the variables in such deductive theory mean only what the relational syntax specifies them to mean. By its appeal to timeless laws and the rigour of logical implication, modern mathematics makes it possible to construct connective links between the present and the future. Its theoretical dynamic, sustained by quantitative conservation, creates what appears to be a modern equivalent of the Greek sense of being.[5]

Mathematics provides a theoretical model for testing the objective significance of normative social theories. But this speculative component must be empirically tested. Since such theories are

hypothetically conceived, verification is indirect, sustained by way
of an epistemic correlation. The objective is to join two factors
which are given by separate ways of knowing.

In determining an experimental correlate, consistency must be
maintained with the original notion that our direct knowledge of
external objects is unreliable. The modality of experience must be
in the domain of pure fact; limited to sense impressions, and
grounded upon what is immediately apprehended, after the manner of oriental wisdom and impressionistic art. This empiric
quality—the real as it is known with immediacy—lies within the
ineffable and emotional aesthetic continuum common to oneself
and to all things. As a primary intuition, it is trans-cultural; independent of value judgments or other relativities of perception.

By joining, through epistemic correlation, the theoretic and
aesthetic components, Northrop asserts a complete philosophical
conception of nature, a mathematical natural science. The systematically related unobserved entities, which designate a conception of ourselves and our universe, constitutes nature as thought.
The immediately apprehended aesthetic continuum constitutes nature in its empirical modality. This modern conception of nature
can be used to objectively test normative social theories which purport to be valid definitions of the good.

The key to evaluating the "living laws" of any society lies in a
distinction between first and second order facts. The latter are
varient beliefs, conceptions of life and value relative to the contingencies of experience. They may be expressed in cultural or
ideological form, such as Western Democracy or Marxist Com-
munism. First order facts, however, are what they are independent
of the beliefs of men. Normative social theories, as second order
facts, may contain premises which are empirically confirmable
statements about first order facts.[6] For example, the laws and customs of patriarchal societies contain assumptions about male and
female nature which have been disproved by modern, experimen-
tally verified, genetic theory.

When the aesthetic component is brought fully to bear all image-
ful differentiations are, as far as possible, removed. We reach an
intuition common to determinate human experience: that all
human beings are, in their essential selves, not only equal but identical. This profound insight voids all laws of status and discrimination.

The explanatory power of mathematical science also suggests

how a new natural law can be formulated for the future of a multicultural world. By joining the theoretical and aesthetic aspects of reality, we define a new meaning of existence and create potentials for a modern morality which can be expressed in universally quantified principles and rules. The cognitive meaningfulness made possible by mathematical physics will make possible a new means of defining the good. We can obtain publically valid propositional meanings which are the same for all human beings.

> The constructs of Western mathematical physics and the new type of cognitive meaningfulness which they provide for the solution of normative questions . . . [give] us positive substantive content for defining a new positive domestic and international law and a reformed living law which is good and just . . .

> Applied to ethics and to law, this theory of cognitive meaningfulness gives the normative concept that moral man and just man is cosmopolitan, or universal, or catholic man—that is, any human individual person whatever standing equally with any other human being as a term in a contractually constructed universal law to which each party to the contract has implicitly or explicitly given his consent. By the legal means of these contractually and axiomatically proposed constructs . . . men who do not know one another empirically and who have no person to person genetically or tribally defined relations with one another can, nonetheless, build a common living law community, a common political nation and a common positive legal system . . .

> . . . . [A]s man in his theories of natural science comes to think of first-order facts about himself and nature in genetics, psychology, astronomy or terrestrial mechanics, in terms of formally constructed cognitive concepts which are the concepts by postulation of universally quantified laws, the possibility is open to the human mind and to its normative imagination of ordering human relations normatively by such conceptual means. . .[7]

Northrop's application of mathematical ordering to the problematic of values provides a heightened sense of equality and universality. The integration of an aesthetic continuum adds a valuable cross-cultural dimension which gives the conception a universal appeal. But it is difficult to find within it any measure of substantive content. Individual freedom and autonomy is affirmed, but the same point has been made by Ethical Idealism[8] and with greater moral force.

If the advantage of Northrop's method lies in its potential for understanding man in terms of modern science, it is of limited usefulness. If the self will be "what experimental physicists, chemists, biologists, and psychologists find him to be"[9] it is becoming clear that such a conception threatens basic civil rights and liberties. Medical experimentation grounded upon Skinnerian models of human nature[10] are illustrative. These conflicts between science and values cannot be resolved within the terms of Northrop's theory, since they invoke qualitative distinctions which cannot be mediated within its frame of reference.

The limitation of Northrop's approach lies in its conception of nature. In a mathematical natural science, nature is constituted by combining the immediately apprehended continuum revealed by the senses with the systematically related, unobserved entities and processes designated by the theoretical postulates. The conception is dynamic in the sense that mathematical operations make possible a timeless extension of ideas. But the theoretical component—nature as thought—has an essentially static quality. Its predictive potential depends upon the total quantitative volume not increasing or decreasing in time. As this occurs, the displacement of the Greek conception of nature is complete:

> The latter consideration makes it possible to put two of the most basic propositions of metaphysics upon an experimental basis. When the basic entities and relations of one's scientific theory obey conservative laws, this is equivalent to asserting what the Greek metaphysical philosophers termed the principle of being. The negate of this metaphysical principle is the principle of becoming. . .[11]

This understanding of nature stands in opposition to the Aristotelian conception in which essential nature was intrinsically related to movement, growth and development. Nature was a way of existing accomplished through progression: being making its way in a world of becoming. The general contrast was between the incipient and the accomplished, as it is embodied in all natural entities.[12]

The aversion to becoming in Northrop's theory reflects a broader antagonism between mathematical and metaphysical interpretations of reality. The conflict is traceable to the defeat of Aristotelian physics in the fourteenth century and the potentials of a universal science of sensible nature made possible by the Cartesian revival of mathematics. In the modern period, mathematics, as a deductive science, has tended not only to rule the lower forms of knowing, but also to replace metaphysics as the highest regulative discipline.[13] Hence the effort to attribute an ontological quality to the theoretical component of Northrop's natural science of man.

But mathematics is essentially a science of quantity, not of being. In its speculative modes, as adopted by Northrop, pure mathematics does not explain essences in themselves. It only understands a "nature" as reconstructed within the exigencies of a formal deduction, and as understood in terms of the relations of order which the forms maintain among themselves. The concepts utilized have a life only in the mind. They are beings of reason. From the aesthetic component of Northrop's theory one may derive some sense of a common nature; but the abstractive component, which is grounded upon mathematical knowledge, cannot yield a substantive theory of human nature.

Modern science was born out of the destruction of Aristotelian physics, and the physics and metaphysics of Aristotle were believed to be so intimately related that they must rise and fall together. The philosophy of Aquinas, which drew significantly from Aristotle's thought, suffered a similar fate. Northrop shares this belief.[14] The assumptions upon which this repudiation of metaphysics is based deserve much closer scrutiny.

In the works of Aristotle there is a mutual interaction between the various treatises, and that dealing with physics had a central importance. But the general field of Being as Being treated in the metaphysics was by no means co-extensive with the physics. The Aristotelian science of Being was explicitly directed towards the universal features of existence. Being was manifested in the motions of sensible reality, but as reflections of transempirical categories which informed all actual and possible existence.[15] Metaphysics was the supreme science, the study of the principles of all reality. Being was understood as the central concept of existence to which all other things that exist were referred.

Aristotle's intention was to establish a univeral science specifically independent of, and superior to, other branches of knowledge. A distinction was maintained between the metaphysics which studies being *qua* being and physics which studied being as movement. He did attempt to provide metaphysical explanations for physical phenomena, and at this point the system was vulnerable. But that failure, spectacular as it was, should not be magnified out of proportion.

The error of Aristotelianism was not that it found an ontology upon a faulty physics. It was rather an unwarranted extension of metaphysics into spheres of reality which were more amenable to other forms of cognition. Such intellectual imperialism, it should be noted, is not exclusively a vice of metaphysicians. The inordinate extensions of mathematics and logic which have occurred in modern thought suggest that a tendency to apply a particular way of knowing beyond its legitimate boundaries is an inevitable aspect of the human condition.

The refinement of Aristotle's metaphysics accomplished by St. Thomas Aquinas has become part of a continuous tradition whose formulations deserve to be considered relevant to the pursuit of knowledge even though they engage ancient principles of thought. It affirms a capacity of the mind to obtain some certitude about extra mental reality. It is this starting point[16] concerning our cognitive powers which provides an alternative to Northrop's conception of human knowledge.

In the Aristotelian-Thomistic critique, an awareness of an active self, and the power of intellection, are joined with sense perception to seize upon an intuition of Being. Here perception involves more than the impingement of sense impressions upon the mind. Something intrudes upon us. This is true even of animal knowledge: A dog is not only stimulated by the variables of sound and smell; he perceives something as friendly or threatening. He seeks or avoids *an object*. The intellect, by comparison, makes judgments of existence.

In human knowledge entities are grasped as being, as something, before their specific natures are understood. In our primordial acts of knowing that which is becomes an object of thought. Before X is known as a plant, an animal or a man, it is first known as an existent, a being. Being is transcendental; at once one and varied. It is found in other entities which differ essentially in their mode of existence from those in which it is first apprehended. And it is trans-sensible. Realized incarnate in some aspect of sensible existence, Being also invokes the order of essences, or the possible real.

Being refers to what exists, or can exist, for itself outside the mind. As the formal object of the intellect, it transcends the order, as well as the disorder, of the senses. And, as a transcendental object Being and its attributes[17] rules our thought, forming a bond between the active intellect and extra mental reality.

Thomism delineates three general types of knowing which correspond with different levels of abstraction: the principles and laws of sensible nature; the universe of quantity as such, and the field of Being. In the first, the objects of knowledge are those which can only be realized in empirical or sensible existence. The second degree, the range of mathematics, deals with objects which, if they are realizable, can only be realized in sensible existence; although its objects can be conceived without reference to the realities of existence. The final level, metaphysics, has for its object a trans-sensible universe of thought. Its object is extra mental existence, but is concepts—substance, cause, etc.—can be realized in non sensible, non empirical existence.

Like mathematics, ontology rises above time. But it does not prescind from the order of existence. The objects of metaphysics are subjects which exist or can exist outside the mind. And metaphysics, to the degree which it attains or reaches essential properties, works within experience. Mathematics constructs entities which have a quantitative essence, deductively constructing an objective world by *a priori* cognition. But it does not grasp essences intuitively from within.

The Aristotelian system was profoundly in error when it sought to perceive "essential" knowledge of physical nature. If, however, the entire development of Aristotelian-Thomistic thought is taken into account, the mistake is not fatal to the general philosophy. In its modern formulations, it carefully circumscribes the capacity of the mind to penetrate or reach essential natures. Jacques Maritain, for example, distinguishes between dianoetic and perionetic intelligibility. In dianoetic intellection the mind, working through the sensible, attains an essence or nature in itself. Beyond the general characteristics of existence, the possibilities of dianoetic knowledge are understood as limited to a cognition of human nature, the know-, ledge of pure spirits, and of God.[18] With corporal natures inferior to man sensible properties, observable or measurable, provide peripheral substitutes. Empirological knowledge bears upon an essence, but is unable to discern an essence in itself.

This approach to metaphysics differs profoundly from Northrop's conception of ultimate reality. For him, the uncertainties of sense perception justify recourse to mathematics as the theoretic determinate of nature. An aesthetic intuition displaces the entitative diversity of existence with an undifferentiated continuum. As a dominant feature, quantitative thought replaces Being.

The Thomistic conception, by contrast, maintains ontology as a field distinct from, and superior to, mathematics. This approach should not be understood as demeaning the value of aesthetic intuition. Not only is it of immense value in its own right; at many junctures an intuition of Being and aesthetic awareness are virtually indistinguishable. but an authentic ontology must be grounded upon Being as an object of intellect; otherwise, the whole metaphysical enterprise becomes distorted.

How Being is understood has important consequences for conceptions of human nature which bear upon a philosophy of law. Within Thomism, it affirms substantial, inherent properties which elevate man above the determinisms of causal nature. It resists, however, the enticements of Idealism. It is fundamental to Thomism that in knowing the mind is confronted with an objective world which has its own consistency. Being, as a transcendental object of thought, provides the bridge between the thinking subject and extra mental reality. In Idealism, cognition is purely immanent. Thought attains nothing but itself. Being, as an object of thought, is constituted by the mind's activity in accordance with its *a priori* cognitive forms. These differences are epistemological, but they also affect one's understanding of the scope of jural cognition.[19]

The comparison between the ontological grounding of human nature espoused by Thomism and that advanced by Northrop is most strikingly revealed in the concept of the person. Its metaphysical foundations has made it possible for Thomism to affirm a sublime conception of the human person. Conceived as a "subsistent individual of a rational nature"[20] the person is here understood as the perfection of nature; capable, through the operations of intellect and moral freedom, of the independence of a whole being.

~

The Thomistic theory of knowledge has other implications for legal philosophy. Thomism affirms a metaphysics; but in so doing it does not deny the merit of other modes of cognition. Because the diverse degrees of knowing are respected there is no intrinsic antagonism between ontological truths and other authentic insights. It has an inclusive dimension which is relevant to the general quest for philosophic and jurisprudential knowledge.

It will be recalled that Northrop, in his search for normative value standards, found certitude in mathematics, while disparaging value assertions derived from lower levels of inquiry. This attitude reflects a prejudice which has arisen out of the developments of modern science. The attraction to higher forms of explanation has engendered an assumption that certitudes can only be obtained through the deductive modalities of logic and mathematics.

The notion of science has, however, a broader significance. As knowledge through causes, it embraces observational as well as deductive ways of knowing. In the first chapter, we saw how inductive knowledge of positive law as developed by the analytical jurists is an integral part of legal philosophy. By such observations intelligible connections were established, at an empirical level, between basic jural phenomenon. Such insights reveal certain universal characteristics of positive law. While supplemented by what are, arguably, more reliably cognitions they nevertheless retain a certain essential validity.

Reflections upon jural experience are now being pursued within a larger framework than was possible within the methodology of nineteenth century empiricism. As we saw, this shift can be seen in the epistemological outlook of Modern Analytical Jurisprudence, particularly as exemplified in the work of H.L.A. Hart. The analytical positivism expressed in THE CONCEPT OF LAW reflects a certain philosophical anthropology: an evolutionary consciousness of human nature which is instinctively felt to be a preferable means of understanding the phenomenon of positive law. And, as the humanistic potentials to be derived from such reflections is high, resistence to abstract modes of cognition is intensified. Hart's challenge to the explanatory power of Kelsen's Pure Theory illustrates these tensions.

The conflict between abstract and concrete modes of cognition is intensified as sociological data becomes increasingly relevant to juristic understanding. As it observes and analyzes man in society, such cognition reveals qualitative riches which are irreducible to quantitative measure. To grasp the intellectual value of such insights requires a sensitivity to the various modalities by which human nature can become intelligible. The potentials of a more profound understanding may be seen through a consideration of the philosophical importance of contemporary Sociological Jurisprudence.

In America, Dewey's aversion towards abstract thought is manifested in the jurisprudential work which has been subject, at least indirectly, to his influence. In Chapter Two we traced its affect upon the policy science methodology of Lasswell and McDougal. Not content with the restrictions of positivism, Sociological Jurisprudence seeks to bring humanistic considerations explicitly into the domain of legal philosophy. The form of explanation is empirological—an application of scientific intelligence to social experience. But ontological considerations are influential. Elements of purpose, value, and authoritativeness permeate the system. The concepts are expressed in a terminology appropriate to socio-experimental inquiry; yet such scholarship reflects a quest for essential being. There is a desire to understand the self and human nature under the circumstances of change and conditional existence.

When the inquiry fails to reach, as beyond the boundaries of its competence, is the constitution of human nature *in itself*. Nor does it attain an adequate philosophical understanding of the central concepts of society, law, and the state. These limitations of sociological knowledge are obviously of great significance. Nevertheless, when viewed within a broad theory of knowledge, the understanding attainable by such modalities are intrinsically entitled to respect. They reveal authentic truths about man *in* society. Stated in formal terms, they reveal a type of knowledge which lies between dianoetic and perinoetic intelligibility. Such observations are scientific, as that term is traditionally understood. They provide, under the force of evidence, stable knowledge. They are subject to supplementation, but not contradiction, by higher reflections through which the ontological bearing of human nature is directly integrated into a scheme of thought.

The validity of cognition at different levels of abstraction is defended by Thomism because it respects the autonomy of the various ways of knowing. For it, being can be grasped upon different planes of experience. This comprehensive structure is absent from Northrop's conception. The intrinsic value of empirico-sociological cognition is missed by Northrop because he treats reflections upon social experience as though they were statements about ultimate or metaphysical reality. As we shall see, his concentration upon higher intellectual cognition also mars his theory of natural law.

B. *NATURAL LAW*

The contrast between Thomism and Northrop's scientific theory involves a competition for supremacy between metaphysical and mathematical modes of cognition. It also engages different conceptions of the good. In its concentration upon speculative, highly abstract certitude, Northrop's thought, in its theoretic component, tends towards an exclusively intellectual understanding of the basic elements of human nature. The good is constituted by one's presuppositions about reality and "there is no such thing as ethics."[21] Here again the contrast with Thomism is fundamental. It bears directly upon the theme of natural law.

In Thomism, being and good are, in one sense, equivalents. Everything that exists possesses some degree of actuality and existence as a perfection is desirable. Moreover, the metaphysics which permeates this philosophy gives a teleological orientation to its basic notions. A given nature is good in the measure that it realizes its fundamental essence. Nevertheless ethics, and the requirements of the practical order, constitute a distinct subject matter within which a theory of natural law is articulated. Here the good is the object of moral freedom rather than a matter of intellectual delight.

As with the general theory of knowledge, Thomistic natural law has been articulated in a manner which draws upon the past. However, in its modern formulations, it makes contact with developments and controversies which have surrounded natural law since the seventeenth century. As we have already seen, the ideals of rational cognition established by DesCartes have had a significant impact upon juristic understanding. In the modern era, the subject of natural law has also been affected by these transformations of thought which extended the range of human reason. The significance of neo-Thomistic natural law can be best appreciated against the background of these developments.

Hugo Grotius was a primary exponent of a rationalistic natural law. The method was one of autonomy; the evidence of human reason being considered in itself sufficient to reveal the structure and substance of basic moral precepts. To establish natural law on scientific foundations, Grotius sought to emulate the standards of internal coherence and necessity being set by the revival of mathematics. Hence, an emphasis upon logical deductions and a corresponding lack of variation in the content of the precepts. This new approach was extended by Pufendorf and Vattel. It marked an identification of natural law with the elaboration of an extensive code capable of regulating the immense contingencies of human affairs.[22]

This conception provoked an extreme reaction, particularly in Kantian ethics. The supremacy of moral law, arising out of an autonomous will, was set over against the pretensions of abstract reason. Two aspects of Kant's system are of present relevance. The concern for moral liberty asserted against rationalism established an antagonism between normative reason and moral freedom. The other distinguishing feature is the sharp contrast maintained between the universe of nature and the ethical realm. In the idealistic tradition, there is a constant opposition between these two worlds.[23] Within modern Thomism, the natural law is distinctively ethical, but understood by reason. Yet it is neither purely moral in the Kantian sense, nor purely rational as in the thought of Grotius. The central idea is again that of nature.

Thomism understands man as part of the universe. Caught up with the determinate laws which govern all life, he is nevertheless unique in his power of intellection and moral freedom. The notion of a community between the natural laws of the physical and moral worlds provides themes of unity and contrast which allow scope to the determinate elements within human nature while maintaining the supremacy of moral perception and choice. Through contact with a broader universe, the full range of human inclinations—the tendency to preserve existence common to all life, those inclinations shared with other animals, and the dispositions proper to human beings—all bear upon an understanding of the meaning and range of natural law.[24]

As a moral science, this theory of natural law assumes some awareness of choice, and a relationship between reason and moral freedom. The will desires happiness, *eudaemonia;* at this level, happiness is seen to consist in the fulfillment of human nature. Natural law is a moral law, *i.e.*, an inner order of precepts which reason can discover and to which the human will should conform in the proper exercise of its freedom. The structure is an ideal order. As acknowledged by conscience, it reveals an essence or intelligible necessities. But it is not, as with rationalism, a detailed code of conduct. Its content is composed of the determinations of what should and should not be done which follow necessarily from the basic principle of the practical order: pursue good and avoid evil.[25]

While it can be justified by reflective thought, natural law is not essentially a system of clear, abstract concepts. Both the extremes of rationalism and pure ethics are avoided. It is a knowledge of moral experience, produced in the intellect through an awareness of the ethical qualities implicit in the dispositions and inclinations of human nature. It is a knowing through congeniality: what is consonant with human nature is understood as being good; what is dissonant, bad.

Human reason knows natural law, but it does not cause it to exist. And it is not known by reason alone. Knowledge of natural law is a way of knowing in which it is impossible to maintain sharp distinctions between intellect and will. For here the intellect is allied with the affective dispositions in a collaborative effort to uncover the unwritten law which guides human destiny.

The cogency of this conception can be appreciated when it is set between the efforts which have been made to establish a rationalistic natural law on the one hand and the effort to establish an autonomous moral law on the other. The Thomistic approach also stands as a rival to the mathematico-logical method of Northrop. Its general import can perhaps be best seen by contrasting it with · theories of natural law as they have been more directly articulated within the field of legal philosophy. Comparison with a theory developed by Professor Hart may bring the deeper meaning of natural law into clearer focus.

Professor Hart's theory uses human vulnerability as a fundamental datum. Upon that premise, reason can perceive the need for rules restricting violence and prohibiting the infliction of harm. From the fact of approximate human equality, we can further conclude that a system of mutual restraint and forebearance is necessary to social life in order that one group or individual may not dominate others. Given the limited resources available, man can also understand the need for rules which make possible the acquisition and exchange of wealth within a stable, coercive framework of laws. Consciousness of the pervasiveness of human fraility and obstinacy leads also to the more general need for a system of sanctions.[26]

Hart's idea of natural law, which draws upon Hobbes and Hume, reflects some of the cognitive assumptions of phenomenology. A confidence in man's ability to grasp essential truths is tempered with a belief that knowledge can only be derived from contingent experience. We can perceive an essence; but it is a whatness circumscribed within spatio-temporal existence. It is a way of knowing dependent upon the great truths of concrete social existence. Natural law formulated within Thomism reflects, by contrast, an ontological awareness. Existence is understood in terms of Being; i.e., of possible, as well as actual, reality. It is not set in opposition to the truths of contingent experience but it asserts potentialities which have profoundly different implications. What is discovered within the Thomistic formulation is an ideal order: an intelligible structure which constitutes a formula for human development rather than a code for survival. And the prescriptions of such a natural law look towards a fullness: not simply life, but an amplitude of existence.

Unless an ontologico-moral perspective is maintained, the order of essential inclinations can be reduced to psychological dispositions. Kelsen posed as an objection to natural law the Hobbesian insight that men, in a state of nature, tend to be violent adversaries.[27] The inclination is obviously not to the good. What he fails to understand is that such physic dispositions must be subject to moral scrutiny. This brings into focus inclinations of a higher order. Primitive facts of propensities towards conflict do not contradict natural law. Rather they draw attention to the requirements of political existence and the structures which make human coexistence possible. Substantive reflections upon the nature of political society come into play which prevent the psychological disposition from being determinative.

Criticism of the Aristotelian-Thomistic conception of natural law also includes the observation that what one historical period considers to be essential may differ from the perceptions of another age. The failure of the Ancients to see that slavery was incompatible with human nature is the standard instance. Of more relevance is the fact that certain values now considered to be indispensable to human dignity and freedom were not acknowledged until the dawn of the modern era. But natural law is essentially evolutionary. Knowledge of it progressively develops in time. No claim is made that cognition of the fundamental principles of human morality was completed at any one stage of human history. As an unwritten law, vitally perceived, our knowledge of it grows with the maturity of moral conscience. To understand that maturity, the ethician must be attentive to the ways that moral awareness manifests itself in time.

Basic moral knowledge first arises in a specific cultural context. But its significance is not limited to any given epoch. Rudimentary apperceptions become subject to universal awareness, in successive ages, in spite of great varieties of interpretation and imperfections of expression. And the content is diverse. In the long perspective of history, man has become progressively aware of differentiations within the substance of the fundamental law which guides moral development. Within this framework, it is possible to attain a whole and coherent view of the principles of social morality.

In primitive societies basic moral rules, mostly negative in character, were observed and the fundamental structures of social life obscurely perceived. In the Ancient and Medieval periods, obligations of commutative and distributive justice were developed as more rudimentary perceptions were refined and the range of social relations extended. In the modern age, there is an explicit consciousness of the value of the individual person; his rights and dignity, as well as a heightened awareness of the nature of political existence. And the knowledge of the basic structure and content is incomplete. It will develop so long as the human species endures.

For a theory of natural law to sustain a diverse content of precepts it must be immersed in time while remaining transcendent in its ultimate justification. Such a methodology is hazardous, since it is extremely difficult to disengage what is timeless from what is culturally conditioned. The temptation to resort to a purely abstract form of knowing is, as Northrop's theory illustrates, strong. But moral knowledge can only attain depth through an interplay between reflection and contingent experience. Indeed, the ideal and existential orders are more intimately linked than is commonly appreciated.

Understanding of the scope of moral law expands with developments in social institutions. Where a society is built upon relation-

ships of kinship, commutative justice cannot be fully realized, because the requisite distinction between individuals is not adequately
developed. And, until some form of political organization is
achieved, a common good cannot be perceived. The hindrance
exists because primitive law is limited to the protection of distinct
family units.[28] An analogous difficulty can presently be observed
on the international plane. Factual interdependence raises issues of
distributive justice which touch the whole of global society, but
considerations of sovereign interest obstruct the evolution of a universal common good.

That close attention to temporal reality is essential to understanding the boundaries and growth of natural law can be seen
most clearly where ethics makes contact with sociology. We have
already acknowledged that sociology as a science is capable of uncovering certain fundamental truths about man as his nature is
understood under conditions of change. On the plane of practical
moral knowledge, standards which are ultimately understood as
part of natural law may first come into consciousness through an
awareness which has a sociological dimension. An ideology can
carry within it essential insights which await their disengagement by
moral reflection.

The problem of justifying moral norms in human nature rather
than society is complicated by advances in the methodology of decision making. Cardozo referred to judges as interpreters of the
"social mind" and other sociologically oriented jurists make a similar convergence between responsible choice and the normativity of
social values. The tendency to believe that an immanent social law
awaits juristic discovery[29] is complemented by the orientation of the
Policy Science school of jurisprudence which virtually defines human dignity as a social process in which values are widely shared.

A case can be made for the proposition that deference to social
reality is essential to responsible decision making. It helps to assure
that the distributed values are those of the community rather than
the legislator, judge or administrator making the choice. But there
are countervailing considerations. As we suggested in Chapter
Two, decisional acts are prudential judgments, implying a choice as
to the requirements of a situation which takes all relevant factors
into account. The corollary of that view is that no norm, either
moral or social, positively determines a particular result.[30] If it is
understood that neither transcendent or immanent norms command decision an atmosphere is established which is conducive to

distinguishing moral precepts derived from a timeless natural law from values which arise within a particular social experience.

Further progress may be made if distinctions are more carefully made between social values and moral precepts. In the Policy Science methodology, the objective for the jurist is to identify the values which people seek to achieve through decisional processes and to use specified values to enhance the goal of human dignity. Recommended procedures for empirically verifying and achieving values further a rational disposition to maximize individual satisfaction on a wide scale. Because human dignity is stated as a primary postulate, the Policy Science process has a firmer moral base than an earlier legal sociology which sought to maximize wants and desires insofar as general order would allow. At the same time, a disposition to identify the good with the realization of social values persists, and it is with reference to this orientation that the boundaries between natural law and sociology are apt to be confused.

This tendency bears some resemblance to Grotius' ambition to identify natural law with all important aspects of human sociability.[31] The transcendent dimensions of moral knowledge were transformed into temporal rules rationally devised. The range of normative regulation was extended as the desire to bring human relations under the control of reason gained a new impetus. The consequences of the contemporary theory are similar. The desire of individuals to realize themselves in society becomes a supreme good which displaces the controls which natural law imposes upon human interactions. The objective of natural law is to discern the rules and principles inscribed in human nature which reveal a universal and certain good. Sociological Jurisprudence aims at the maximization of human values as governed by a commitment to human dignity. The objectives do not converge; however they should not be set in opposition. The empirical mode of grounding value judgments has unique advantages. Rooted in inquiry and reappraisal, the process of clarifying and implementing values given in experience checks propensities towards moral dogmatism and promotes the practical attainment of human dignity. However the postulation of basic values and the subjective justification which it entails leaves the grounding of human dignity, as well as the ordering of human values, within substantial foundations. There is no specific attention to the duties which life in society imposes. A value such as power, for example, cannot be rationally measured unless firm principles of justice and right govern its use. And other

specified values, such as well being, affection, wealth, are all desires whose concrete realization requires guidance from moral principles derived from a higher order of human development.[32]

The relationship between natural law and sociology can be intimate in other respects. This is especially true of the dimensions of
morality which bear upon the nature of community. In contemporary awareness, the necessity of learning to live together is a good
of paramount importance.[33] Yet the accomplishment of the objective is dependent upon an understanding of the structures and
nuances of community life which only sociology can perceive. The
dependence of justice upon sociological insight is particularly acute
where matters of equality are at issue, as the sociologist has precise
instruments for uncovering patterns of discrimination which make
the requisite moral norms operative.[34]

Essential principles of morality make up the content of natural
law, even though our knowledge of them is conditioned by cultural
experience. However, further difficulty would appear to invalidate
any claims that immutable, universal precepts can survive the encounter with experience. Because of the progressive increase in
both the quality and quantity of moral claims, it would seem impossible to determine which, if any, have transcendent significance.
We may have, at best, a natural law with a changing content. The
difficulty is itself a product of history. It was provoked by claims of
the late scholastics and the proponents of a rationalistic natural law
who unduly extended the certitudes of moral reason. From the point
of view of neo-Thomism, the subject of natural law, in its direct
bearing upon legal philosophy, is concerned with the precepts of
social life which flow in a necessary fashion from the primary inclination to do good and avoid evil.[35] Furthermore, knowledge of
these norms develops as conscience becomes more aware of the
essential requirements of human interaction.

If these qualifications are kept in mind, it is possible to perceive
continuities and additions which slowly build the moral life of society. These connections between points of ethical awareness can
help to resolve uncertainties. For example, the principle that fraud
or deception is incompatible with the purposes of human sociability
has a very long history. What is significant is that the effort to resist
deception is continuous, subject to refinement in its meaning and
scope. At an earlier period, only the most explicit misrepre-
sentations were proscribed within a narrow range of human transactions. In contemporary life an effort is made to reach more subtle

forms, in a wide variety of circumstances.[36] Similar developmental observations could be made about other moral duties. The phenomenon of genocide not only shocks the conscience; it reinforces prescriptions against murder. The progress of history deepens our understanding of precepts which, at an earlier period, were less forcefully perceived. Temporal developments which clarify the structures of political existence affect the moral principles which sustain the fabric of government. The principle of obedience to legitimate authority has a persistent relevance; however an evolving comprehension that the people are the source of such authority draws other ethical norms into prominence. As we have suggested in earlier chapters, accountability for the use of delegated power[37] has become of primary importance for legal as well as political philosophy.

The pluralism and diversity of moral precepts is also relevant to the assertion that an immutable natural law is made relative by the exigencies of history. Here confusion is generated by a failure to observe a distinction between contradiction and adjustment. Essential precepts are not intrinsically opposed, although their mutual bearing upon a concrete situation can make the burden of ethical choice difficult. Some concrete verification of this analysis can be gathered from general experience.

An effort to acknowledge the relevance of competing values is a mark of sound judgment. Attempts by the Supreme Court to strike a balance between freedom of expression and the traditional values protected by defamation laws[38] is illustrative. The difficulties are more painfully apparent in the controversy over abortion. What the antagonists perceive from their perspective as a simply case of right is in fact a collision between an enduring principle that innocent life must be preserved and a more contemporary consciousness of the value of human privacy. A failure to acknowledge the latter principle may possibly lead to an infringement of personal rights, but to ignore the former value is equally offensive to moral conscience.

This approach to the diversity of moral principles has advantages over the methodology of idealism which is prone to ethical reductionism. Rather than collapse all values into an undifferentiated moral norm,[39] Thomistic realism acknowledges a plurality of essential precepts and remains in contact with the complexities of existential choice.

We shall return to the theme of judgment and its relation to natural law. However at this juncture it is appropriate to draw attention to other ways in which this tradition has relevance to the concerns of legal philosophy.

~

A dynamic understanding of nature and vital contacts with the processes of history allows the natural law tradition to make a valuable contribution to that search for the good which gives an ethical dimension to legal philosophy. Natural law also makes an indispensable contribution to the quest to understand the nature of law. Interacting with legal history, it has developed a comprehensive definition of law which draws its diverse manifestations into a coherent and hierarchical whole.

The Roman jurists had some conception of a tripartite division of law. Although the elements were expressed in a confusing manner, certain distinctive features did emerge. As formulated in the CORPUS JURIS CIVILIS, *Ius Naturale* was attributed to a will superior to any lawmaker, embodying a justice which human authority ought to express but which it does not make. The concept of *ius gentium,* a law of nations, reflected the cosmopolitan elements in Roman law, encompassing broader jural principles which were devised to facilitate human contact. *Ius civile* was the particular law of the state.

During the medieval period, this trichotomy was subjected to theological and philosophical refinement. The idea of natural law was clarified, and given an elevated meaning in Aquinas' definition that natural law was the rational creatures' participation in the eternal law.[40] The obligations which it entailed were elaborated, and its supremacy over other forms of law affirmed. Reflection also sought to clarify the distinction between natural law and *ius gentium;* an undertaking of considerable difficulty, since this intermediate form straddled the immutable and contingent realms.

In the theocentric atmosphere of medieval society the priority of natural law was affirmed with a spirit of absolute moral vigor. Supremacy was a natural consequence of its divine character. But natural and positive human law were never understood as being essentially opposed, either in content or authority. If a positive rule commanded what was intrinsically unjust, it would not be law but violence. But no fundamental antagonism between the two orders was implied.

The extent of compatability between natural law and human lawmaking has been greatly obscured in the modern age. There is a strong tendency to view transcendent law in terms of norms which impose restrictive obligations upon the will, rather than as a measure of what should be done in the proper exercise of freedom. Kelsen's Pure Theory of Law gives this inclination its highest expression. His effort to draw an antithetical relationship between natural and positive law[41] results from a desire to attribute supremacy to human enactments. This impulse towards a purely secular humanism, expressed in a logico-deductive form of thought, fails to grasp the complementary relationships which exist between natural and positive law. Beyond a firm minimum of hierarchical supremacy, the inter-relationship between the forms of law can be understood harmoniously. Each is a measure of human acts, involving some form of obligation[42] although only positive law, as an expression of political authority, carries coercive force. The autonomy of positive law is preserved; but it is neither the exclusive nor, as Kelsen maintained, the supreme form of law.

Kelsen's tendency to pose issues deductively also led him to express the relationship in terms of an assumed subordination of positive law which was inimical to the freedom of human will. Conflict was posed in terms of a personified natural law standing over against a positive legal order which symbolized creative human will. But there is a fundamental unity between natural law, the law of nations and positive law. They are joined by a common human disposition to pursue the good:

> *Natural law* deals with the rights and the duties which are connected in a *necessary* manner with the first principle: "Do good and avoid evil" . . . *Jus gentium* or the *Law of Nations* . . . is intermediary between natural law and positive law . . . because it is *known* not through inclination, but through the *conceptual exercise of reason,* or through rational knowledge; in this sense it pertains to positive law . . . But as concerns its content, *jus gentium* comprises both things which belong also to natural law . . . and things which . . . are beyond the content of natural law (because they are *only* rationally inferred and not known through inclination). In both cases *jus gentium* or the common law of civilization deals, like natural law, with rights and

duties which are connected with the first principle in a *necessary* manner . . .

Positive law . . . the body of laws . . . in force in a given social group, deals with the rights and duties which are connected with the first principle, but in a *contingent* manner, by virtue of the determinate ways of conduct set down by the reason and the will of man when they institute the laws or give birth to the customs of a particular society . . .

But it is in virtue of natural law that the laws of nations and positive law take on the force of law, and impose themselves upon the conscience. They are a prolongation or an extension of natural law, passing into objective zones which can less and less be sufficiently determined by the essential inclinations of human nature. *For it is natural law itself which requires that whatever it leaves undetermined shall subsequently be determined . . .* [43]

This general conception does not postulate an absolute content of natural law standing over in opposition to the intrinsic relativity of positive law. Legal rules directly contrary to moral law are proscribed; but there is a general deference to positive lawmaking. Natural law claims a *limited* supremacy. However obnoxious this may appear, it constitutes a foundation upon which conscience can justify its refusal to submit to the absolutist pretentions of sovereign power.

The interconnectedness between the three forms of law is one of congruence rather than dependence. The separate and autonomous sphere of each is respected as are the modalities by which they arise and become operative. The uniqueness of the common law compared, for example, with the civil law system can be fully accommodated within the general frame. Preservation of jural independence can be seen even more clearly with respect to the *ius gentium*.

Primary moral principles, and the conclusions necessarily drawn from them, were considered to be within the domain of natural law. The primary distinction was one of authorship. Natural law was a reflection of Creative Wisdom. *Ius gentium* was a human creation, responsive to the influence of natural law. Unlike the precepts of natural law, the content of *ius gentium* was not understood as being, in all particulars, essential for moral rectitude. But it was in harmony with natural circumstances. The laws of diplomatic exchange were illustrative. A further important distinction was that while natural law would not tolerate evil, *ius gentium* may. The general acceptance, by civilized peoples, of rules permitting prescriptive rights of property, or the general effect of statutes of limitation, are illustrative.

The range of *ius gentium* was extensive, since it was understood as covering both international relations and general juridical principles recognized by the majority of mankind. When Suarez sought to provide the moral foundations for sovereign state relations *ius gentium,* understood as the common rules of international intercourse, was responsive to that need.[44]

Confusion between natural law and *ius gentium* begins to develop with the work of Grotius. A "law of nature" was evoked indiscriminately, to be proven *a priori* by demonstrating its necessary agreement or disagreement with a rational and social nature; to be proved *a posteriori* by a probable conviction "that that is according to the law of nature which is believed to be such among all nations, or among all those that are more advanced in civilization."[45] As Del Vecchio recognized, the change deprived natural law of its absolute value,[46] as well as hopelessly confusing the distinction between natural law and *ius gentium*. The Thomistic conception preserves the integrity of each jural sphere. In retaining *ius gentium* as a viable category, it also keeps its conception of law in touch with present realities.

As an intermediate form of law, *ius gentium* or the law of nations draws within its ambit the general procedural and substantive principles of justice recognized by reasonably mature legal systems.[47] In addition, it gives jural significance to some of the normative statements expressed within the context of global society, such as the Universal Declaration of Human Rights. While not capable of coercive implementation, they influence legal decisions in a variety of international and national situations. One may, as a strict positivist, prefer to treat these norms as but *sources* of law; yet jural comprehension is inhanced when *ius gentium* and positive law are viewed in a dynamic interrelation.

The evolving importance of *ius gentium* may also influence its relationship with natural law. Traditionally, insofar as moral norms were known through inclination, rather than through the conceptual exercise of reason, they were properly within the province of natural law. A natural law precept for example, the prohibition of murder, may also appear as part of a law of nations but only because reason, of itself, derives such a conclusion from natural principles prohibiting the infliction of harm. As the growth of general principles of civilization is understood more as the expression of moral conscience, a strict distinction between these two forms of law may not be possible. The norms of *ius gentium* as they are embodied in Universal Declaration, or as recognized by the major legal systems, manifest moral conviction as well as the affirmative exercise of reason. The crucial distinction between pure normative immanence and a conception which understands moral awareness as including a transcendent dimension remains. Natural law, with its higher ontological framework, will retain its distinctiveness. We shall also look towards an evolving law of nations for jural guidance. This shift in emphasis is consonant with the pluralism of modern civilization, and the insights which concentrate morality within human consciousness and conscience.

The tripartite Thomistic conception of law establishes a definitional frame within which varied forms of jural understanding can find adequate expression. The reality and legitimate competence of state positive law is affirmed without allowing it to exhaust the meaning of law. The quest for a common law of civilization is ratified and encouraged. And transcendent moral law is acknowledged without intruding upon the autonomy of the other jural spheres.

⁓

This all encompassing definition possesses great explanatory power. As it broadens our understanding of law, it should also contribute a stabilizing dimension to our decisional abilities. Yet the problems of concrete choice are so complex that it is difficult to draw meaningful connections between general knowledge and the contingencies of life. In particular, the inclusion of natural law within the scope of jural cognition does not displace the concrete uncertainties aroused by the need to make practical choices:

> Quite apart from the stock philosophical difficulties, there are often—and I would say typically—deep perplexities about

how we are to act. We thirst, no doubt immaturely, for some sure guide, some certain set of rational principles, that anywhere and at any time will lift this anxiety—arousing perplexity from our shoulders and give us, at least in certain essentials, a sure guide as to how we ought to live and die and how we ought to order our society. Natural law seemed to give us such a guide; it seemed to provide us with a rational foundation for such a certitude on fundamental moral matters. But there is a fly in the ointment. To give natural moral law conceptions a ghost of a chance of being intellectually respectable, we must relativize them . . .Yet when this is done the natural law loses much of its allure and loses its apparent advantage over, say, a pragmatic moral theory such as John Dewey's. If a *'jus naturale more geometrico* is scarcely possible,' and if we must rely on the judgment and wisdom of the jurist and moral agent, we will lose that cettainty, that absoluteness that natural moral law conceptions seemed to provide.[48]

These are authentic difficulties which force attention upon the existential elements of action. Insofar as relativity is invoked, the quoted remarks repeat the objection concerning moral pluralism which we have already considered. Of greater importance is the unfavorable reference to the "judgment and wisdom" of the decisional actor.

The criticism refers to difficulties encountered in the practical order, yet it bears some analogy with the speculative aspirations which we noted at the beginning of this chapter. The mathematical trend of modern thought seeks to establish stable connections between the highest abstractions and concrete experiences. Justice Cardozo's lament that "they do things better with logarithms"[49] symbolizes this unique yearning for decisional certitude. Such a disposition accentuates the contrast between the objectivity of impersonal science and the biases of individuals.

A *"jus naturale more geometrico"* may have been the ideal of seventeenth century rationalism, but it does not represent the attitude of the Aristotelian-Thomistic tradition. Possibilities of practical certitude are here affirmed, but with reference to the personal qualities of the decision maker rather than precise determinations of law. Deliberation and choice are the essence of decision, and they call for practical wisdom rather than scientific demonstration.[50]

Natural law is a part of moral knowledge. It must be supplemented by virtues of justice, courage and prudence.

Through their development we learn to judge what it is right to do in concrete circumstances. In such a conception, there are potentials for certitude, but they lie within the realm of personal excellence, realized as we acquire a stable disposition which perfects the exercise of moral freedom. This understanding of the relationship between the speculative and practical realm leads Thomism to affirm that lawmaking is an act of prudence.[51]

A perfected ability to make right decisions becomes the moral ideal. The emphasis upon personal virtue protects the freedom of the decision maker without giving license to the moral impulses of an autonomous ego. It also provides a model of sound judgment.

Where a judge has discretion it must be exercised in a manner compatible with authoritative legal rules and principles. And institutional restraints quite properly prevent a judge from directly basing his decision upon competing social policies. However, adjudication is inevitably influenced by demands and values which are operative in the larger community. Sociological Jurisprudence provides abundant evidence of the extent to which all decisional processes have a societal dimension.

Much valuable work has been done which helps to delineate the boundaries of adjudicatory competence.[52] Yet the proper balance between legal and social considerations in such cases eludes precise determination because it depends upon an assessment of intangibles by the one responsible for choice. Insofar as the judgement is not subject to review, the personal character of the judge must provide the ultimate measure.

This is not to suggest arbitrary choice nor the secretive implementation of personal value preferences. Thomism does not endorse the idea that a public official may impose his own view of right conduct upon the community. But in placing the decisional act within the framework of moral choice,[53] it affirms those qualities of creative decision making which have always been a hallmark of a sound and progressive jurisprudence.

C. *CONCLUSION*

The Thomistic theory of law, and conceptions of human nature which it implies, is rooted in ontological forms of explanation. Drawing upon metaphysics, it affirms the power of thought to attain essential truths which bear upon the field of legal philosophy. It thus moves beyond the experiential and logical ways of comprehending jural reality, without setting itself in opposition to these other cognitive modalities.

Modern legal philosophy attempts to comprehend the nature of law from different angles of intellectual vision. From the time of Austin and his followers, jurists have utilized various inductive and deductive modes of thought in attempting to penetrate the meaning of law. No single way of knowing or cognitive procedure has prevailed. There is a persistent tension between experiential and abstract thought; however, the juristic mind, intent on deeper understanding, tends towards higher forms of explanation.

A struggle between logical and empirical cognition marks the history of legal positivism. The conflicts of Pure Theory with Sociology of Law reflects preferences for abstract over concrete modes of knowing. Comparable tension can be observed in the efforts to define justice. In the idealism of Del Vecchio, and in the social contract theories of Rawls, the *a priori* modality of Kantian ethics has become the predominate form of explanation. At the summit of speculative thought, the legal philosophy of F.S.C. Northrop illustrates how inexorable is the desire to reach ultimate levels of jural knowledge.

The Thomistic theory is in integral continuity with the ascending disposition to make the phenomenon of law fully intelligible. Cognitive in the deepest sense, it reveals an ultimate structure which makes possible the understanding of law as a meaningful whole. Its triparte definition of law provides a general frame which is responsive to the whole of juristic experience. It thus completes the quest for comprehensive understanding which we have traced through the observational and deductive modes of modern jurisprudence.

While making possible the comprehension of law in its widest significance, Thomism also respects and affirms the authentic jural insights which have been attained through other ways of knowing. If it is critical, it is so only to the degree that it questions the adequacy, rather than the intrinsic competence, of each particular approach. No invidious comparisons are made between the cognitive presuppositions which sustain the various jurisprudential theories. There is no gratitious intrusion of metaphysics, nor reference to complexities which can be adequately resolved by other forms of understanding.

Thomism is relevant in the degree to which other forms of jural explanation are found to be insufficient. This is true with respect to ultimate questions of human nature, as explained in the present chapter, where ontology directly competes with mathematical cognition. But the philosophical perspective which is characteristic of Thomism has significance for other fundamental questions which pervade the discipline. The concept of sovereignty was intrinsic to the establishment of modern jurisprudence, and its presence raised issues of power and authority which have occupied all of the literature. Each subsequent theory developed new insights; but when we have exhausted the non-metaphysical modes of inquiry, analysis remains incomplete. There remains the need to pursue, upon a philosophical plane, reflections upon the nature of the state, its place within society, and its relation to the people, who retain the ultimate right to govern.[54]

A feeling that something further can be said is apparent with respect to other essential attributes of jural definition. The complexities of distributive justice, for example, can only be fully comprehended within a theoretical conception which affirms both the independent value of the human person and his authentic relationship to a wider community. Thomism can make a positive contribution to these difficult problems. As a supplementary insight it contributes to our understanding of the nature of law, bringing to completion what has been imperfectly perceived by other ways of knowing.

Thomism has an additional advantage in that it moves with relative facility between the speculative and practical domains. As we noted earlier in our appraisal of Northrop's theory, Thomism avoids the basic error of equating the good with purely intellectual understanding.[55] An explicitly moral orientation informs the theory of natural law and continues throughout all subsequent reflections upon the realm of action. There are interactions between reason and volition, as well as between certainty and contingency, which have important implications for the practical concerns of jurisprudence.

The protection of human rights engages cognitive and operational energies. In pursuing that objective, modern legal philosophy tends to move between extremes of practical action and abstract thought. Sociological instrumentalism seeks to establish rights in concrete existence by promoting the widest sharing of human values. It is a laudable objective; however, insufficient attention is given to the need for antecedent justification. To inquire into the consequences of actual violation[56] is useful, but a deeper grounding is required to restrain offenses to human dignity. And, in a world of antagonistic ideologies, implementation understood as self realization is unpersuasive.

Critical reflection is indispensable to the establishment of objective values. The solution of idealism is also inadequate. While it raises the question of personality to the plane of abstract thought, it confines knowledge of other selves to the contents of consciousness. Thomism places the question of human rights within an ontological context which attributes substantive content to the extra-mental reality of other persons.[57] The *alteritas* indispensible to justice is preserved through a cognitive enterprise which transcends the relativities of culture. And, since the universe of social as well as individual reality is affirmed, an intellectual framework is established which makes it possible to comprehend the dynamic relationship between the person and society. Further, both the right and the good are included as integral to total comprehension. Refusal to admit either element inevitably leads to significant distortions, as we have noted in our survey of Rawls' theory of justice.

It may be objected that Thomism relies upon a teleological conception which is inimical to the modern spirit. Yet it has been clearly demonstrated[58] that the liberal psychology and political theories which maintain this aversion do not do justice to the structure of personality. If we wish to fully understand the phenomenon of personality we must be open to its transcendent aspirations. Moreover, an adequate philosophy of law must include some of the substantive ends of civilization within its scope. Profound humanistic tendencies actually influence the development of legal and social policy; they should be taken into account and subject to philosophical discipline instead of being dogmatically excluded from the province of jurisprudence.

Aspirations for the realization of values continue to make their impression upon legal philosophy, and efforts towards their implementation necessarily imply some form of ethical orientation. Inevitably, at critical junctures, choices must be made between a teleological and deontological conception of law. A rigorous morality derived from Kantian ethics now dominates the subject of justice. It exalts the autonomous ego, but its reliance upon imperatives and its affinity for Rousseauistic political theories threatens the very moral freedom which it seeks to protect. Understood as a purposive ethic, Thomism is viewed with suspicion because an awareness of finalities is thought to be a threat to individual liberty.

However, its inclusion of ends is matched by an aversion to the use of legal coercion as a means of realizing the highest goals of the human spirit.[59] If its philosophy of law were better understood it should compare favorably with ethical traditions which are only apparently more conducive to freedom.

In a teleological ethic, the focus is upon what should be done with our moral freedom. Stressing *should* rather than *ought*, Thomism accentuates elements of deliberation and choice which can be overlooked when duty and normative obligations predominate. The contrasting emphases have a broad influence upon the problems of jurisprudence. As law becomes increasingly understood as a decisional phenomenon, the moral qualities of jural action will gain in importance. Here the vitality of Thomism, as well as its jurisprudential relevance, is demonstrable. For its conception of the good, provoked by reflections upon human nature and natural law, turns increasingly towards the realm of action and culminates in the practical virtue of prudence.

~

It may be appropriate, in ending these reflections, to make some observations upon the relation between natural law and the quest for a stable world order. We have seen how modern legal philosophy has sought to justify international law in spite of the absence of political institutions. For H.L.A. Hart, the decentralization of international life is not a decisive obstacle to jural understanding. The prevailing system, which stresses the consent of states, is intelligible in terms of the stage of human evolution which it manifests. The lack of global law making and enforcing machinery also does not deter the sociological jurist. For he can observe a factual restraint contributing to order: the compliance with jural norms in the practice of national and transnational officials. For Kelsen, the constructive power of abstract logic makes possible the projection of an international legal order of cognitive supremacy over national will.

These approaches to the problem of international law are not only incomplete; they are fundamentally flawed. They are incapable of measuring the deeper anarchy within the world community; the absence of restraint where vital issues are at stake; the ineffectiveness of voluntary dispute settlement and the balances of terror which mark a fragile truce between contentious powers. Moral sensibility recoils at the possibilities of human destruction inherent in the present situation, while jurisprudence is unable to make a formative contribution to lasting peace. What is often overlooked is the extent to which present impotency is directly linked with the separation of questions of human nature and natural law from their metaphystical foundations.

Since the time of Grotius, there has been a continuing effort to establish juridical relationships between nations without the institution of political authority. This effort of autonomous reason reaches its highest expression in the thought of Kelsen, who, as we have seen, constructs a theoretical international law as if it represented a superior normative order. The result is a radical disjuncture between thought and reality.

The underlying premises of this trend of thought includes conceptions of human nature. There are psychological assumptions concerning the aggressive instincts derived mainly from Hobbesian psychology. There is also an aversion to teleological interpretations of human life. A classical expression can be seen in the work of Spinoza who, following the formation of national states, transferred the Hobbesian *jus naturale* to international relations.[60] What is lacking is any positive idea of an inclination towards political society which might provide an impetus towards fundamental reconstruction.

Lockean political theory is more optimistic about transitions from "a state of nature" to political society. But, as it shares the anti-metaphysical bias, it does not reach the deeper potentials of humanistic development. The ideas of human nature and natural law preserved by the Thomistic tradition may provide the requisite momentum towards universal change. For it comprehends the tendency towards political organization as an integral dynamic of natural law; part of the propensity towards growth and fulfillment which characterize a metaphystical conception of human nature.[61] By again making contact with this tradition legal philosophy may perhaps make a vital contribution to world civilization and gain that preeminence as an explanatory discipline which is its enduring ambition.

Notes

Chapter One

1. H. Cairns, Legal Philosophy From Plato To Hegel Ch. 1 (1949). "... The tendency of jurisprudence, which had broken with theology in the sixteenth century... was towards complete independence. Jurisprudence, the analytical jurist insisted, was a wholly self-sufficient science...." *Id.* at 2. See also the title *Analytic Jurisprudence* in I, The Encyclopedia Of Philosophy, 109 et seq. (1967). For the general intellectual development, see A. Whitehead, Science And The Modern World (1925) and H. Butterfield, The Origins Of Modern Science Ch. 6 (Rev. ed. 1957).

2. J. S. Mill, IV Dissertations And Discussion, *Political, Philosophical, and Historical* 161 (1868).

3. Of Commonwealth in III The English Works Of Thomas Hobbes *1915 (W. Molesworth,* ed. 1839). The empirical characterization I owe to H. Cairns, Legal Philosophy From Plato To Hegel Ch. VII (1949).

4. Quoted in J. Bentham, The Limits Of Jurisprudence Defined 3–4 (C. Everett ed. 1945).

5. W. Blackstone, Commentaries On The Laws Of England, Intro. Sec. 2.

6. J. Bentham, A Fragment On Government, Ch. L, XIV-XXI in I Works Of Jeremy Bentham (J. Bowring, ed. 1843).

7. *Id.,* XVI-XLVIII: I Works 270–271. For Bentham's theory of utilitarianism see The Principles Of Legislation, Ch. 1, I Works, 1. Compare J. S. Mill, Utilitarianism (1861). For a general discussion, see W. Davidson, Political Thought From Bentham to J. S. Mill (1915); E. Patterson, Jurisprudence, Ch. 16 (1953).

8. Ch. XI, XXXI; I Works at 276.

9. J. Bentham, Of Laws In General (H.L.A. Hart ed. 1970). Interest in Bentham's contribution to jurisprudence has undergone a revival in recent years. More extensive studies can be found in Hart, *Bentham on Sovereignty,* 2 The Irish Jurist 327 (1967); D. Lyons, In The Interest Of The Governed: A Study Of Bentham's Philosophy Of Utility And Law (1973), *Logic and Coercion in Bentham's Theory of Law,* 57 Cornell L. Rev. 335 (1971); Olivecrona, *The Will of the Sovereign: Some Reflections on Benttham's Concept of 'Law,'* 20 AmJ. Jur. 95 (1975).

10. J. Austin, The Province Of Jurisprudence Determined, Ch. 1 (H.L.A. Hart, ed. 1954). This volume contains the first six Lectures together with an essay on the Uses of the Study of Jurisprudence. Austin's Jurisprudence, an earlier two volume work printed in several editions, contains all the lectures as given by Austin and the outline of the unfinished course. Primary references will be to The Province.

Austin took pains to restrict positive law to general commands. For Bentham, expressions of will derived from sovereign power were laws, but his definition would encompass all volitions, whether general or particular, which emanated from sovereign authority. Some comparison between Bentham's and Austin's concept of law can be found in D. Lyons, In The Interests Of The Governed (1973).

Biographical sketches of Austin may be found in: *Introduction* to The Province (H.L.A. Hart, ed., 1954) and F.J.C. Hearnshaw, The Social And Political Ideas Of Some Representative Thinkers Of The Age Of Reaction And Reconstruction VIII (1932).

11. Province, Lec. V, pp. 126–140. The theocentric aspects of Austin's jurisprudence are examined in Murphy, *Austinian Natural Law*, 39 U. Detroit L. Rev. 650 (1961).

12. Lec. VI, pp. 193–212. The sovereign was not in obedience to a further superior. Austin felt that this negative emphasis constituted an improvement upon Bentham's view.

13. *Ibid.;* 294–306. As the duties of the subject are grounded upon Divine Law, positive law and positive morality, the hypothesis of an original compact was unnecessary. *Ibid.*; 306 et seq. Cf. 336–344.

14.

"A positive law may be defined generally in the following manner: ... Every positive law (or every law simply and strictly so called) is set, directly or circuitously, by a sovereign individual or body, to a member or members of the independent political society wherein its author is supreme. In other words, it is set, directly or circuitously, by a monarch or sovereign number, to a person or persons in a state of subjection to its author." Province at 350.

15. See *The Uses of the Study of Jurisprudence,* in The Province Of Jurisprudence Determined 363. Compare I Austin's Jurisprudence Ch. XI (R. Campbell, ed. 1885).

16. J. S. Mill, IV Dissertations at 167 (1868).

17. Compare H. Maine, Early History Of Institutions (1884) at 343:

"[T]o Bentham, and even in a higher degree to Austin, the world is indebted for the only existing attempt to construct a system of jurisprudence by strict scientific process and to found it, not on *a priori* assumption, but on the observation, comparison, and analysis of the various legal conceptions...

See also T. Holland, The Elements Of Jurisprudence, Ch. 1, 5–9 (13th ed. 1924). Holland, who is explicit about the empirical method, also shifts analytical attention from commands to the concept of rule. Other examples of this analytical method can be seen in W. Markby, Elements

OF LAW (1871); H. TERRY, LEADING PRINCIPLES OF ANGLO AMERICAN LAW (1887); J. SALMOND, JURISPRUDENCE (10th ed. 1947). For a general summary, see Kocourek, *The Century of Analytical Jurisprudence Since John Austin,* in 2 LAW: A CENTURY OF PROGRESS, *1835–1935,* 195 (1937).

The general import of this empirical mode of knowing will be discussed in Chapter Five, *infra.*

18. PROVINCE, Lec. VI, pp. 245 et seq. Compare J. SALMOND, ON JURISPRUDENCE Appendix I (11th ed. 1957). Austin's ideas also had an influence upon Continental legal philosophy, particularly in the work of Solmo, and later upon Hans Kelsen. See the general discussion in L. FULLER, THE LAW IN QUEST OF ITSELF 26–41 (1940). However, it is within the English speaking world that its potentials as an empirical mode of jurisprudence have been most fully realized. Kelsen's Pure Theory of Law will be considered separately, in Chapter Three.

19. J. C. GRAY, THE NATURE AND SOURCES OF LAW, Ch. 3, § § 175–179 (1909).

20. See GRAY, op. cit. § 180; H.L.A. HART, THE CONCEPT OF LAW 70–76 (1961).

21. Austin believed that the thesis of a sovereign people depended upon proof that all the members of the society jointly founded the government. See THE PROVINCE Ch. VI, esp. 336. But that is to ask for more precision than the subject will allow. In Chapter V of the Lectures, Austin makes a strong case for the importance of a determinate number in the identification of *legal* authority; he was mistaken, however, in looking for the same exact standards of proof in matters of political authority. As Dewey once observed, the result of Austin's method is that sovereignty is identified with only part of the body politic, with no adequate reason given for such supreme power. Dewey, *Austin's Theory of Sovereignty,* IX POL. SCIENCE Q. 31, 41 (1894).

Dewey believed that the organs of government exist to give expression to social forces. In our conception there is a reliance upon political philosophy rather than sociology. For a general analysis, see J. MARITAIN, MAN AND THE STATE, Ch. 1 (1950).

22. Marshall, C. J. in McCulloch, v. Maryland, 17 U.S. (4 Wheat.) 316, 4 L.Ed. 579 (1819). Compare E. S. MORGAN, THE BIRTH OF THE REPUBLIC, 143 (1956), R. PALMER, I THE AGE OF THE DEMOCRATIC REVOLUTION 3–24 (1959). The concept of autonomy is a more accurate description of ultimate political authority. Sovereignty refers to a supreme power separate and above those who are ruled.

23. II AUSTIN'S JURISPRUDENCE, Lec. XXXVII, XXXVIII (1878).

24. J. SALMOND, JURISPRUDENCE, Ch. 2 § 17 (10th ed. 1947). Austin preferred codification as a remedy for the imperfections of judicial lawmaking. See Lec. XXXIX.

25. THE NATURE AND SOURCES OF LAW, Ch. IV; V.

26. *Ibid.*; Ch. V §§ 266–276. Compare AUSTIN, *op. cit.,* Ch. XXXVIII, §§ 924–931.

27. E. ROSTOW, THE SOVEREIGN PREROGATIVE, 88 (1962). And see White, *The Supreme Court's Public and the Public's Supreme Court,* 52 VA. Q. REV. 370 (1976).

28. E.g., McCloskey, *Reflections on the Warren Court,* 51 Va. L. Rev. 1229 (1965). I explore the persistent aspects of this problem in my article *The Supreme Court and Democratic Theory,* 17 Syracuse L. Rev. 642 (1966).

29. Province, Ch. VI, pp. 257 et. seq.

30. Wechsler, *Toward Neutral Principles of Constitutional Law,* In Principles, Politics And Fundamental Law, 1, 14 (1961). Compare A. Bickel, The Least Dangerous Branch (1961). Referring to standing to sue, the Supreme Court, in a recent decision stated:

> "In essence the question of standing is whether the litigant is entitled to have the court decide the merits of the dispute or of particular issues. This inquiry involves both constitutional limitations on federal court jurisdiction and prudential limitations on its exercise...In both dimensions it is founded in concern about the proper—and properly limited—role of the courts in a democratic society..."

Warth v. Seldin, 422 U.S. 490, 498 (1975).

31. Youngstown Sheet and Tube v. Sawyer, 343 U.S. 579 (1952). Compare Austin, Province, at 265.

32. 395 U.S. 486 (1969).

33. 418 U.S. 683 (1974).

34. Province at 254.

35.

> "Nor would a political society escape from legal despotism, although the power of the sovereign were bounded by legal restraints. The power of the superior sovereign immediately imposing the restraints, or the power of some other sovereign superior to that superior, would still be absolutely free from the fetters of positive law. For unless the imagined restraints were ultimately imposed by a sovereign not in a state of subjection to a higher or superior sovereign, a series of sovereigns ascending to infinity would govern the imagined community. Which is impossible and absurd." *Id.*

36. *See* The Province, Lec. V., pp. 165–171 where Austin quotes extensively from Locke's Essay on Human Understanding on the subject of moral relations.

37. Of Commonwealth, Ch. 26; III Works 253.

38. D. Hume, A Treatise Of Human Nature, Part II, Sec. II.

39. Province Lec. V, at 190.

40. M Walzer, Obligations, 11 (1970). See also Wasserstrom, *The Obligation To Obey,* 10 U.C.L.A. L. Rev. 780 (1962).

41.

> "The existence of law is one thing; its merit or demerit is another. Whether it be or not be is one inquiry; whether it be or be not conformable to an assumed standard is a different inquiry. A law, which actually exists, is a law, though we happen to dislike it..." Province, 184. See also, 185, 190.

Blackstone's position was that no human laws should be allowed ("suffered") to contradict the revealed laws of nature. Commentaries Introduction § 2. If we were ordered, or empowered to commit murder by the human law we are bound, he asserted, to disobey the positive rule or permission. Bentham saw in this a "dangerous maxim" which might "impel a man by the force of conscience to rise up in arms against any law whatever that he happened not to like..." A FRAGMENT ON GOVERNMENT, Ch. V § XIX. As for the case of murder, it is killing under certain circumstances, and Bentham argued that it was for the civil law to define the situations in which the taking of a life would or would not be proper.

Austin agreed with Blackstone's general point that we are personally obliged to conform to the Divine mandate as a superior rule; but insisted that a human enactment which conflicts with the Divine order *is a law,* i.e., positively binding. "[A]n exception, demurrer, or plea, founded on the law of God was never heard in a Court of Justice from the creation of the world down to the present moment." PROVINCE, at 185.

42. See T. HOLLAND, JURISPRUDENCE, Ch. VI (4th ed. 1887), where concern with purpose is dropped once the establishment and enforcement of legal rights is put at the center of analytical thought.

43. L. FULLER, THE MORALITY OF LAW, 197 (rev. ed. 1969). See also, Fuller, *Human Interaction and the Law,* 14 AM. J. JUR. 1, (1969).

44. Objections are considered by Professor Fuller in Chapter V of the revised edition of THE MORALITY OF LAW. Dworkin, *Philosophy, Morality and Law—Observations Prompted by Professor Fuller's Novel Claim,* 113 U. PA. L. REV. 668 (1964) is one of the more important critiques.

45. The Pure Theory of Law shall be considered in Chapter Three, *infra.*

46. The transition from "old" to "new" analytical thought is surveyed in Summers, *The New Analytical Jurists,* 41 N.Y.U. L. REV. 861 (1966). Professor Hart's basic work is THE CONCEPT OF LAW (1961). It has been reprinted (1972). The new edition contains a bibliography of critical writings. Among his earlier writings, the following should be consulted: DEFINITION AND THEORY IN JURISPRUDENCE (1953), Hart's inaugural lecture at Oxford, reprinted in 70 LAW QUART. REV. 37 (1954); *Are There Any Natural Rights,* 64 PHIL. REV. 1975 (1955); and *Analytical Jurisprudence in Mid-Twentieth Century: A Reply to Professor Bodenheimer,* 105 U. PA. L., REV. 953 (1957). The Oliver Wendell Holmes Lecture, delivered at Harvard School in April, 1957, is published as *Positivism and the Separation of Law and Morals,* in 71 HARV. L. REV. 593 (1958).

THE CONCEPT OF LAW covers the essential legal categories developed by Kelsen's PURE THEORY OF LAW. The contrasting labors of these two jurists illustrates the tensions between abstract and concrete forms of cognition—which is a principle theme of this study. Hart's aversion to logical explanations has been consistent. See, e.g. *A Logician's Fairy Tale,* 60 Philosophical Review 198 (1951); *Kelsen's Doctrine of the Unity of Law,* in ETHICS AND SOCIAL JUSTICE, 171–199 (Kiefer and Munitz, eds. 1970). For a contemporary assessment of the influence of positivism, see OXFORD ESSAYS IN JURISPRUDENCE, *Second Series* (Simpson, ed. 1973).

In the present section, emphasis will be placed upon the work of H.L.A. Hart which is the most systematic of the work of modern analytical jurisprudence. Reference to other jurists whose work is in the same general area will be made as appropriate, both in this section and the entire book.

47. H. MAINE, ANCIENT LAW. See S. AMOS, THE SCIENCE OF LAW (8th ed. 1896). See also F. SAVIGNY, OF THE VOCATION OF OUR AGE FOR LEGISLATION AND JURISPRUDENCE, (Hayward, trans. 1831).

48. H.L.A. HART, THE CONCEPT OF LAW, Ch. V (1961).

49. P. de CHARDIN, THE PHENOMENON OF LAW, (1959). de Chardin notes the movement of thought from observation of external data to inwardness of perception: "In its early, naive stage, science, perhaps inevitably, imagined that we could observe phenomena in themselves as they would take place in our absence . . . They are now beginning to realize that even the most objective of their observations are steeped in forms or habits of thought . . . Object and subject marry and mutually transform each other in the act of knowledge . . ." *Id.,* at 32.

The tendency towards a philosophical anthropology in modern thought is explained in Martin Buber's essay *What Is Man* in BTWEEN MAN AND MAN 118 et seq. (R. Smith trans. 1955). For application to the problems of history see ORTEGA Y GASSET, THE MEANING OF HISTORY (1961) AND E. KAHLER, OUT OF THE LABYRINTH (1967).

50. Dickinson, *Legal Rules, Their Function In The Process of Decision,* 79 U. of PA. L. REV. 833, 843–844 (1931); quoted in MODERN THEORIES OF LAW 10 (1933). Compare Holmes, *The Path of the Law,* 10 HARV. L. REV. 457 (1896).

51. See THE CONCEPT OF LAW, Ch. VI.

52. For a brief explanation of the legal realist movement, see *infra,* p. 37. It will be discussed more fully in Chapter Two.

53. E. LEVI, AN INTRODUCTION TO LEGAL REASONING Ch. 1 (1948). Compare Goodhart, *Determining the Ratio Decidendi of A Case,* 40 Yale L. J. 161 (1930).

54. THE CONCEPT OF LAW, 119–120.

55. Dworkin, *Hard Cases,* 88 HARV. L. REV. 1057 (1975). See also Dworkin, *The Model of Rules,* 35 U. CHI. L. REV. 14 (1967), *reprinted in* LAW, REASON, AND JUSTICE (G. Hughes, ed. 1969), and *Judicial Discretion,* 60 J. PHIL. 624 (1963).

56. 88 HARV. L. REV. at 1089–1090; TAKING RIGHTS SERIOUSLY Ch. 4 (1977).

57. This must be distinguished from the independent question whether there are legal principles and policies, as well as legal rules, within the corpus of law. Dworkin deals with this broader jural material in his earlier writings. See The *Model of Rules,* 35 U. CHI¡ L. REV. 14 (1967). See further, Hughes, *Rules Policy and Decision-Making,* in LAW, REASON AND JUSTICE, 101 (G. Hughes, ed. 1969); Greenawalt, *Discretion and Judicial Decision: The Elusive Quest for the Fetters that Bind Judges,* 75 COL. L. REV. 359 (1976); Note, *Dworkin's 'Rights Thesis,'* 74 MICH. L. REV. 1167 (1976).

58. *Hard Cases,* Part V.

59. *Supra,* pp. 13–15.

60. White, *The Supreme Court's Public and the Public's Supreme Court,* 52 VA. Q. REV. 370 (1976); Murphy, *The Supreme Court and Democratic Theory,* 17 SYRACUSE L. REV. 642 (1966).

61. Hart, *Law in the Perspective of Philosophy: 1776–1976,* 51 N.Y.U.L. REV. 538, 551 (1976). On the subjectivity of judicial decisions compare B.

CARDOZO, THE GROWTH OF THE LAW 85–86 (1924). This point will be developed more fully in Chapter Two.

62. For a classic expression, see United States v. Morris, 25 Fed. Cas. 1323 (C.C.D. Mass. 1851).

63. See Scheflin, *Jury Nullification: The Right to Say No*, 45 S. CAL. L. REV. 168 (1972); M. KADISH & S. KADISH, DISCRETION TO DISOBEY 40–72 (1973).

64. A good example is Maki v. Frelk, 40 Ill.2d, 193, 239 N.E.2d 445 (1968). See also Comment, *Should the Court or Legislature Decide?*, 21 VAND. L. REV. 889 (1968). On the general question of judicial innovation, see R. KEETON, VENTURING TO DO JUSTICE (1969).

The principle of primary jurisdiction in administrative law is somewhat analogous, although it involves the postponement of judicial decision.

65. J. SALMOND, ON JURISPRUDENCE, §§ 77–80 (11th ed., G. Williams, ed. 1957).

66. See W. HOHFELD, FUNDAMENTAL LEGAL CONCEPTIONS AS APPLIED IN LEGAL REASONING (1920). Kocourek's ideas appear in his book JURAL RELATIONS (1928). Professor Gobel's emphasis upon power is explained in *A Redefinition of Basic Legal Terms*, 35 COL. L. REV. 535 (1935). See also Williams, *The Concept of Legal Liberty*, 56 COL. L. REV. 1129 (1956). There is a good collection of the general literature in J. HALL, READINGS IN JURISPRUDENCE, CH. XI. J. SALMOND, JURISPRUDENCE, Ch. 10, and J. STONE, LEGAL SYSTEMS AND LAWYERS REASONINGS, Ch. 4 should also be consulted. The major claim that Hohfeldian analysis is an exercise in logic is made by Pound. See Volume 4 of JURISPRUDENCE (1959).

67. W. JAMES, ESSAYS IN RADICAL EMPIRICISM (1912). James contrasted his method with that of English empiricism which he characterized as an atomization of isolated facts and perceptions. In his philosophy, no directly experienced elements were to be excluded. Any kind of relation experienced was as real as a perceived discrete entity. We shall explain in Chapter Two how this methodology as developed by Dewey has influenced the policy science form of jurisprudence.

68. A. N. WHITEHEAD, SCIENCE AND THE MODERN WORLD, Ch. III (1925).

69. See G. PATON, JURISPRUDENCE, Ch. X (1946).

70. See J. AUSTIN, HOW TO DO THINGS WITH WORDS (1962). For a convenient review of philosophical understanding of the structure of language, see G. WARNOCK, ENGLISH PHILOSOPHY SINCE 1900 (1958). Summers, *The New Analytical Jurists*, 41 N.Y.U. L. REV. 861 (1961) contains valuable insights.

71. H.L.A. HART, THE CONCEPT OF LAW 80–81 (1961).

72. J. BENTHAM, THE LIMITS OF JURISPRUDENCE DEFINED 57 (C. Everett, ed. 1945).

73. THE CONCEPT OF LAW Ch. I-V; *Definition and Theory in Jurisprudence*, 70 L.Q. REV. 37 (1954).

74. See, generally, W. TWINING, KARL LLEWELLYN AND THE REALIST MOVEMENT (1973), Gilmore, *The Age of Anxiety*, 84 Yale L. J. 1022 (1975). The realist movement will be considered more fully in Chapter Two.

75. H.L.A. HART & A. M. HONORE, CAUSATION IN THE LAW (1959).

76. McBoyle v. United States, 283 U.S. 25 (1931).

77. Compare the majority and dissenting opinions in Gooding v. Wilson, 406 U.S. 18 (1972).

78. Professor Hall's theory appears in GENERAL PRINCIPLES OF CRIMINAL LAW (2 Vol. 1960). For Professor Hart's views, see PUNISHMENT AND RESPONSIBILITY, Ch. 1, 2 (1968). For Hall's replies to Hart's criticism, see FOUNDATIONS OF JURISPRUDENCE 87–100 (1973).

79. I am here indebted to Professor Wasserstrom's article *H.L.A. Hart and Doctrines of Mens Rea and Criminal Responsibility,* 35 U. Chi. L. Rev. 92 (1967).

80. Hart, *Legal Responsibility and Excuses* in PUNISHMENT AND RESPONSIBILITY at 37 (1968).

81. See Morris, *Verbal Disputes and the Legal Philosophy of John Austin,* 7 U.S.C.L. REV. 27, 36–40 (1959). The significance of theorizing is also recognized in McBride, *The Essential Role of Models and Analogies in the Philosophy of Law,* 43 N.Y.U. L. Rev. 53 (1968). See also Bodenheimer, *Modern Analytical Jurisprudence and the Limits of its Usefulness,* 104 U. PA. L. REV. 1080 (1953) which contains a relevant criticism of Hart's views and the reply by Professor Hart in 105 U. PA. L. REV. 953 (1957).

82. CONCEPT OF LAW, Ch. II.

83. See Walker v. The City of Birmingham, 388 U.S. 307 (1967).

84. Hill. *Legal Validity and Legal Obligation,* 80 Yale L.J. 47 (1970).

85. J. FEINBERG, SOCIAL PHILOSOPHY, 58–59 (1973). In the analytical tradition the shift in emphasis from a conception of Laws as Commands can be seen in Holland's JURISPRUDENCE, Ch. VII (4th ed. 1888). Among modern analysts the importance of the protection of rights by the judiciary is championed by Professor Ronald Dworkin.

86. THE CONCEPT OF LAW at 94. (emphasis added).

87. Cohen, Book Review, 71 MIND 395 (1962).

88. Horizontalism refers to all reflections about the nature of international law which accept decentralization as a given *datum.* See, further my essay *Some Reflections Upon Theories of International Law,* 71 COL. L. REV. 447 (1970).

89. THE CONCEPT OF LAW, Ch. 10.

90. J. CASTANEDA, LEGAL EFFECTS OF UNITED NATIONS RESOLUTIONS 168–171 (1969). The normative potentials of these resolutions will be considered further from a sociological perspective in Chapter Two.

91. The pervasive instabilities in global life are understood by competent political scientists. Inis Claude, Professor of Government at the University of Virginia, has described the power dynamic of international relations in terms painfully similar to those reported by Hobbes in the LEVIATHAN. In the present circumstances:

> "The competition of states for power coupled with their capacity and inclination to make use of power against each other, is perpetually dangerous, sporadically disastrous, and potentially catastrophic; it makes the multistate system, ultimately and all too often proximately, a war system. It produces mistrust, fear, insecurity, rivalry and waste,"

The United Nations, 27th Session, Introduction, 14 HARV. INT'L. L. J. 517, 519 (1973). The internal instability of states, which has international repercussions, is also documented. *Id.* at 523.

92. CONCEPT OF LAW, Ch. 10, § 3–5. The incapacity of Hart's theories to reach these fundamental questions is probably an aspect of its evolutionary character. Such doctrines tend to insist upon the evanescence of evil in the ongoing evolutionary process. Herbert Spencer's theories were a primary example of this mentality in the Nineteenth Century.

Criticisms of horizontal ordering in international affairs are not a claim that treaties and customary rules are worthless. International agreements, in particular, are productive of much good. The Geneva Conventions, for example, have proven to lessen much of the suffering connected with armed conflict. The point made here is that without effective political authority, on a global scale, the fundamental instabilities will persist.

93. THE PROVINCE OF JURISPRUDENCE DETERMINED, Lec. VI.

CHAPTER TWO

1. A. COMTE, POSITIVE PHILOSOPHY, 2 Vols. (H. Martineau trans. 1893). A sociological tendency can be perceived in earlier writers, especially in Montesquieu and his SPIRIT OF THE LAWS. See R. ARON, I MAIN CURRENTS IN SOCIOLOGICAL THOUGHT (R. Howard and H. Weaver trans. 1965). The sense of an organic relationship between positive law and social reality is also found in the work of the historical jurists, such as von Savigny.

The basic connection between sociology and legal philosophy is explained in G. GURVITCH, SOCIOLOGY OF LAW (1942) and N. TIMASHEFF, AN INTRODUCTION TO SOCIAL SCIENCES (E. Shils and H. Finch trans. 1949). General summaries of the influence of Sociology can be found in G. HUGHES, JURISPRUDENCE, Ch. 5 (1955) and J. STONE, SOCIAL DIMENSIONS OF LAW AND JUSTICE (1966). An extensive bibliography can be found in R. DIAS, A BIBLIOGRAPHY OF JURISPRUDENCE, Ch. 18 (1970). THE SOCIOLOGY OF LAW (R. Simon, ed. 1968) and V. AUBERT, SOCIOLOGY OF LAW (1969) contain representative collections of interdisciplinary readings.

2. *Les Regles de La Me'thode Sociologique,* 120–1 in EMILE DURKHEIM: SELECTED WRITINGS 100–101 (A. Giddens, ed. 1972). See also R. NISBET, THE SOCIOLOGY OF EMILE DURKHEIM (1974).

The idea of an order being imposed should be corrected by the insight that social life requires the active participation of each person, thereby creating the mutual expectations which make social life possible.

The explanation of social life offered by Durkheim was modified by Duguit, who, by shifting from an external to an internal perspective, found that social phenomena are facts of individual consciousness. Human communities are "primary, irreducible and spontaneous" but they come into existence because individuals desire to prolong life and are aware that in isolation this is impossible. If man wishes to continue his existence, lessen suffering and have his needs satisfied, he must act in conformity with social laws of solidarity which are designed to preserve these objectives. The state of consciousness remains individual even when becoming more social because it is only in society that one's individuality is expanded. *Theory of Objective Law Anterior to the State,* in MODERN FRENCH LEGAL PHILOSOPHY, Ch. IX (Mod. Legal Phil. Series VII, 1916).

3. *Theory of Objective Law Anterior to the State,* in MODERN FRENCH LEGAL PHILOSOPHY, Ch. X, p. 288 (Mod. Legal Phil. Series, VII, 1916). See also LAW IN THE MODERN STATE (1919). Compare R. von IHERING, LAW AS A MEANS TO AN END, Ch. 8 (Mod. Legal Phil. Series V, Husik trans. 1921) which provides a general explanation of the emergence of law out of social conflict.

4. E. ERLICH, SOCIOLOGY OF LAW (W. Moll trans. 1936). Following von Gierke, Ehrlich uses the concept of Association as the primary phenomenon, and he divides it into genetic and voluntary forms. The concept designates any social relationship which is structured or "ordered" through an equilibrium of forces operative within it. Ehrlich's use of the dominative model is a valuable tool of analysis. Unfortunately, it can lend itself to ideological ends especially since the ideas of domination and subjection have become part of Marxist terminology.

An association can be of a dominative or collaborative type. Hauriou's theory of the institution expands this distinction and is a valuable improvement over earlier models of group life. His theory refers to an idea of enterprise or function to be fulfilled, where organized power is put to the service of the idea for its realization and where there exists a "communion" within the group with respect to the idea. *Theory of the Institution,* in THE FRENCH INSTITUTIONALISTS, 93 et seq. (A. Broderick ed. Twentieth Cent. Legal Phil. Series, Vol. VIII, 1972).

5. The basic study on the relationship between tort law and automobile insurance is the so-called COLUMBIA REPORT: Columbia University Council for Research in the Social Sciences, Report by the Committee to Study Compensation for Automobile Accidents (1932). Other studies include L. GREEN, TRAFFIC VICTIMS—TORT LAW AND INSURANCE (1958) and A. EHRENZWEIG, FULL AID INSURANCE FOR THE TRAFFIC VICTIM (1954). The general development is reviewed in R. KEETON and J. O'CONNELL, BASIC PROTECTION FOR THE TRAFFIC VICTIM (1965) and 2 F. HARPER and F. JAMES, THE LAW OF TORTS, Ch. XIII. On Products Liability, see *Id.* Ch. XXVIII.

6. H. MARCUSE, ONE DIMENSIONAL MAN (1964). See also Murphy, *Social Criticism and Legal Philosophy: Some Reflections on Law and the New Politics,* 45 ST. JOHN'S L. REV. 39 (1970).

7. 32 N.J. 358, 161 A.2d 69 (1960).

8. Compare Gregg v. Georgia, 428 U.S. 153 (1976) with Woodson v. North Carolina, 428 U.S. 280 (1976) and Roberts v. Louisiana, 97 S.Ct. 1993 (1977). For a general discussion see L.M. FRIEDMAN, THE LEGAL SYSTEM, Ch. IV, V (1975).

9. See Brennan *State Constitutions and the Protection of Individual Rights,* 90 HARV. L. REV. 489 (1977).

10. E.g. Harlan, J. in Poe v. Ullman, 367 U.S. 497, 539–555 (1961) (dissenting opinion). See also the joint opinion of Justices Stewart, Powell, and Stevens in Gregg v. Georgia, 428 U.S. 153 (1976).

11. 347 U.S. 483 (1954).

12. 392 U.S. 409 (1968). Compare Runyon v. McCrary, 427 U.S. 160 (1976) interpreting 42 U.S.C. § 1981. The concurring opinion of Mr. Justice Stevens in Runyon is instructive.

13. For a more extended analysis of this problem see E. BODENHEIMER, POWER, LAW & SOCIETY (1973).

14. Glendon, *Marriage and the State: The Withering Away of Marriage*, 62 VA. L. REV. 663 (1976).

15. For a basic study, see Held, *Persons, Male and Female*, in I EQUALITY AND FREEDOM, International and Comparative Jurisprudence, 135 (G. Dorsey, ed. 1977). See also Wasserstrom, *Racism, Sexism, and Preferential Treatment: An Approach to the Topics*, 24 UCLA L. REV. 518 (1977).

16. See the discussion in R. NISBET, TWILIGHT OF AUTHORITY 252–260 (1975).

17. Compare Nisbet, *op. cit.*, with R. NOZICK, ANARCHY, STATE AND UTOPIA Ch. 7–8 (1976).

18. Compare Hauriou's theory of an institution *supra*, Note 4, suggesting transitions from dominative to collaborative relationships.

19. See the discussion, *supra*, Ch. 1, p. 48.

20. See R. FALK, THE STATUS OF LAW IN INTERNATIONAL SOCIETY Part Two (1970) and his essay *The Interplay of Westphalia and Charter Conceptions of International Order* in I THE FUTURE OF THE INTERNATIONAL LEGAL ORDER 32 (R. Falk and C. Black ed. 1969).

21. See the discussion in Murphy, *Limitations Upon the Power of a State to Determine the Amount of Compensation Payable to an Alien Upon Nationalization,* in III THE VALUATION OF NATIONALIZED PROPERTY IN INTERNATIONAL LAW (R. Lillich ed. and cont. 1975). The perception of customary law as an order imposed by capital exporting western states upon an undeveloped, largely colonial, world has been articulated by the Soviet jurist G. Tunkin in his Hague lectures *Co-existence and International Law* in (1958) III ACADE'MIE DE DROIT INTERNATIONAL, RECUEIL DES COURS. The ideas are restated in Tunkin, *Remarks on the Juridical Nature of Customary Norms of International Law,* 49 CALIF. L. REV. 419 (1961) and THEORY OF INTERNATIONAL LAW (W. Butler, trans. 1974). Such insights do not of course depend upon an ideological bias. E.g. Fatouros, *International Law and the Third World,* 50 VA. L. REV. 783 (1964).

The general influence of Marxism upon international law should be noted, as it reflects the force of an ideology which bears comparison with Sociology of Law. Marx inverted the Hegelian dialectic. Instead of absorbing reality into the logical entities of the mind, he forced logic into the flow of reality. The purpose of conceptualization was then to reflect the antagonisms and contradictions which reveal the true movement of history. This epistemology provides a powerful weapon for understanding social structures. What a naive sociology conceives as a relation of forces — of general facts of domination and subjection — the Marxist perceives as a material development: the inexorable passage of man through successive stages of exploitation and reaction.

Basic themes such as national liberation, self-determination, and sovereignty over natural resources have, for the Marxist, a significance which is understandable only if his unique "Sociology of Law" is taken into account. This is also true of basic foreign policy such as "Peaceful Co-existence" which in orthodox terms means that the emancipatory struggle has passed from a revolutionary to an evolutionary stage. See generally, C. FRIEDRICH, THE PHILOSOPHY OF LAW IN HISTORICAL PERSPECTIVE Ch. XVI (1958); G. TUNKIN, THEORY OF INTERNATIONAL RELATIONS (W. Butler, trans. 1974); Chaumont, *Cours General De Droit International Public* (1970) I RECUEIL DES COURS 339. Compare: E. MCWHINNEY, PEACEFUL CO-EXISTENCE AND SOVIET UNION INTERNATIONAL LAW (1964) and J. HAZARD, COMMUNISTS AND THEIR LAW (1969).

22. The pervasive influence of sociology upon jurisprudence is reflected in the distinction between Sociology of Law and Sociological Jurisprudence. In the former, there is an emphasis upon the phenomenon of group life and an appraisal of its effects upon our understanding of law. The latter concentrates upon the proximate relationship between sociology and decisional responsibility. The distinction is averted to by Ehrlich in Chapter One of SOCIOLOGY OF LAW; Compare Pound, *Sociology of Law and Sociological Jurisprudence*, 5 U. TORONTO L.J. 1 (1943).

23. The general development of Pound's Sociological Jurisprudence can be traced through several of his major essays and books. In a paper read before the American Bar Association in 1906 he vividly portrayed the gap between popular expectations and the legal regime developed by judges and lawyers *The Causes of Popular Dissatisfaction With the Administration of Justice*, 40 AM. L. REV. 729 (1906). In *The Scope and Purpose of Sociological Jurisprudence*, 24 HARV. L. REV. 591 (1911); 25 *Ibid.* 140, 489 (1912), the primary influences of Ihering and Hegel are acknowledged and potentials of an American jurisprudence explored.

For a critical assessment of Pound's view of nineteenth century adjudication see H. Morris, Book Review, 13 STAN. L. REV. 185 (1960).

24. The theory of interests is explained in OUTLINES OF LECTURES ON JURISPRUDENCE Part IV (5th ed. 1943); *A Survey of Social Interests*, 57 HARV. L. REV. 1 (1943) and III JURISPRUDENCE §§ 80–99 (1959).

Pound first sought to base the theory on social instincts but later adopted the simpler method of observing what demands were in fact made upon the legal order. The recognition of interests was considered to be a matter of ethical obligation as well as social necessity. He adopted William James' view that the good consisted in recognizing demands. III JURISPRUDENCE at 16.

25. An historical and philosophical exposition of the nature of law was given in the Storrs Lectures of 1921, published by AN INTRODUCTION TO THE PHILOSOPHY OF LAW (Rev. ed. 1954). The interplay between a sociological jurisprudence and analytical positivism is strongly expressed in SOCIAL CONTROL THROUGH LAW (1942). See also II JURISPRUDENCE, Ch. 9, 10 (1959).

A fuller analysis of rights, powers, conditions and other juristic conceptions can be found in IV JURISPRUDENCE, Ch. 21-27; V, 28-32. Pound's analysis of *precept*, understood as divisible into rules, principles, precepts describing conceptions and precepts prescribing standards (SOCIAL CONTROL THROUGH LAW at 44-45, II JURISPRUDENCE, p. 124-132) should be compared with Dworkin, *The Model of Rules,* 35 U. Chi. L. Rev. 14 (1965), *reprinted in* Law, Reason And Justice (G. Hughes, ed. & Cont. 1968).

26. In his Jurisprudence (4th ed. 1888), the analytic jurist Thomas Holland referring to the ambiguities inherent in words such as Jus Droit and Recht, states "[A] coherent science cannot be constructed upon an idea which has complex or shifting meanings. One or the other meaning must be chosen, and when chosen must be made the sole foundation of the edifice. It is, therefore, a piece of good fortune that when we say in English that Jurisprudence is the science of law we are spared the ambiguities which beset the expression of that proposition in Latin, German, and French and have greatly obscured its exposition in those languages." *Id.* at 14.

27. John Chipman Gray placed stress upon judicial creativity The Nature And Sources Of Law, Pt. 11. This probably influenced Pound who was his student. Gray is also considered, along with Justice Holmes, as the first sociological jurist in America. See H. Laski, *The Political Philosophy of Justice Holmes,* in Studies In Law And Politics Ch. VI (1932).

28. III Jurisprudence. For a detailed analysis of the postulates see E. Patterson, Jurisprudence § 4.60 (1953) and *Roscoe Pound on Jurisprudence,* 60 Col. L. Rev. 1124 (1960). Compare, J. Kohler, Philosophy Of Law (Mod. Legal Phil. Series, Vo. XII 1914).

Pound recognized the importance of administrative processes, particularly when they involved adjudication methods. He was anxious to assert the value of judicial review of agency action. See R. Pound, Administrative Law (1942).

29. There are good critical studies of the Theory of Interests in E. Patterson, Jurisprudence Ch. 18 § 461 (1953). Allen, *Justice and Expediency,* in Interpretations Of Modern Legal Philosophy 15 (J. Sayre, ed. 1947) and J. Stone, *A Critique of Pound's Theory of Justice,* 20 Iowa L. Rev. 531 (1935); The Social Dimensions Of Law And Justice, Ch. 4 § 4 (1966) and Human Law And Justice, Ch. 9 § 6 (1965). Stone's criticisms were taken into account by Pound in the *Magnum Opus,* III Jurisprudence at 11–15. For Stone's reaction see *The Golden Age of Pound,* 4 Sydney L. Rev. 1 (1962); Trends In Jurisprudence In The Second Half Century, 13 (1967). Stone's doubts that the theory of interests can be successfully applied to the conditions of either a mass society or a society experiencing a revolutionary transition are important. See further, L. M. Friedman, The Legal System 150–154 (1975).

For a more general evaluation of Pound's jurisprudence, see the section entitled *The Pre-Emptive Roscoe Pound,* in H. Reuschlein, Jurisprudence Its American Prophets 103–154 (1951). There is a perceptive review of Jurisprudence by Professor Morris in 13 Stanford L. Rev. 185 (1960) which is reprinted in More Essays In Legal Philosophy 43 (R. Summers ed. and contrib. 1971). More particularized studies of interests, placing emphasis upon their psychological and cultural origins, can be found in F. Beutel, Experimental Jurisprudence Ch. 111 (1957); A. Ross, On Law And Justice, Ch. 17 (1959).

An interesting biography of Pound D. Wigdor, Roscoe Pound (1974) draws parallels between Pound's botanical experience and the development of his jurisprudence. The technique of observing the interaction of the organism and its environment, together with a scientific teleology which results in stable plant equilibrium, bears some relationship to the elements of sociological jurisprudence.

30. For Pound's mature views on the subject of reasoned judgment see the small volume R. POUND, LAW FINDING THROUGH EXPERIENCE AND REASON (1960).

31. For an application of this approach to the question of whether a norm of non-discrimination exists in international law, see the dissenting opinion of Judge Jessup in the South West Africa Cases, Second Phase, Judgment (Ethiopia v. South Africa; Liberia v. South Africa), [1966] I.C.J. 4, 325–442.

32. In his Carpentier lectures Mr. Justice Cardozo attempted to develop the implications of a balancing test for judicial decision making. The quality of legal justice was embedded in a "social mind" which reflects the values which social man attaches to his interests. Moral, economic, and cultural values, as well as precepts of utility, were to be "ascertained and assessed and equilibrated . . . the thought and the will and the desires of society as the judge perceives and interprets them supplying the measure and scale . . ." THE PARADOXES OF LEGAL SCIENCE 54–55 (1928). Yet personal responsibility remained, because the final estimate of comparative valuation ". . .[w]ill be shaped for the judge, as it is for the legislator, in accordance with an act of judgment in which many elements cooperate . . . by his experience of life; his study of the social sciences; at times, in the end, by his intuitions, his guesses, even his ignorance or prejudice . . ." THE GROWTH OF THE LAW, 85–86 (1924). See also, THE NATURE OF THE JUDICIAL PROCESS (1921). Cardozo was influenced by the French Jurist Francois Gény who had introduced a sociological orientation into the judicial process.

Compare the claims for judicial autonomy of Professor Dworkin which we examined in Chapter One. And see also Fletcher, *Fairness and Utility in Tort Theory,* 85 HARV. L. REV. 537 (1971).

33. See the symposium, HUGO BLACK AND THE SUPREME COURT (S. Strickland, ed. 1967).

34. Studies which analyze some of the issues of judicial process discussed in the text include R. WASSERSTROM, THE JUDICIAL DECISION (1961) and Wechsler, *Toward Neutral Principles of Constitutional Law,* 73 HARV. L. REV. 1 (1959), reprinted in PRINCIPLES, POLITICS AND FUNDAMENTAL LAW (1961). For a pessimistic view of the court's policy making see A. BICKEL, THE SUPREME COURT AND THE IDEA OF PROGRESS (1970). A defense of judicial activism can be found in Wright, *Professor Bickel, The Scholarly Tradition, and The Supreme Court,* 84 HARV. L. REV. 769 (1971).

35. The proposal of allocation of comptencies appears in Fried, *Two Concepts of Interests: Some Reflections on the Supreme Court's Balancing Tests,* 76 HARV. L. REV. 755 (1963). A more recent articulation is Tribe, *Towards A Model of Roles in the Due Process of Life and Law,* 87 HARV. L. REV. 1 (1973). The general preference is for a broader protection of individual liberty through an affirmation of private decisional authority. This method should be compared with an opposite tendency which would restrain judi-

cial discretion by an invocation of strict construction, E.g. Bork, *Neutral Principles and Some First Amendment Problems,* 47 IND. L. J. 1 (1971).

36. Developments in the controversy over abortion demonstrate the importance of recognizing relevant interests. Compare Roe v. Wade, 410 U.S. 113 (1973) with Maher v. Roe, 432 U.S. 464 (1977).

Proposals for the allocation of competencies in constitutional law bear some resemblance to methods which have been found wanting in the conflict of laws field. Choice of law rules were expressed in the first Restatement of Conflicts as jurisdictional precepts which could be rigorously applied to extremely complex cases. These rules were objectionable because they failed to meet the demands of justice in particular cases and were not responsive to the policy concerns of the various states whose interests were affected. The older rules are being replaced by rules and principles designed to promote more careful analysis of the relevant interests and competing analogies. See D. CAVERS, THE CHOICE OF LAW PROCESS (1965); *Comments on Babcock v. Jackson,* 63 COL. L. REV. 1212 (1963).

37. The restraints which organized society brings to bear against an individual raise some extremely difficult questions of moral and political philosophy. Courts, whose constitutional duty is to protect the individual from arbitrary power, quite properly have a preference for liberty; but this legitimate bias should not be generalized into jurisdictional rules which evade the ethical complexities of concrete cases. For a review of the moral issues see J. FEINBERG, SOCIAL PHILOSOPHY, Ch. 2 (1973).

38. Compare Dworkin, *Hard Cases,* 88 HARV. L. REV. 1057 (1975) *reprinted in* TAKING RIGHTS SERIOUSLY (1977) which draws a distinction between arguments of principle intended to establish an individual right and arguments of policy intended to establish a collective goal. The general thesis, which we reviewed in Chapter One, is that judicial organs should make decisions on the basis of legal right rather than social or economic policy. Dworkin uses various forms of utilitarianism as models of a policy approach. This should be compared with Pound's use of policy as a choice between conflicting general interests. Pound's category of *general* interests also elevates the policy decision. Dworkin tends to treat goals with a demeaning tone.

39. Lepaulle, *The Function of Comparative Law (With A critique of Sociological Jurisprudence),* 35 HARV. L. REV. 838, 839 (1922).

40. In an important but neglected essay *Social Order and Political Authority.* 23 AM. POL. SC. REV. 293 (1929), Professor John Dickerson expressed concern over the decline of customary norms and the increase of social conflict. Conflict has become intense because changes in the environment evoked varied forms of reaction; a diversity which was easily multiplied in a pluralistic industrial society. There were universal interests in security, but the problematic of social order arose because of the immense variations of demands at the periphery of social life. The adjustment of conflict in such circumstances seem to require a plan or scheme of order emanating from an impartial central authority.

41. J. DEWEY, THE QUEST FOR CERTAINTY 213 (1929).

The principal works consulted include LOGIC, THE THEORY OF INQUIRY (1938); THE QUEST FOR CERTAINTY (1929); HUMAN NATURE AND CONDUCT

(1922) and THE RECONSTRUCTION OF PHILOSOPHY (1920). M. WHITE, THE ORIGIN OF DEWEY'S INSTRUMENTALISM (1943) traces the development of Dewey's thought. S. HOOK, THE QUEST FOR BEING, Ch. 3 (1951) contains a defense of Dewey's ethical naturalism. It may be compared with the critique in J. MARITAIN, SOCIAL PHILOSOPHY, Ch. 14 (1964).

42. See Dewey's contribution to MY PHILOSOPHY OF LAW 73 (1941), and his *Logical Method and Law,* 10 CORNELL L. Q. 17 (1924). There is a good general assessment in E. PATTERSON, JURISPRUDENCE, Ch. 17 (1953). Professors Patterson and Dewey jointly taught a seminar on Legal Philosophy at Columbia.

43. Llewellyn, *Some Realism About Realism,* 44 HARV. L. REV. 1222, 1250 (1931), *reprinted in* JURISPRUDENCE 42, 68 (1962). *Some Realism* was written in reply to Pound's criticisms of the realist movement *The Call For A Realist Jurisprudence,* 44 HARV. L. REV. 697 (1931).

Llewellyn was an important legal philosopher. While sensitive to social data, he retained a conviction that the judicial process was of itself intelligible. This belief is evidence in his study of the appellate process THE COMMON LAW TRADITION (1960). For a more general assessment of the realist movement see White, *From Sociological Jurisprudence to Realism: Jurisprudence* and *Social Change in Early Twentieth-Century America,* 58 VA. L. 999 (1972). See the recent study by W. TWINING: KARL LLEWELLYN AND THE REALIST MOVEMENT (1973). And see G. GILMORE, THE AGES OF AMERICAN LAW (1977); *The Age of Anxiety,* 84 Yale L. J. 1022 (1975). A more general bibliography can be found in 4 ENCYCLOPEDIA OF PHILOSOPHY 420 (1967).

44. In this section the philosophy of John Dewey is highlighted to demonstrate a general influence of a leading thinker. It is not intended to prove a specific causal connection between his work and that of sociologically oriented jurists.

45. Lasswell and McDougal, *Legal Education and Public Policy: Professional Training in the Public Interest,* 52 YALE L.J. 203 (1943). These ideas are expanded in McDougal, *Law As A Process of Decision: A Policy-Oriented Approach to Legal Study,* 1 NAT. L. FORUM 53 (1956). Basic essays are collected in STUDIES OF WORLD PUBLIC ORDER (1960) and McDOUGAL AND FELICIANO, LAW AND WORLD MINIMUM PUBLIC ORDER: THE LEGAL REGULATION OF INTERNATIONAL COERCION (1961). The structure and objectives of the policy science method is explained in H. LASSWELL, A PREVIEW OF POLICY SCIENCES (1971).

More recent publications include: *Trends in Theories About Law: Comprehensiveness in Conceptions of Constitutive Process,* 41 GEO. WASH. L. REV. 1 (1972); Lasswell and McDougal, *Criteria For A Theory About Law,* 44 S. CAL. L. REV. 362 (1971): McDougal, Lasswell, and Reisman, *Theories About International Law: Prologue To A Configurative Jurisprudence,* 8 VA. J. INT'L. L. 188 (1968); McDougal, Lasswell and Reisman, *The World Constitutive Process of Authoritative Decision,* 19 J. LEG. ED. 253 (1967). An extensive bibliography, and defense of the "New Haven Approach" can be found in Moore, *Prolegomenon To The Jurisprudence of Myres McDougal and Harold Lasswell,* 54 VA. L. REV. 662 (1968). See also *The Writings of Myres S. McDougal* in 84 YALE L. J. 965 (1975).

46. E.g. Professor Falk's critical essay *McDougal and Feliciano on Law and*

Minimum World Public Order in LEGAL ORDER IN A VIOLENT WORLD 80
(1968). And see Allott, *Language, Method and the Nature of International Law,*
XLV Brit. Y. B. INT'L. L. 79 (1971).

47. The emphasis which the McDougal-Lasswell school places upon the
rationality ofconduct viewed in light of the context in which it occurs has
led to the objection that reasonableness is equated with legality. The pre-
dictability which rules promotes, is replaced by the subjectivity of decisional judgment. See Fischer, Book Review, SCIENCE 658 (1962).

48. It would be instructive to compare the General Assembly Declaration on the establishment of a new International Economic Order, Res.
3201 (S-VI), 13 Int'l Leg. Mat. 715 (1974) with the value orientation of
scholars devoted to the policy science jurisprudence.

49. Principles and procedures of interpretation are stated in THE IN-
TERPRETATION OF AGREEMENTS AND WORLD PUBLIC ORDER (1967) by
McDougal, Lasswell, and an associate James Miller. For critical reactions,
see the Panel on Treaty Interpretation, (1969) Proceedings of The American Society of International Law, 108–140 which includes Professor
McDougal's response, and Fitzmaurice, *Vae Victis or Woe to the Negotiators!,*
65 A.J.I.L. 358 (1971). Compare further, Rest. Foreign Relations Law of
the United States § 146 (1965) with Vienna Convention on the Law of
Treaties, Arts. 31–32 *Adopted,* May 22, 1969 in 8 Int'l Leg. Mat. 679 (1969).

50. Fitzmaurice, *op. cit.* at 372.

51. See the criticism by Lepaulle, cited above at Note 39.

52. THE QUEST FOR CERTAINTY Ch. X; RECONSTRUCTION IN PHILOSOPHY
Ch. VIII, IX. and see *The Concept of Value,* in 16 International Encyclopedia of the Social Sciences 283 (1968).

An extensive critique of this approach to the problem of values will be
found in Chapter Five.

This approach to the problem of values should be compared with that of
Durkheim, who developed a neo-naturalism which mediated between
philosophical idealism and reductionism. He believed that moral and religious experiences were distinctive. But he could not accept the theory of a
noumenal self in a unilateral relationship to society for whom social existence was not a primary factor in explaining moral obligation. Such explanations could not be reconciled with Durkheim's own understanding of
social phenomena. Man is a being in society; not absorbed by social relations, but nevertheless born into a community of selves who have shared
conceptions of the good. These shared meanings permeate the *milieu* and
penetrate the consciousness of each individual life. This "conscience collective" has phenomenological connotations. The individual is aware of these
cultural norms, and they obtain a certain representation in conscience
and/or consciousness. One becomes aware that they are not one's own
values, but rather a means by which society lives and acts within us. These
moral rules have an imperative character: awareness of them is coupled
with a sense of their being obligatory. Beyond this realm of public moral
rules and values we are also aware, according to Durkheim, of a realm of
moral ideals personal and distinct to ourselves, and it is these which make
us an individual. See E. WALLWORK, DURKHEIM, Ch. 2 (1972).

Durkheim's conception of publicly shared moral rules may bear some resemblance to Dewey's conception of democratic values. Basic moral principles, developed through inquiry, become in Dewey's conception the shared experiences of the community. Conditions for enlightened valuation are best attained in a democratic society, where a sense of common interests is balanced by a spirit of inquiry. Here there is a fund of moral experience which provides a stable base for valuation but which, if uncritically accepted, would become norms of blind acceptance.

These basic values are secure, but can be modified by experience; they are stable but not static. When we submit what we know to public tests, and explore consequences in new contexts, there may be revisions but not absolute relativity.

53. In their paper *Human Rights and World Public Order: A Framework for Policy-Oriented Inquiry,* 63 A.J.I.L. 237 (1969) Professors McDougal, Lasswell, and an associate, Lung-chu-Chen, refer to the global demands for human dignity as being formulated at sufficiently high levels of abstraction to allow for great diversity in the modes of implementation. Certain minimal values, however, such as freedom from torture, and freedoms of thought, conscience, and religion are considered as being indispensible to a dignified human existence and therefore immune from derogation. Compare Hook, *Reflections On Human Rights,* in ETHICS AND SOCIAL JUSTICE (H. Kiefer and M. Munitz, ed. 1970).

In a national community there is some likelihood that widely shared common values can be discovered through contextual inquiry. On the international plane where competing ideologies and diverse cultures interact, the prospects for the discovery of common values diminish. The dangers of subjectivity of value selection are therefore greater at the global level of decision making.

54. See CH. PERELMAN, THE IDEA OF JUSTICE AND THE PROBLEM OF ARGUMENT (1963).

55. See *supra,* Ch. 1, § C.; Dworkin, *Hard Cases,* 88 HARV. L. REV. 1957 (1957), *reprinted in* R. DWORKIN, TAKING RIGHTS SERIOUSLY (1977). Professor Dworkin's effort to exclude policy considerations from judicial decisions is not fully successful. Judges act upon the assumption that their responsibility is to implement legal rights; yet, in important decisions where basic values are in conflict, judges also strive to adjust the conflict. The result, in sociological terms. constitutes public policy. For a recent illustration see Mitchell v. W.T. Grant Co., 416 U.S. 600 (1974).

56. THE QUEST FOR CERTAINTY, at 262 (1929). Compare RECONSTRUCTION IN PHILOSOPHY 164.

57. ON LIBERTY, Ch. III, 104–106 (1885). The fact that Mill was objecting to the burden of custom does not detract from the present relevance of his idea.

58. Compare J. DABIN, *General Theory of Law* in THE LEGAL PHILOSOPHIES OF LASK, RADBRUCH AND DABIN, 341, 373–82 (IV Twent. Cent. Legal Phil., K. Wilk, trans. 1950). In the jurisprudence of Geny (which had a considerable influence upon the thought of Justice Cardozo) sociological data held a dominant position. By identifying law with the exercise of a virtue of judgment, Dabin brought all the elements of decision into clearer perspective. The general point is that one whose moral

faculties are well formed will be able to perceive his proper role and the requirements of the concrete situation. See my paper, *Justice and Judgment,* 23 BUFFALO L. REV. 565 (1974), Mulvaney, *Political Wisdom,* (1973) MED. STUDIES 294. The significance of prudence will also be considered in Chapter Four, *infra.*

CHAPTER THREE

1. The conditions of legal philosophy in the late Nineteenth Century are surveyed in K. BASU, THE MODERN THEORIES OF JURISPRUDENCE, Lec. IV (1929) and J. Charmont, *Recent Phases of French Legal Philosophy* in VII MODERN LEGAL PHILOSOPHY (1916). Charmont was critical of the sociological movement in jurisprudence because he believed it gave social reality an undue prominence. And, because of the pragmatic temperament which it expressed, expediency was being substituted for legality. The felt need was for some form of ideal law. As we observed in the last chapter, Sociological Jurisprudence, particularly as espoused by Lasswell and McDougal, has become explicitly value-oriented. The difficulties of attaining a decisive separation between positive law and sociology are, of course, as acute today as they were in the Nineteenth Century.

2. KANT, THE CRITIQUE OF PURE REASON (Modern Library, ed. 1949); N. KEMPSMITH, A COMMENTARY TO KANT'S CRITIQUE OF REASON (Rev. ed. 1962). F. COPLESTON, A HISTORY OF PHILOSOPHY, Vol. VI, Pt. IV provides a good general summary. There are studies of Kant's Legal Philosophy in E. BODENHEIMER, JURISPRUDENCE, Ch. IV (1962); H. CAIRNS, LEGAL PHILOSOPHY FROM PLATO TO HEGEL, Ch. VII (1949) and C. FRIEDRICH, THE PHILOSOPHY OF THE LAW IN HISTORICAL PERSPECTIVE, 125–130 (2nd ed. 1963).

3. G. DEL VECCHIO, THE FORMAL BASES OF LAW, p. 99 in X *Modern Legal Philosophy Series* (S. Risle, ed. 1969). For Stammler's neo-Kantian conception, see R. STAMMLER, THE THEORY OF JUSTICE (Husik, trans. 1925) and the study by Morris Ginsberg in MODERN THEORIES OF LAW 38 (1933). Del Vecchio's philosophy of law opposes logical form to juridic empiricism. For a later formulation see PHILOSOPHY OF LAW (8th ed., Martin trans. 1953). The works of both Stammler and Del Vecchio are summarized in Bodenheimer, *op. cit.,* Ch. IV. See also, R. POUND, I. JURISPRUDENCE § 15 (1959); E. PATTERSON, JURISPRUDENCE, Ch. 14 (1953). Del Vecchio's theory of justice will be considered in Chapter Four of this study.

4. See generally, F. COPLESTON, A HISTORY OF PHILOSOPHY, Vol. 7. Schelling sought to make nature conform to the demands of reason. Moving beyond the Kantian idea that the intellect imposes forms upon nature, Schelling believed that the absolute in the ideal order is the absolute in the real. The absolute, or eternal essence in the idea, was objectifying itself in nature, realizing itself through philosophical reflection as an identity of real and ideal; of nature and spirit.

Following Hegel, a reaction set in against metaphysical idealism. The thought of Herbart, Schopenhauer and the Marburg School which were part of this reaction all had an influence upon Kelsen. Kelsen's thought aspires to a pure, dispassionate, rationality, in the spirit of Spinoza, but it is never free of the influence of metaphysical idealism. The Pure Theory is an example of a thought process progressively determining its object. The legal order is personified in such a way as to suggest that an absolute essence, law, is realizing itself in and through man.

5. THE PURE THEORY OF LAW, 204 (M. Knight, trans. 1969). The Pure Theory is a translation of REINE RECHTSLEHRE (Rev. ed. 1960). Basic English works relied upon include *The Pure Theory of Law,* 50 LAW Q. REV. 474 (1934); 51 *Id.* 577 (1935); *The Function of the Pure Theory of Law* in 2 LAW A CENTURY OF PROGRESS 231 (1937); *The Pure Theory of Law and Analytical Jurisprudence,* 55 HARV. L. REV. 44 (1941); GENERAL THEORY OF LAW AND STATE (1945) and PURE THEORY OF LAW (1967). WHAT IS JUSTICE? (1957) contains a collection of Kelsen's essays in moral, political, and legal theory. A more recent collection is HANS KELSEN ESSAYS IN LEGAL AND MORAL PHILOSOPHY (O. Weinberger, 1973). There is a general bibliography in R. METALL, HANS KELSEN, LEBEN UND WERK (1969). A limited bibliography of English publications is published in *A Tribute to Hans Kelsen,* 59 Cal. L. Rev. 609–619 (1971). The basic general study of Kelsen's thought is W. EBENSTEIN, THE PURE THEORY OF LAW (1945). A bibliographical sketch by M. P. Golding appears in 4 THE ENCYCLOPEDIA OF PHILOSOPHY 328.

Hans Kelsen died at Berkeley, California, in April, 1973. Memoria include Akzin, *Hans Kelsen — In Memoriam,* 8 Israel L. Rev. 323 (1973), Gross, *Hans Kelsen,* 67 AM. J. INT'L L. 491 (1973).

6. The extensive causal inquiries which are part of Sociological Jurisprudence are examined in Chapter Two, *supra,* § C.

7. Arguments for the superiority of the normative sciences are based upon anthropological as well as philosophical material. Kelsen placed particular emphasis upon the evolution of consciousness and the tensions between freedom and determination. See his SOCIETY AND NATURE, A SOCIOLOGICAL INQUIRY (1943) and *Causality and Imputation* in WHAT IS JUSTICE? at 324. See also *The Natural Law Doctrine Before the Tribunal of Science,* Part V, in WHAT IS JUSTICE?

8. PURE THEORY OF LAW at 4.

9. Kelsen's evaluation of natural law thinking is a mixture of epistemological criticism and character study. It was his conviction that the intellectual activity of great moralists is rooted in their personal life. Their reflections on the nature of the good arise out of some profound moral experience. In the case of Plato, Kelsen argues, a pedagogical desire to shape the political lives of men was linked to erotic frustration. *Platonic Justice* in WHAT IS JUSTICE? 82. Character analysis is also used to explain the persistence of natural law thinking. It is interesting to note that Kelsen was a member of the Vienna Psychoanalytic Society. See 3 VIENNA PSYCHOANALYTICAL SOCIETY MINUTES (Numberg & Federn, ed. 1974).

The textual summary of Kelsen's position on natural law is drawn from the appendix to GENERAL THEORY OF LAW AND STATE and Kelsen's essay on natural law in CRITICA DEL DERECHO NATURAL (Elias Dias ed. 1959); *The Idea of Natural Law* in ESSAYS IN LEGAL AND MORAL PHILOSOPHY, Ch. II.

Reference is also made to W. EBENSTEIN, THE PURE THEORY OF LAW, Ch. III.

The problem of natural law, extending a discussion of Kelsen's *critique,* will be considered in Chapter Five, *infra.*

10. See generally, Kelsen, *The Pure Theory of Law and Analytical Jurisprudence,* 55 Harv. L. Rev. 44 (1941).

11. THE NATURE AND SOURCES OF LAW at 12.

12. [1966] I.C.J. 7.

13. THE PURE THEORY OF LAW, IV, § 29.

14. *Supra,* Ch. One, § C.

15. A valuable, earlier evaluation of the Pure Theory of Law is Lauterpacht, *Kelsen's Pure Science of Law,* in MODERN THEORIES OF LAW 105 (1933). Specific valuations of Kelsen by Hart can be found in a book review *Kelsen Visited* in 16 U.C.L.A. L. REV. 722 (1963) and the essay *Kelsen's Doctrine of the Unity of Law* in ETHICS AND SOCIAL JUSTICE 171 (Kiefer and Munitz, ed. 1970).

16. Golding, *Kelsen and the Concept of a Legal System,* in MORE ESSAYS IN LEGAL PHILOSOPHY 69 (Summers, ed. 1971) and J. RAZ, THE CONCEPT OF A LEGAL SYSTEM (1970) contain valuable insights into the relative contributions of Bentham, Austin, Kelsen and Hart.

17. On legal duties, legal rights, and sanctions see HOLLAND, JURISPRUDENCE, Ch. VI; Raz, *op. cit.,* Ch. IV; Hall, FOUNDATIONS OF JURISPRUDENCE, Ch. V and *Justice in the Twentieth Century,* in 59 Cal. L. Rev. 752 (1971). Hart, *Bentham On Legal Rights* in OXFORD ESSAYS IN JURISPRUDENCE (Second Series, Simpson, ed. 1973) provides interesting reflections upon the correlation of rights and duties.

The definition of law as a coercive order is defined in GENERAL THEORY OF LAW AND STATE, Part One, I(B); PURE THEORY, Ch. I, especially part 5. See also, *Ibid.,* I.6(e), which discusses dependent legal norms. Compare Dabin, *General Theory of Law,* Ch. One, Section Three in THE LEGAL PHILOSOPHIES OF LASK, RADBRUCH AND DABIN (Vol. IV, Twentieth Century Legal Philosophy Series, Wilk, Trans. 1950).

18. "When we think that a person is bound in justice to do a thing, it is an ordinary form of language to say that he ought to be compelled to do it ..." J.S. MILL, UTILITARIANISM, Ch. V, pp. 59–60 (O. Piest, ed. 1957). Compare, DABIN, *op. cit., supra,* Pt. III, Ch. 2 §§ 224–225.

19. 369 U.S. 186, 208 (1967). And see R. DWORKIN, TAKING RIGHTS SERIOUSLY (1977), discussed in Chapter One, *supra,* § C.

20. For Kelsen's criticisms of the economic foundations of liberalism, see *Foundations of Democracy* in 66 Ethics 1 (Supp. 1955); WHAT IS JUSTICE?, *passim;* GENERAL THEORY OF LAW AND STATE, Part One, I.A.(c) and Part Two IV. Specific critiques of Marxism appear in THE POLITICAL THEORY OF BOLSHEVISM (1948) and THE COMMUNIST THEORY OF LAW (1955). See also, *Democracy and Socialism* (Conference on Jurisprudence and Politics, Univ. of Chicago Law School 4/30/54); *Law and Morality* in ESSAYS IN LEGAL AND MORAL PHILOSOPHY, Ch. IV.

21. G.A. Res. 217A (III) of 10 December, 1948. Marxist conceptions of human rights are defended in a collection of essays SOCIALIST CONCEPT OF HUMAN RIGHTS (Budapest 1966). Morris Ginsberg's ON JUSTICE IN SOCI-

ETY (1973) contains reflections on the political freedoms expressed in the Declaration of Human Rights. See also, the essays on human rights in ETHICS AND SOCIAL JUSTICE. For a comparative analysis, see my study *Ideological Interpretations of Human Rights,* in 21 DePaul L. REV. 286 (1971).

22. EBENSTEIN, THE PURE THEORY OF LAW, Ch. II, p. 63. See also, KELSEN, *Causality And Imputation,* in WHAT IS JUSTICE? In his PURE THEORY OF LAW, Ch. 2 Ebenstein contrasts a causal inquiry "who did the act" with a normative quest "to whom are we to legally attribute the act."

Formal attribution has positive value as it widens the scope of legal responsibility and can be a useful aid to the creation of remedies. It can also be a valuable way of protecting and promoting civil rights. The effort to link harmful behavior to some form of "state action" is illustrative. See Mulkey v. Reitman, 62 Cal.2d 529, 413 P2d 825 (1966). Attribution as collective responsibility gives rise to very difficult moral problems. See Black, *The Erosion of Legal Principles in the Creation of Legal Policies,* 84 Ethics 93 (1974).

23. Compare KELSEN, GENERAL THEORY OF LAW AND STATE, Ch. X with GRAY, THE NATURE AND SOURCES OF THE LAW.

24. See Bivens v. Six Unknown Fed. Narcotics Agents, 403 U.S. 388, 403 (1971) (Harlan, J. Concurring).

25. THE PURE THEORY OF LAW, 351. Our textual discussion here is a critique of Ch. VIII of THE PURE THEORY.

26. See L. FULLER, THE MORALITY OF LAW, and THE ANATOMY OF LAW, Part Two.

27. E.g. Scenic Hudson Preservation Conf. v. Fed. Power Com'n., 354 F.2d 608 (2nd Cir. 1965).

28. Quoted in KLUBACK, WILHEM DILTHEY'S PHILOSOPHY OF HISTORY 52–53 (1956). See also DILTHEY, THE ESSENCE OF PHILOSOPHY (S & W. Emery trans. 1954). Dilthey understood the Kantian period against the background of the history of philosophy. He believed that one recurring theme was the movement towards vital life whenever the limits of philosophy as general knowledge were reached. Fichte and Schelling, he argued, were vainly trying to prove a systematic unity in the structure of logic and the universe. The Kantian project of the logical completeness of knowledge was only an academic idea; the true task was to relate knowledge to the essential aims of human reason.

Two movements outside of the Kantian tradition were important: the rise of sociology and psychology. Comte had understood the essential relationships between the human sciences, he had only failed to provide them with a philosophical base. The predominance of psychology was significant, because it emphasized the reality of consciousness and inner experience. The science of psychology was bound up with a general trend, exemplified by the works of Montaigne and Shakespeare, to explain the experience of life in terms of one's psychological awareness of that experience. Out of such reflections there develops a general view of life.

Upon this basis, Dilthey argued, a systematic approach to the experience of life can be built. The relation between the mind and concrete data is one of reciprocity. In reaction to external stimuli we appreciate, distinguish, and reason. The mental processes are activated in a teleological context;

we are, as von Ihering insisted, constantly engaged in a search for means to ends. At the center of our mental structure, inclination and feeling are cooperatively at work, and from here "the depths of our being are stirred" THE ESSENCE OF PHILOSOPHY 35. This is the experience of life.

29. Rickert criticized Dilthey's method as being too subjective. In his search for universal, objective values, Rickert placed an emphasis upon culture, and called the historical sciences *Kulturwissenschaft,* in preference to Dilthey's term *Geisteswissenschaft* (science of mind or spirit).

The influence of these perceptions upon historical studies can be seen in the work of Ortega Y Gasset. See. e.g., THE MODERN THEME. For a purposive study of legal history see W. HURST, LAW AND THE CONDITIONS OF FREEDOM IN THE NINETEENTH CENTURY UNITED STATES (1956). The effect of these developments on the thought of Max Weber is summarized in PARSONS, ESSAYS IN SOCIAL THEORY PURE AND APPLIED Ch. V (1949). There is a general review of the reaction to neo-Kantian thought in Copleston, *A History of Philosophy,* Vol. 7 Ch. XXIII. The philosophy of N. Hartmann is summarized in 3 THE ENCYCLOPEDIA OF PHILOSOPHY 421.

30. Radbruch's legal philosophy tried to overcome some of the strictures of legal positivism but with a tragic lack of success. His basic work is translated in THE LEGAL PHILOSOPHIES OF LASK, RADBRUCH AND DABIN (Wilk, trans. 1950). For a general summary, see Bodenheimer's JURISPRUDENCE 131–134. Radbruch's thought will be considered further in Chapter Four. On Recaséns-Siches, see his *Human Life, Society and Law* in LATIN AMERICAN LEGAL PHILOSOPHY (Ireland, trans.) and *The Logic of the Reasonable as Differentiated from the Logic of the Rational,* in ESSAYS IN JURISPRUDENCE IN HONOR OF ROSCOE POUND 192 (R. Neuman, ed. 1962). Recaséns-Siches, who is greatly influenced by Hartmann, draws some valuable distinctions between values and other objects of thought. And he defines reason as "every intellectual operation which brings us in contact with reality" *The Logic of the Reasonable* 208. Hartmann's philosophy has also influenced the thought of Julius Stone. See His Hague Lectures, *Problems Confronting Sociological Inquiries Concerning International Law* (1956) 89 Recuil Des Cours.

31. On Dewey's conception of reason as immanent intelligence, see RECONSTRUCTION IN PHILOSOPHY, Ch. IV. The general development of Dewey's thought involved a turning from idealism. M. WHITE, THE ORIGINS OF DEWEY'S INSTRUMENTALISM Ch. 7 (1943). Dewey's thought, and its influence upon Sociological Jurisprudence is more fully examined in Chapter Two, *supra.*

For more recent reflections upon the structure of practical life see Frankel, *The Philosophy of Practice,* in ETHICS AND SOCIAL JUSTICE 1 (Keefer and Munitz, ed. 1970) and the essay by Bubner in 83 ETHICS 224 (1973). For the position of Pure Theory on questions of value and purpose, see EBENSTEIN, *op. cit.,* Ch. III, especially pp. 55 et seq.

32. THE PURE THEORY OF LAW, at 199. On validity see Ch. V *passim.*

33. See Golding, *Kelsen and the Concept of a Legal System* in MORE ESSAYS ON LEGAL PHILOSOPHY 69 (R. Summers, ed. 1971).

34. Kelsen's attempt to confine the cognition of norms to a theory of logical derivation should be compared with the analysis by von Wright in

Norm And Action. This study in deontic logic conceives of the law of the state as prescriptions, *i.e.*, as commands, permissions and prohibitions, usually manifesting the will of authorities that subjects behave in a certain way. Promulgation is included, to make the will known, and a sanction attached to make it effective. A concrete understanding of norms is also found in J. Raz, The Concept Of A Legal System (1970). Kelsen's view of validity, and its emphasis upon delegation, parallels the concept of validity as applied to deductive argumentation in theories of logic. Compare, e.g. W. Salmon, Logic Ch. 2 (1963).

Further criticisms of Kelsen's conception can be found in Raz, *op. cit.,* Golding, *Kelsen and the Concept of a Legal System,* in More Essays In Legal Philosophy 69 (R. Summers, ed. 1971) Hughes, *Validity and the Basic Norm,* 59 Cal. L. Rev. 695 (1971). For the controversy between Kelsen and Professor Stone, see 17 Stanford L. Rev. 1128 (1965). There is a defense of Kelsen's theory of validity in Finch, Introduction To Legal Theory, Ch. 6 (1970). For a more general discussion see S. Munzer, Legal Validity (1972); *Validity and Legal Conflicts,* 82 Yale L. J. 1140 (1973); J. Hall, The Foundations Of Jurisprudence, Ch. V.

Olivecrona believed that the prescription character of law could be understood in the same way as any other social phenomena, *i.e.*, in terms of facts, and the causal relation between one set of facts and another. He also advanced beyond Holmes' theory. The binding force of legal norms was not reducible to the unpleasant consequences which would follow a breach of the rules. He also, however, disagreed with Kelsen. The oughtness of law arouses imperative emotions; the psychological effect is that we feel ourselves to be under a legal obligation. K. Olivecrona, Law As Fact (1939). Ross held that law was valid only if adhered to and felt to be binding. A. Ross, On Law And Justice, Ch. 1, 13 (1959).

If a particular norm is permenantly inefficacious, it is deprived of its validity by *desuetudo.*

35.

> "... [t]he science of law can state no more than: the subjective meaning of the acts by which legal norms are created can be interpreted as their objective meaning only if we presuppose in our juristic thinking the norm: 'one ought to obey the prescriptions of the historically first constitution'.
>
> The science of law does not prescribe that one ought to obey the commands of the creator of the constitution. The science of law remains a merely cognitive discipline ....." Pure Theory, at 204.

The textual summary of Kelsen's view of political authority and its relations to philosophical relativism is drawn from: General Theory Of Law And State, Part Two, IV(B); Foundation Of Democracy, in 66 Ethics 1 (Supp. 1955); *Democracy and Socialism* 63. And see *Why Should Law Be Obeyed in What Is Justice?* 257. Compare the critique of liberal political theory in R. Unger, Knowledge And Politics (1975).

36. For basic material on authority, see Friedrich, *Authority, Reason and Discretion,* in Nomos I, Authority (Friedrich, ed. 1958); J. Maritain, Man

AND THE STATE, Ch. 3, The Policy Science methodology of Lasswell and McDougal, considered in Chapter Two, is strongly oriented towards authoritativeness, because of its insistence that decisions be correlated with prefered community values and policies.

The idea of a reciprocal structure for authority is drawn from the work of Professor Fuller. In his criticism of Hart's rule of recognition, which applies, *a fortiori* to Kelsen's Pure Theory, Fuller points out that recognition contains no suggestion of reciprocities, or rightful expectations on the part of the citizen that could be violated by the lawgiver. There is no tacit provision that the authority conferred can be withdrawn for abuses. THE MORALITY OF LAW, Ch. 3, 137–139 (Rev. ed. 1969). For its relevance to Austinian views of sovereignty see Ch. One, pp. 21–23. The ideas of reciprocity, in Professor Fuller's thought, is primarily connected with procedural morality; it is used here to imply the need for substantive as well as procedural communications.

37. Among the reasons for judicial decision, adherence to precedent, and to principles of fairness generally accepted in the community, are of paramount importance. Insofar as other values or social purposes are involved, it is impossible to determine their structure or content in advance. Professor Dworkin's review of THE JUDICIAL DECISION in 75 ETHICS 47 (1964) contains valuable reflections upon this general problem. Dworkin quite properly points out that even if a community does have some overriding goals, its courts may not be authorized to look to them as a measure of the rules which they adopt. As organs of adjudication, their basic standards may be limited to those which relate to the redress of injuries. See further, TAKING RIGHTS SERIOUSLY (1977).

38. See Ch. 1, § B. See also, § C. which includes a critique of Professor Dworkin's theory of judicial autonomy. The basic material is drawn from my study *The Supreme Court and Democratic Theory*, 17 SYRACUSE L. REV. 642 (1966). It should be noted that the Supreme Court can only in a qualified sense be understood as a coercive organ. Its major constitutional decisions, designed to affect substantial transformations within the nation, are dependent for their implementation upon public support. Kelsen feared that allowing for acceptance of the content of a law within the definition of law would constitute an endorsement of individual anarchy. PURE THEORY, 218, n. 82. It is not here advocated that, by subjective whim, each individual should only comply with these decision which please him. The central idea is a moral reflection upon a sociological fact: the court needs the active cooperation of innumerable public officials and citizens; the overall tempo of that cooperation is a function of the authoritativeness of decisional patterns. See ROSTOW, THE SOVEREIGN PREROGATIVE 89 (1962); McCLOSKEY, *Reflections On The Warren Court*, 51 VA. L. REV. 1229, 1260 (1965). On public assent, compare E. CAHN, THE SENSE OF INJUSTICE, Part V.

39. WHAT IS JUSTICE?, Ch. 1; ESSAYS IN MORAL PHILOSOPHY, Ch. 4.

40. It may be recalled that for Dewey, moral knowledge was a species of empirical knowledge and that values of democracy could only develop in a community context. Some of the factors causing an absence of general consensus are identified by Professor White in his article *The Evolution of*

Reasoned Elaboration: Jurisprudential Criticism and Social Change, in 59 Va. L. Rev. 279 (1973). That article includes reflections upon democratic theory which in some measure parallel those in the text. Compare also, J. HALL, LIVING LAW OF DEMOCRATIC SOCIETY, Ch. 2 (1949) with J. MARITAIN, MAN AND STATE, Ch. V (1950). The relevance of concrete moral experience will be considered further in Chapter Four, in our critique of Rawl's theory of justice.

41. On the State, PURE THEORY, Ch. VI; General Theory, Part Two. Kelsen's thought here shows the influence of the methodology of modern science which tends to dissolve concepts into nonsubstantive relations. His treatment of other central concepts, such as personality is similar. The conception of the State here expressed should be compared with the idea of sovereignty which formed the background for Austin's jurisprudence and which was evaluated in Chapter One. On Hegel's theory of the State, see FRIEDRICH, *op. cit.*, Ch. XV.

42. On attribution, compare the theory of state action in constitutional law, e.g. Williams v. United States, 341 U.S. 97 (1951). For a discussion of attribution in international theory, see R. Ago, *(Fourth) Report On State Responsibility for Injuries to Aliens,* (1972), 2 Y.B. INT'L L. COMM'N 71, U.N. Doc. A/CN.4/Ser. A/1972/Add. 1 (1972).

43. See *supra,* Chapter Two, § C.

44. E.g. Molitor v. Kaneland Community Hospital, 18 Ill.2d 11, 163 N.E.2d 89 (1959). The dissenting opinion of Mr. Justice Davis is particularly *apropos.*

45. J. MARITAIN, MAN AND THE STATE, Ch. 1 (1950).

46. PURE THEORY OF LAW, Ch. VII; I.6; GENERAL THEORY OF LAW, AND STATE Part Two, Ch. VII. LAW AND PEACE IN INTERNATIONAL RELATIONS (1948). Here, as in his theory of the state, Kelsen was anxious to deflate metaphysical pretensions. The general background, especially the prevalence of voluntarist positivism, is surveyed in C. de VISSCHER, THEORY AND REALITY IN PUBLIC INTERNATIONAL LAW, Ch. 3 (Corbett trans. 1957); H. LAUTERPACHT, THE FUNCTION OF LAW IN THE INTERNATIONAL COMMUЄ NITY, Ch. 20 (1933); J. STONE, LEGAL CONTROL OF INTERNATIONAL CONЄ FLICT, Ch. 2 (1954).

47. Triepel's theory is the primary expression of this view.

48. The autolimitation theory is traceable to Jellinek and his followers. See the summary in LAUTERPACHT, THE FUNCTION OF LAW IN THE INTERNATIONAL COMMUNITY, Ch. VI, § 14.

49. Those who postulate the primacy of national law, and conceive of international law as delegated therefrom have, according to Kelsen, a subjectivist epistemology. To conceive a universe, they start from the sovereign self; the world is for them internal: "an idea and will of the self" (Pure Theory, at 344). An objective world view, out of which is born the primacy of international law, begins with the reality of the external world in order to conceive the self. Within this framework the ego is not understood in isolation, but as one with other selves who are an essential part of the given world. To these epistemologies there are corresponding emotional dispositions.

Those who stress the primacy of the national legal order are prone to the ideologies of imperialism. They identify themselves, and their increased self-consciousness, with the expansion or affirmation of sovereign independence. These personalities are apt to confuse the meaning of sovereignty. They fail to carefully distinguish between the idea of highest legal authority and freedom of sovereign action.

These confusions can only be dispelled by the calm logic of rational thought. Assuming the primacy of the national legal order, it is consistent to maintain that the state, having recognized international law and made it a part of its national law, has itself restricted its sovereignty. Once recognized, international law is valid for that state to the same degree as if it were valid as a supranational legal order. The norms of international law include the principle of *pacta sunt servanda*; therefore no international norm can be excluded on the basis that it is incompatible with sovereignty. As for the freedom of action of the state, it can only be determined on the basis of the content of international law.

Those who favor the primacy of international law are also guilty of biases which flow from emotional preference. Motivated by pacificism, they tend to narrow the range of sovereign discretion beyond what a dispassionate analysis of the content of international norms will allow. Anxious for the advance of universal order, they tend to assume an effective legal order which cannot, unfortunately, be verified.

The recognition of international law should not be confused with the related question of recognition of states and governments, although analytically there are parallels. See Lauterpacht, Recognition In International Law (1947).

Pacta Sunt Servanda, is considered by Kelsen to be a norm of customary international law which authorizes states to regulate their conduct by treaty. Compare, The Vienna Convention on the Law of Treaties, Art. 26. In the Pure Theory, *pacta sunt* has a broader prescriptive purpose as is evident from the above discussion concerning national sovereignty. However, it cannot easily be used to support obligations based upon customary international law. See the discussion in Stone, *op. cit.*, Ch. 2, VII and Kunz, *The 'Vienna School' and International Law*, 11 N.Y.U.L.Q. Rev. 370. (1934). It has also been questioned whether *pacta sunt* should be treated as an *a priori* hypothesis or a legal rule generated by state practice, Lauterpacht, *op. cit.*, Ch. 20, 117. It is not, like the *grundnorm*, a strict presupposition, but as a construct of obligation it seems to serve a similar function.

Kelsen's thought should be compared with that of Verdross, originally a member of the Vienna School who deviates from Kelsen on crucial points. Verdross would ground the obligations or international law upon general principles insofar as they have not been changed by positive rules, reserving an inviolability for some principles from which no derogation would be allowed. Verdross also would make the cognition of international law more concrete; rather than limiting definition to the sources of norms, he would comprehend international law as the law of a certain community, i.e., a presupposed community of states. It would then be understood that international law was created, almost exclusively, by the cooperation of states. Verdross, *On the Concept of International Law*, 43 A.J.I.L. 435 (1949). Compare Dabin, General Theory Of Law, Ch. 1, § 39–40, which perceives customary international law as a composite of social rules which evidence a desire for coordination and organization.

50. On the monist and dualist conceptions generally, see Collected Papers of HERSCH LAUTERPACHT, I GENERAL WORKS 213–14 (E. Lauterpacht ed. 1970). On individual and collective responsibility see id. 391–393. Problems of the binding force of international law within the United States are analyzed in McClure, *World Rule of Law: Next Steps by Individual States* (World Rule of Law Book Series 10) 37 Notre Dame L. Rev. 2 (1961). Compare LAUTERPACHT, *op. cit.*, Ch. 2.

In the primacy of international law aspect of Pure Theory, international and national law are treated as an inseparable whole. However, if one legal system provides that rules of a description satisfied by another are valid, it does not follow that the rules form a single system. A national legal system may be valid *according to* international law, without having its validity *derived from* international law. Hart, *Kelsen's Doctrine of the Unity of Law* in ETHICS AND SOCIAL JUSTICE, 171 (H. Kiefer and M. Munitz, ed. 1968) Kelsen's failure to grasp this distinction may be traceable to his inability to fully acknowledge the reality of distinct legal systems. Hart's essay also contains valuable observations on the problem of conflicts of norms.

51. On the Austinian position, compare the discussion *supra*, Chapter One. And see LAUTERPACHT, THE FUNCTION OF LAW IN THE INTERNATIONAL COMMUNITY, Ch. 20 §§ 10–13. On horizontalism, see HART, THE CONCEPT OF LAW, Ch. 10, § § 3–5 (1961) and my study, *Some Reflections Upon Theories of International Law*, 70 Col. L. Rev. 447 (1970). The need for empirical verification of a presumed basic norm is stronger in the international environment than in national law, where organs of government exist. Validity in the international realm needs a supplementation which Professor Stone calls "positivity", i.e., a measure of the actual degree of effectiveness as manifested in acts of observance. See his Hague Lectures, *Problems Confronting Sociological Inquiries Concerning International Law* [1956] RECUEIL DES COURS. Compare the work of Professor Falk, applying sociological insight to international law, discussed *supra*, Chapter Two of the present work.

A sociological perspective also brings a concreteness to the structure of international society. The emergence of nations from colonial domination has stimulated reflection upon the subjective roots of sovereignty. No longer the expression of abstract will, it expresses the emergence of peoples whose aspirations to self-determination provide the content of sovereignty. Charmont, *Cours General De Droit International Public*. Premiere Partie [1970] I, RECUEIL DES COURS 343. On this view, the state remains at the center of international law, but the task of the jurist is to coordinate human beings rather than transcendental entities.

52. The reconciliation model is discussed in Haas, *Collective Security and the Future of the International System,* in 1 THE FUTURE OF THE INTERNATIONAL LEGAL ORDER, 226 (C. Black and R. Falk ed. 1969). And see, Franck and Chesler, *'At Arms Length, The Coming Age of Collective Bargaining In International Relations Between Equilibrated States'*, 15 Va. J. INT'L. L. 579 (1975). Compare KELSEN, THE LAW OF THE UNITED NATIONS (1964), and

PEACE THROUGH LAW (1944) where compulsory adjudication is advocated. The conciliatory authority of the Security Council is emphasized in my paper *The Obligation of States to Settle Disputes By Peaceful Means*, 14 Va. J. INT'L. L.57 (1973). Its roots in the institutions and practices of the League of Nations are explored in *The Conciliatory Authority of the Council of the League of Nations*, 15 Duq. L. Rev. 199 (1977).

CHAPTER FOUR

1. H. KELSEN, WHAT IS JUSTICE 4 (1957). Compare *What is Justice*, in ESSAYS IN LEGAL AND MORAL PHILOSOPHY (O. Weinberger, ed. 1973).

2. H. KELSEN, GENERAL THEORY OF LAW AND STATE (I 20th Cent. Legal Phil., A. Wedberg, trans. 1945) at 14. See also Part One, Ch. I.A; H. KELSEN, THE PURE THEORY OF LAW (M. Knight, trans. 1967) Ch. 11. Compare A. ROSS, ON LAW AND JUSTICE Ch. 11, 12 (1959).

3. The basic ideas of Arnold Brecht are to be found in POLITICAL THEORY (1959) Part Four, exp. Ch. X, XII. There is further elucidation in a later essay *The Ultimate Standard of Justice*, in (Nomos VI) JUSTICE 62 (C. Friedrick & J. Chapman, ed. 1963).

4. The writings of Julius Stone are legion. Part Two of THE PROVINCE AND FUNCTIONS OF LAW (1950) analyzes the basic theories of justice. Further review appears in J. STONE, HUMAN LAW AND HUMAN JUSTICE Ch. 10 (1965) Chapter 11 contains an elaboration of Stone's own theory. The works, J. STONE, LEGAL SYSTEMS AND LAWYERS REASONING (1964) and SOCIAL DIMENSIONS OF LAW AND JUSTICE (1966), are also relevant.

5. See H.L.A. HART, THE CONCEPT OF LAW Ch. VIII (1961).

6. The Magnum Opus is RECHTSPHILOSPHIE (1932) translated in IV 20th Century Legal Philosophy Series, THE LEGAL PHILOSOPHIES OF LASK, RADBRUCH AND DABIN (K. Wilk, trans. 1950).

7. After the Second World War, Radbruch modified earlier preferences for legal certainty and order. In a conflict between justice and legal security, a positive rule, violative of justice to an intolerable degree, becomes, in effect a 'lawless' law and must yield to the requirements of justice. The degree to which his earlier views were modified is a matter of controversy. Compare Fuller, *American Legal Philosophy at Mid-Century*, 6 J. LEG. ED. 457, 481 (1954) with Wolf, *Revolution or Evolution in Gustav Radbruch's Legal Philosophy*, 3 NAT. L. FORUM 1 (1958). See also J. STONE, HUMAN LAW AND HUMAN JUSTICE, Ch. 8, §§ 6–11 (1965).

8. Kelsen framed the evolution of man in terms of a conflict between the rational and emotional elements of consciousness. There is some irony in the fact that, through a concentration upon human feelings, Edmund Cahn developed a substantial challenge to Kelsen's views. This American legal philosopher expressed a "sense of injustice;" a mixture of empathy and reason which reflected operative demands for human dignity and equality. Predictable outrage would follow from abuses of authority such as judicial favoritism, uneven treatment of like offenses, cruel punishment, or sup-

pression of inquiry; reactions which evidence the innate disposition of human beings to fight justice. Cahn's basic theory is expressed in THE SENSE OF INJUSTICE (1964). See also THE MORAL DECISION (1955) and the collection of essays CONFRONTING INJUSTICE (L. Cahn, ed. 1962). Cahn's views bear some relation to those of John Stuart Mill. See UTILITARIANISM, Ch. 5, where the instinctive elements of justice are emphasized.

9. *Man and Nature: Transcendental Parallelism,* in MAN AND NATURE, 4–5 (A. Campbell trans. 1969). The basic English reference to Del Vecchio's work are: PHILOSOPHY OF LAW (8th ed. O. Martin, trans. 1963): THE FORMAL BASIS OF LAW, published as Vol. X in the Modern Legal Philosophy Series of the Association of American Law Schools; JUSTICE (A. Campbell trans. 1956) and MAN AND NATURE (A. Campbell trans. 1969), a collection of selected essays.

Del Vecchio's thought reveals the influence of the Eighteenth Century philosopher of history, Giabattista Vico. Vico was one of the first modern thinkers to conceive of history as the work of man's spirit; a work in which he creates, not an extrinsic order, but his own ideal being in its existential concreteness. Vico gave considerable attention to the study of juridical processes and the connections between positive law and man's ethical aspirations. A. R. CAPONIGRI, TIME AND IDEA (1953) is a good general study of Vico's theory.

For the Kantian ethics, see H.J. PATON, THE CATEGORICAL IMPERATIVE (1948) and THE MORAL LAW (Groundwork of the Metaphysics of Morals) (1936). For a general review of idealism, including its approach to ethical questions, see W. E. HOCKING, TYPES OF PHILOSOPHY, Ch. 19–29 (3rd ed. 1959). It will be recalled from Chapter Three that Kelsen's Pure Theory of Law is a continuation of the intellectual dimensions of Kantian philosophy. A criticism of Kantian ethics by Kelsen can be found in his essay *Justice et Droit Naturel* in LE DROIT NATUREL, I, 12 (1959).

10. G. DEL VECCHIO, MAN AND NATURE 8 (1969).

11. C. FRIED, AN ANATOMY OF VALUES 49 (1970).

12. The thought of Fried summarized in the text is in the tradition of ethical idealism. His exposition of the principle of morality includes within its scope all actions which significantly affect other persons. In his work there are analyses of love and friendship as well as the obligations of justice. The ideal of Kantian morality is expressed with much greater concreteness in Fried's work than in Del Vecchio's. For Fried's general conception see AN ANATOMY OF VALUES Ch. IV (1970), and *Right and Wrong - Preliminary Considerations*, 5 J. LEGAL STUDIES 165 (1976). His notion of a right of privacy should be compared with Del Vecchio's 'right to solitude.' See AN ANATOMY OF VALUES Ch. IX, and *Privacy*, in LAW REASON AND JUSTICE, 45 (G. Hughes, ed. 1969).

The tradition of moral idealism was also reflected in the thought of Morris Cohen. See his *Philosophy and Legal Science,* 32 CO L. REV. 1103 (1932); D. HOLLINGER, MORRIS R. COHEN AND THE SCIENTIFIC IDEAL (1975).

13. AN ANATOMY OF VALUES at 51.

14. The principle ideas appear in the C. PERELMAN, THE IDEA OF JUSTICE AND THE PROBLEM OF ARGUMENT(J. Petrie, trans. 1963). See also, C. PERELMAN and L. OLBRECHTS-TYTECA, THE NEW RHETORIC: A TREATISE

On Argumentation (J. Wilkinson & P. Weaver, trans. 1969). Perelman's approach should be compared with A. J. Ayer's emotive theory of values. See Language, Truth And Logic Ch. VI (1936). See also, C. Stevenson, Ethics And Language (1944). S. Shuman, Legal Positivism (1963) contains proposals for transcending an emotive theory of ethics. He emphasizes a general duty to justify jural actions by reasons which have a public aspect and reflect perceptions of a shared world.

15. "An ethics is not a set of prudential rules indicating the most expedient way of getting what we want: if it were, it would be a branch of economics. An ethics is concerned with the difference between right and wrong; it is concerned with a *standard* or 'norm' of some sort for our behavior toward which we stand in the relation of 'ought' obligation, duty." W. E. Hocking, Types Of Philosophy 201 (3rd ed. 1959).

16. For the basic Thomistic explanation of prudence as right reason in the performance of actions see Summa Theologica, I.II. Q. 57 Art. 4. Central to Aquinas' thesis is the idea that, for practical wisdom, the actor's will must be formed by the moral virtues. For a fuller discussion, see my paper *Justice and Judgment,* 23 Buffalo L. Rev. 565 (1975); Mulvaney, *Political Wisdom,* (1973) Med. Studies 294. J. Dabin, *General Theory of Law* in The Legal Philosophies Of Lask, Radbruch And Dabin §§ 123–130 (K. Wilk, trans. 1950) specifically incorporates prudence into legal philosophy.

17. C. Fried, An Anatomy Of Values at 60–61. When the problem of justice is considered as a part of political theory, an assumed social contract makes the pursuit of justice obligatory. See the discussion of Rawl's theory of justice, *infra.*

In idealism, a distinction is maintained between the external character of knowledge and the interior basis of moral understanding. Fried makes such a distinction in An Anatomy Of Values. With moral ends "the point of encounter is a certain form of interactions between agent and object—as in acts of justice or love. The end of knowledge, by contrast, requires the agent to abstract from his own characteristics as much as possible, so he sees his object just as it is... *Id.* at 89. This distinction reinforces the criticism which we have made in the text. Further, although the obligations of justice are, in idealism, distinguished from optional relations of love and friendship, the deeper vocation to be a moral person is essentially a subjective choice.

For a further development in the thought of Charles Fried, see *The Lawyer As Friend: The Moral Foundations of the Lawyer—Client Relation,* 85 Yale L. J. 1060 (1976).

18. Traditional philosophy defined knowledge in terms of a correspondence of the mind with objective reality; modern epistemology virtually equates reality with thought. Since Descartes, subjectivity has become, for a large segment of philosophy, the only true source of objectivity valid knowledge. The external world exists, but only insofar as the incarnate self has relations with it and invests it with meaning. Phenomenologically, the transcendental thinking subject *constitutes* reality. There are very good reasons for these philosophical developments, but it is questionable whether assumptions that all moral knowledge is self given can establish

values upon these secure foundations which they so obviously require. We shall return to this question in Chapter Five.

19. DEL VECCHIO, PHILOSOPHY OF LAW, Systematic Treatise, Sec. II.; *On the State Character of Law,* in MAN AND NATURE 134 et seq.

20. Compare the discussion in Hobbes' political theory in Chapter One, A. *supra.*

21. THE SOCIAL CONTRACT, Bk. One, Ch. 6.

22. See E. CASSIRER, ROUSSEAU, KANT & GOETHE (1945).

23. A THEORY OF JUSTICE at 587. There is a full length study of a THEORY OF JUSTICE by BRIAN BARRY, THE LIBERAL THEORY OF JUSTICE (1973). Among the countless reviews of Rawls' book, those of importance to the present study include: Dworkin, *The Original Position,* 40 UNIV. CHIC. L. REV. 500 (1972); Feinberg, *Justice, Fairness and Rationality,* 81 YALE L.J. 1004 (1972); Fried, *Book Review* in 85 HARV. L. REV. 1691 (1972); Hampshire, in *The New York Review of Books,* Feb. 2, 1972 at 34; Hart, *Rawls on Liberty and Its Priority,* 40 UNIV. CHIC. L. REV. 534 (1972); McBride, *Social Theory Sub Specie Aeternitatis: A New Perspective,* 81 YALE L.J. 980 (1972); Murphy, *Distributive Justice,* 17 AM. J. JURISPRUDENCE 153 (1972); Choptiany, *A Critique of John Rawls's Principles of Justice,* 83 ETHICS 146 (1973); Hare, *Rawls's Theory of Justice,* 23 PHILOSOPHICAL QUART. 144 (1973); Nagel, *Rawls on Justice,* 82 PHILOSOPHICAL REV. 220 (1973); and Nozick, *Distributive Justice,* in 3 PHILOSOPHY AND PUBLIC AFFAIRS, 45, 78 (1973). See also READING RAWLS (N. Daniels, ed. 1977).

24. A THEORY OF JUSTICE, § 66.

25. *Id.,* § 39.

26. *Id.,* § 31. (The Four Stage Sequence).

27. Compare the discussion in Chapter Two, *supra.*

28. A THEORY OF JUSTICE, Ch. V.

29. See J. NYERERE, UJAMAA - ESSAYS ON SOCIALISM (1968) and the comments on the *Arusha Declaration* in Bienan, *An Ideology for Africa,* (1969) FOREIGN AFFAIRS 545. Mention should also be made of the phenomenon of religious socialism. See MARTIN BUBER, *The Life of Dialogue,* Ch. VIII (Friedman, ed. 1959).

30. E.g. H. MARCUSE, ONE DIMENSIONAL MAN.

31. A THEORY OF JUSTICE, § 42.

32. See *Id.,* § 43, § 47.

33. *Id.,* § 17, pp. 104, §§ 48, 66. For the Rawlsian distinction between the right and the good see A THEORY OF JUSTICE, Ch. VII, where goodness is defined as rationality in one's conception of a plan of life. Taking into account general facts about human desires and abilities, as well as the necessities of social interdependence, the list of primary goods can be accounted for by the conception of goodness as rationality (the thin theory; § 61–62). For the conception of moral goodness, principles of right and justice are introduced, and integrated into the contractarian thesis. There is then a full theory of goodness as rationality (§ 66).

So conceived, the good possesses both a descriptive and a prescriptive character. The dimension of right gives it an imperative quality. For a general analysis of the nature of the good in this branch of contemporary philosophy see McIverny, *The Poverty of Prescriptionism,* 17 AM. J. JUR. 80 (1972).

34. § 68.

35. Compare B. BARRY, THE LIBERAL THEORY OF JUSTICE (1973) Ch. 10, 11.

36. Kauper, *The Higher Law and the Rights of Man in a Revolutionary Society* in 18 Law Quadrangle Notes, University of Michigan Law School, No. 29, 15 (1974).

37. A THEORY OF JUSTICE, Ch. VI.

38. A THEORY OF JUSTICE at 515–516. Compare E. CASSIRER, THE QUESTION OF JEAN JACQUES ROUSSEAU (P. Gorg, trans., 1954) at p. 55:

> ... To him [i.e. Rousseau] freedom did not mean arbitrariness but the overcoming and elimination of all arbitrariness, the submission to a strict and inviolable law which the individual erects over himself. Not renunciation of and release from this law but free consent to it determines the genuine and true character of freedom. And that character is realized in the *volonte generale,* the will of the state. The state claims the individual completely and without reservations. However, in doing so it does not act as a coercive institution but only puts the individual under an obligation which he himself recognizes as valid and necessary, and to which he therefore assents for its sake as well as for his own.

39. E.g. Chapter Three, § B. Validity and the Basic Norm.

40. Compare Shapiro v. Thompson, 394 U.S. 618 (1969) with Dandridge v. Williams, 397 U.S. 471 (1970). The general influence of Rawls' ideas upon constitutional law can be seen in Michelman, *Foreword: On Protecting the Poor Through the Fourteenth Amendment,* 83 HARV. L. REV. 7 (1969).

41. The Thomistic conception of the Person and Society is drawn primarily from MARITAIN, THE PERSON AND THE COMMON GOOD (1947). These ideas are reflected in theories of distributive justice. See DABIN,*General Theory of Law,* Part Three, II. On the notion of the common good as an ethical datum see MARITAIN, *op. cit.,* Ch. IV; Y. SIMON, A GENERAL THEORY OF AUTHORITY Ch. 2 (1961). Simon's reflections on individual fulfillment should be compared with Rawls' idea of a social union. For a juridical exposition of the temporal common good, see DABIN, *op. cit.,* Part Two, II, Sections 1–3. Rawls' understanding of the common good is restricted to the maintenance of conditions which are equally to everyone's advantage.

42. E.g., J. S. Mill:

> ... [t]he utilitarian standard of what is right in conduct is not the agent's own happiness but that of all concerned ... [U]tility would enjoin, first, that laws and social arrangements should place the happiness or (as, speaking practically, it may be called) the interest of every individual as nearly as possible in harmony with the interest of the whole; and secondly that education and opinion, which have so vast a power over human character, should so use that power as to establish in the mind of every individual an indissoluble association between his own happiness and the good of the whole...

UTILITARIANISM, p. 22 (Library of Ideas, O. Piest, ed. 1957).

43. Dabin, General Theory, Part Three, Ch. II, § 234.

44. R. NOZICK, ANARCHY, STATE, AND UTOPIA 149–150 (1974).

45. *Id.,* at 152.

46. Compare Bakke v. The Regents of the Univ. of Calif., 132 Cal. Rptr. 680; 553 P.2d 1152 (1976).

47. *Supra,* Ch. One, § C. See also Professor Dworkin's defense of the right to be treated as an equal in TAKING RIGHTS SERIOUSLY Ch. 6 (1977).

48. E.g. Village of Euclid v. Ambler Realty Co., 272 U.S. 365 (1926).

49. On this, see the recent decision of the Supreme Court of the United States, Young v. American Mini Theaters, 96 S.Ct. 2440 (1976).

50. A conception of individual liberty is inevitably qualified by general consideration of social existence. And freedom from the domination of others is insufficient for the fulfillment of liberty; there is also a dimension of collaborative effort with others which is necessary to make freedom meaningful. On this, see the seminal article by Fuller, *Freedom, A Suggested Analysis,* 68 HARV. L. REV. 1305 (1955). Further, while liberty should normally include freedom from the actions of groups, there are also many instances where the individual needs groups to protect his interests and to give him the power leverage which he does not individually possess. The labor union is the obvious example but larger groups such as the nation can be included. *In Natural Law Restated: An Analysis of Liberty* in HUMAN RIGHTS 55 (E. Pollack ed. 1971) Professor De Cervera attempts to reconcile the two notions: freedom from, and freedom with, the group within an indeterminate ideal criterion of freedom. The primacy of liberty understood as freedom from coercion would suggest, however, that the two concepts should be analyzed in a more dialectic manner. This approach is suggested by Raymond Aron's AN ESSAY ON FREEDOM (1970). Aron's book contrasts the Marxist perspective with the Western values of political and intellectual freedom.

CHAPTER FIVE

1. See *supra,* Chapter Two. The quest for a deeper order beneath the various strata of social life is stated forcefully in G. GURVITCH, SOCIOLOGY OF LAW (1942).

2. F.S.C. NORTHROP, THE COMPLEXITY OF LEGAL AND ETHICAL EXPERIENCE, Ch. XVIII (1959); *Contemporary Jurisprudence and International Law,* 61 YALE L.J. 623 (1952); THE LOGIC OF THE SCIENCES AND HUMANITIES, Ch. 1 (1947).

3. THE COMPLEXITY OF LEGAL AND ETHICAL EXPERIENCE Ch. V-VIII.

4. THE LOGIC OF THE SCIENCES AND THE HUMANITIES at 296.

5. *Id.,* Ch. IV-VI; See also, F.S.C. NORTHROP, MAN, NATURE AND GOD (1962).

6. F.S.C. NORTHROP, THE MEETINGS OF EAST AND WEST, Ch. XII (1950); THE LOGIC OF THE SCIENCES AND HUMANITIES, VI-IX.

7. THE COMPLEXITY OF LEGAL AND ETHICAL EXPERIENCE 270–271.

8. Compare the influece of Kantian ethics on theories of justice in Chapter Four, *supra.*

9. The Meetings Of East And West at 464.

10. See generally, J. Katz, Experimentation With Human Beings (1972) and the symposium of *Daedalus,* Spring, 1969. And see Kaimowitz v. Department of Mental Health, Civil No. 19, 434 (Cir. Ct. Wayne Co., Mich. July 10, 1973).

11. The Logic Of The Sciences And The Humanities at 117.

12. See Y. Simon, The Tradition Of Natural Law (1965).

13. J. Maritain, The Degrees Of Knowledge, 41–43 (1959).

14. The Meeting Of East And West Ch. VII. "Since there is not a major concept in Aristotle's metaphysics which does not appear in his physics, this . . . [requires] the rejection of the Aristotelean philosophy and its attendant medieval Thomistic theology. The modern world, once it was forced by Galilei's analysis and experiment to replace Aristotelean physics . . . was required thereby to rear its philosophy also on attendantly new foundations . . ." The Logic Of The Sciences And The Humanities, 27–28. See also Nielsen, *Thomistic Theory of Natural Law,* 4 Nat. L. Forum 44 (1959).

15. J. Owens, The Doctrine Of Being In The Aristotelean Metaphysics (Rev. ed. 1963).

16. In addition to giving metaphysics a more secure theocentric orientation Aquinas developed his own metaphysical insights. He maintained that the principle in virtue of which something is a being was to be called *esse* the act of existing. For representative texts see Selected Writings Of St. Thomas Aquinas (R. Goodwin, trans. 1965); An Introduction To The Metaphysics Of St. Thomas Aquinas (J. Anderson, trans. 1953). See also, J. Maritain, An Introduction To Philosophy (1962).

17. The textual material is drawn from J. Maritain, The Degrees Of Knowledge, Ch. I, IV. The primary principle is that of identity. Every being is what it is. This principle guards the pluralism of existence against a Parmenidian or Hegelian monism. As each being is what it is, it is not what others are. Transferred to the logical order, the principle becomes one of non-contradiction. Here it can be breached by imaginative reconstruction. But, upon the ontological plane, the principle of identity is unshakeable. It is meta-logical, universally communicable; transcending every species, genus, or category.

18. The Degrees Of Knowledge, Ch. V. Within this framework, the general idea of science is operative. The object of science or scientific knowledge is the intelligible necessities discoverable either by observation or deductive modes of thought. Insofar as this conception has Aristotelian roots it is not as Popper charges, an "essentialist" view of knowledge. It does not treat the intuitive view of essences as the only form of reliable knowledge. The Open Society And Its Enemies, Ch. II. Nor is it accurate to define modern science as essentially provisional in its methodology. The progress of science is not one in which all scientific theories must always remain hypotheses. Sciences such as sociology and sociology of law (see Chapter Two) are based upon fundamental observations which have a sufficiently stable constancy to qualify as authentic knowledge. Similarly, analytical legal positivism is built upon well established linkages which have been perceived between basic jural phenomena.

The more important tensions are those *within* the experimental sciences. Empirometric forms of explanation compete with the inclination to understand phenomena by empiriological modalities. Sciences which are inductive in their methodology tend to resist mathematical explanations of the sensible within their field of inquiry. They do not wish to substitute quantitatively reconstructed entities for the qualitatively determined objects which observation makes possible. This conflict in the biological sciences (see 190 SCIENCE 773 (1975)) is intelligible when the degrees of knowing affirmed by Thomism are taken into account.

19. Compare the influence of idealism upon the development of the concept of Justice, *supra,* Ch. IV.

20. T. AQUINAS, SUMMA THEOLOGICA, I.Q. 29, Art. 3 (affirming the definition of Boethius).

21. THE LOGIC OF THE SCIENCES AND THE HUMANITIES at 296.

22. H. GROTIUS, DE JURE BELLI AC PACIS, *Prolegomena,* (Carnegie endowment ed. 1944); J. PUFENDORF, DE JURE NATURAE ET GENTIUM (Carnegie endowment ed. 1964). See generally, A.P. d'ENTREVES, NATURAL LAW (1951).

23. See Chapter Four, *supra,* § B.

24. SUMMA THEOLOGICA, I, II. Q. 94 Art. 2; Y. SIMON, THE TRADITION OF NATURAL LAW, Ch. 3–5 (1965).

25. See generally, J. MARITAIN, MAN AND THE STATE, Ch. IV (1950); J.C. MURRAY, WE HOLD THESE TRUTHS, Ch. 13 (1960). H. ROMMEN, THE NATURAL LAW (1947). Rommen tends to interpret the dynamic element of natural law in a voluntaristic rather than ontological, manner. See his essay *In Defense of Natural Law,* in LAW AND PHILOSOPHY 105 (S. Hook, ed. 1964) and the comment by W. Friedmann in the same volume.

26. H.L.A. HART, THE CONCEPT OF LAW Ch. IX (1961).

27. See LE DROIT NATUREL (1959).

28. Fay, *Toward A Thomistic-Anthropological View of the Evolution of Obligation,* 7 NAT. L. FORUM 38 (1962); Mead, *Some Anthropological Considerations Concerning Natural Law,* 6 NAT. L. FORUM 51 (1961).

29. Llewellyn's enthusiasm for 'immanent law' as something pre-existing which awaits human discovery is discussed in W. TWINING, KARL LLEWELLYN AND THE REALIST MOVEMENT, 223–224 (1973).

30. Natural Law does not regulate contingencies, and, from a Thomistic view, the exercise of the virtue of prudence determines the content of a legal rule. DABIN, *General Theory of Law,* III, §§ 123–130 in LEGAL PHILOSOPHIES OF LASK, RADBRUCH AND DABIN (IV, Twentieth Century Legal Philosophy Series, K. Wilk, trans. 1950). However, while natural law does not positively command a particular decision, positive law is proscribed from contradicting the essential precepts of Natural Law. *Id.* § 203. We shall discuss the relationship between positive law and natural law further in the text, *infra.*

31. Compare, *Dabin, op. cit.* §§ 212–214.

32. See Little, *Toward Clarifying the Grounds of Value Clarification: A Reaction to the Policy-Oriented Jurisprudence of Lasswell and McDougal,* 14 VA. J. INT'L. L. 451 (1974) for a general review of the basic issues.

33. In a speech prepared for delivery on April 13, 1945, President

Franklin Roosevelt had written: "Today, we are faced with the pre-eminent fact that if civilization is to survive, we must cultivate the science of human relationships—the ability of all peoples of all kinds to live together and work together in the same world at peace . . ." Quoted in R. HISCOCKS, THE SECURITY COUNCIL IN THEORY AND PRACTICE 53 (1974).

34. Compare the discussion of SOCIOLOGY OF LAW Ch. II, *supra.*

35. Natural law covers personal as well as social morality, but for juristic purposes, emphasis is placed upon the duties which life in society imposes. Dabin, *op. cit.* § 206.

36. For an illustration, see S.E.C. v. Capitol Gains Research Bureau, 375 U.S. 180 (1964).

37. For a general discussion of accountability with reference to the exercise of judicial power, see Chapter One, *supra.* See also J. MARITAIN, MAN AND THE STATE, Ch. 1 (1950).

The question of public accountability for the use of power is of great importance to Western-Marxist dialogue. See the discussion between George F. Kennen and Dr. Adam Schaff, a member of the Polish United Workers Party Central Committee in ON COEXISTENCE, 26 (Occasional Paper, Center for the Study of Democratic Institutions, 1965).

38. See A. BRECHT, POLITICAL THEORY Ch. X, XII (1959); *The Ultimate Standard of Justice* in VI NOMOS (C. FRIEDRICH & J. CHAPMAN, ed. 1963).

A preference for fundamental rights over other values has been advocated. See the discussion in Greenawalt, *Discretion and Judicial Decision: The Elusive Quest for the Fetters That Bind Judges,* 75 COL. L. REV. 359 (1975).

39. The tendency to reduce the diversity of moral precepts to unitary norms of human dignity is evident in the work of Del Vecchio. See, e.g. his JUSTICE, Ch. XI (1952).

40. SUMMA THEOLOGICA, I. II. Q. 91, A. 2. On the medieval period generally, see A.P. d'ENTREVES, NATURAL LAW, Ch. 2 (1951).

41. Kelsen's views on the natural law are summarized in Chapter Three, A *supra.* Basic sources include: *Natural Law Doctrine and Legal Positivism,* Appendix to GENERAL THEORY OF LAW AND THE STATE (1945); and his contribution to LE DROIT NATURALE (1959). See also, PURE THEORY OF LAW, Ch. II, III (1950) and *The Idea of Natural Law; The Contradiction of Natural Law,* in ESSAYS IN LEGAL AND MORAL PHILOSOPHY (O. Weinberger, ed. 1973).

42. "Law, even though without a sanction, is not entirely void of effect. For justice brings peace of conscience, while injustice causes torments and anguish . . ." H. GROTIUS, ON WAR AND PEACE *Prolegomena* 20.

43. J. MARITAIN, MAN AND STATE, 97–99 (1950).

44. See F. SUAREZ, DE LEGIBUS, AC DEO LEGISLATORE, in SELECTIONS FROM THREE WORKS (Carnegies Endow. trans. 1944).

45. DE JURE BELLI AC PACIS BK. I. Ch. 1, § 12.

46. THE FORMAL BASES OF LAW, 119.

47. See W. FRIEDMANN, THE CHANGING STRUCTURE OF INTERNATIONAL LAW 196 (1964) where three types of general principles are elucidated. Compare: Rest. Foreign Relations Law, § 165(1).

48. K. Nielson, *The Myth of Natural Law,* in LAW AND PHILOSOPHY 122, 124 (S. Hook, ed. 1964).

49. B. CARDOZO, THE PARADOXES OF LEGAL SCIENCE 1 (1928).

50. Cf. ARISTOTLE, NICHOMACHEAN ETHICS BK. VI, Ch. 5.

51. DABIN, *General Theory of Law*, Part Two, Section 3. Compare AQUINAS, SUMMA I-II Q. 49–59; J. PIEPER, PRUDENCE (1959). See also Murphy, *Justice and Judgment*, 23 BUFFALO L. REV. 565 (1974).

52. See R. DWORKIN, TAKING RIGHTS SERIOUSLY (1977). See also, Greenawalt, *Discretion and Judicial Decision: The Elusive Quest for the Fetters That Bind Judges*, 75 COL. L. REV. 359 (1975).

53. Compare B. CARDOZO, THE NATURE OF THE JUDICIAL PROCESS 103–113 (1921). Greenawalt, *op. cit.* 394–399.

54. See, generally, J. MARITAIN, MAN AND STATE Ch. 1 (1950).

55. *Supra,* pp. 217–218.

56. See S. Hook, *Reflections on Human Rights,* in ETHICS AND SOCIAL JUSTICE 252 (H. Kiefer and M. Munitz, ed. 1970).

57. Compare our critique of idealistic ethics, *supra,* Chapter Four at 166–167.

58. R. UNGER, KNOWLEDGE AND POLITICS (1975). Professor Unger also rejects what he understands to be objective theories of human nature. He seeks to mediate between objective and subjective views through a moderate form of Hegelianism. The 'good' becomes the "... manifestation and development of individual and universal human nature. .." (*Id.,* at 239) upon the stage of history. The idea of a human nature as an essence separate from social experiences, and antithetical to human choice is not, as he suggests, the heritage of the Aristotelean-Thomistic tradition. It is traceable to late scholasticism and the work of Suarez. See E. GILSON, BEING AND SOME PHILSOPHERS (1949).

Unfortunately, Professor Unger's thought tends towards the same "essentialist' errors which he would repudiate. He divides the concept of personality into a universal and particular aspect. The former represents sociability and the abstract self; the latter, the unique self of talents and capacities. But the individual tends to be absorbed in the whole. Thus "... the particular good [of the self] is the development of the unique set of talents and capacities *through which the species nature of mankind takes a concrete form in him* (*Id.,* emphasis supplied).

59. See J. DABIN, GENERAL THEORY, Part Two, II § 3.

60. TRACTATUS POLITICUS, Ch. III, 11–13.

61. E.B.F. MIDGLEY, THE NATURAL LAW TRADITION AND THE THEORY OF INTERNATIONAL RELATIONS (1975).

Table of Cases

Index